BUSINESS ECONOMICS IN A RAPIDLY-CHANGING WORLD

THE FINANCIAL CRISIS: ISSUES IN BUSINESS, FINANCE AND GLOBAL ECONOMICS

BUSINESS ECONOMICS IN A RAPIDLY-CHANGING WORLD

Additional books in this series can be found on Nova's website under the Series tab.

Additional E-books in this series can be found on Nova's website under the E-books tab.

BUSINESS ECONOMICS IN A RAPIDLY-CHANGING WORLD

THE FINANCIAL CRISIS: ISSUES IN BUSINESS, FINANCE AND GLOBAL ECONOMICS

BARBARA L. CAMPOS
AND
JANET P. WILKINS
EDITORS

Nova Science Publishers, Inc.
New York

For permission to use material from this book please contact us:
Telephone 631-231-7269; Fax 631-231-8175
Web Site: http://www.novapublishers.com

LIBRARY OF CONGRESS CATALOGING-IN-PUBLICATION DATA

The financial crisis : issues in business, finance and global economics /
editors, Barbara L. Campos and Janet P. Wilkins.
p. cm.
Includes bibliographical references.
ISBN 978-1-61209-281-2 (hardcover)
1. Financial crises--History--21st century. 2. International
finance--History--21st century. 3. Globalization--History--21st century.
I. Campos, Barbara L. II. Wilkins, Janet P.
HB3722.F545 2011
330.9'0511--dc22

2010048385

Published by Nova Science Publishers, Inc. † New York

CONTENTS

Preface		**vii**
Chapter 1	Causes of the Financial Crisis *Mark Jickling*	**1**
Chapter 2	Greed without Trust: Financial Crisis and the Break-Down in Spontaneous Order *Michael Devaney*	**9**
Chapter 3	Elements for an Effective Management of a Business Corporation Crisis Situation *Jorge Morales Pedraza*	**17**
Chapter 4	A Contribution to the Positive Theory of the Public Debt *Emanuele Canegrati*	**53**
Chapter 5	An Analysis of the Determinants of Credit Default Swap Spread Changes Before and During the Financial Turmoil *Antonio Di Cesare and Giovanni Guazzarotti*	**69**
Chapter 6	Insolvency of Systemically Significant Financial Companies: Bankruptcy vs. Conservatorship/Receivership *David H. Carpenter*	**103**
Chapter 7	Financial Market Intervention *Edward V. Murphy and Baird Webel*	**117**
Chapter 8	The Debt Limit: History and Recent Increases *D. Andrew Austin and Mindy R. Levit*	**127**
Chapter 9	Economic Stimulus: Issues and Policies *Jane G. Gravelle, Thomas L. Hungerford and Marc Labonte*	**147**
Commentary	Global Operations Management *Rui Yang Chen*	**169**
Index		**173**

PREFACE

This book examines the financial crisis and the effect it has had in the global business, finance and economic sectors. Topics discussed include the causes of the financial crisis; the elements needed for the management of a business corporation crisis; global operations management; an analysis of the public debt; the history and recent increases in the debt limit and the various issues and policies surrounding the economic stimulus.

Chapter 1 – While some may insist that there is a single cause, and thus a simple remedy, the sheer number of causal factors that have been identified tends to suggest that the current financial situation is not yet fully understood in its full complexity. This report consists of a table that summarizes very briefly some of the arguments for particular causes, presents equally brief rejoinders, and includes a reference or two for further reading. It will be updated as required by market developments.

Chapter 2 – In his *Theory of Moral Sentiments* Adam Smith observed the cupidity of man but never regarded it as something that could be changed. Rather than alter man's nature, he believed greed could be harnessed to create efficient mechanisms for producing desired social behaviors given man's moral limitations. Markets are one method for harnessing greed to create social benefit, but a complex market system can only operate efficiently in the presence of trust. When trust in markets is withdrawn greed alone is not sufficient to maintain "spontaneous order." This paper examines the role of greed and trust enforcement in the context of the financial crisis.

Chapter 3 – Obviously, any business corporation hopes not to face, under any circumstance, a situation that could cause an important interruption of its business activities, particularly if this situation could origin an extensive covering of the media and the public anger.

A crisis is an abnormal situation, or even perception, which is beyond the scope of everyday business and represents a real threat to the operation, safety and reputation of any business organization. A crisis situation disrupts the way an organization conducts business and attracts significant new media coverage and/or public scrutiny. Typically, these crises have the capacity to have negative financial, legal, and moral repercussions on the business corporation, especially if they are not dealt with in a prompt and effective manner.

A crisis management is defined as the intervention or co-ordination by individuals or teams before, during or after an event to resolve the crisis, minimize losses or otherwise protect the organization; in other words the way in which a crisis situation is managed during its evolution by the top management of a business corporation. It is considered a process designed to prevent or reduce to the minimum possible the damage a crisis can inflict on a business corporation activity and to its stakeholders. When a crisis occurred there is no other choice that to handle it properly with the purpose to reduce to the minimum the negative impact that it can cause to the business corporation activities.

For the better handling of a crisis situation is better to divided it in different phases. These phases are the following:

1) pre-crisis phase;
2) crisis response phase;
3) post-crisis phase.

The pre-crisis phase is concerned with prevention and preparation of the business corporation to handling a crisis situation in the best way possible. The crisis response phase is the one during which the top management of a business corporation must respond to a crisis situation. The post-crisis phase looks for ways to better prepare the business corporation for the next crisis. In this phase the top managers of a business corporation should fulfills all commitments adopted during the crisis.

Chapter 4 – Are social security transfers associated with public debt? In this paper the authors discuss a probabilistic voting model, where two office- motivated candidates must choose a debt issuance policy in order to win the election. Under the assumption that the political power of a cohort depends positively on the level of leisure, the authors demonstrate that, in equilibrium, the burden of debt, represented by the taxes levied to repay it, is borne by the younger cohort. Furthermore, the tax system induces the old to retire and allows them to receive a positive social transfer, paid by the young.

Chapter 5 – This paper analyzes the determinants of credit default swap spread changes for a large sample of US non-financial companies over the period between January2002 and March 2009. In the authors' analysis they use variables that the literature has found to have an impact on CDS spreads and, in order to account for possible non-linear effects, the theoretical CDS spreads predicted by Merton model. The authors show that their set of variables is able to explain more than 50% of CDS spread variations both before and after July 2007, when the current financial turmoil had its onset. The author also document that since the beginning of the crisis CDS spreads have become much more sensible to the level of leverage while volatility has lost its importance. Using a principal component analysis the author also show that since the beginning of the crisis CDS spread changes have been increasingly driven by a common factor. Although the variables the author use explain a significant part of the common behavior of CDS spread changes much of it still remains unexplained.

Chapter 6 – This report first discusses the purposes behind the creation of a separate insolvency regime for depository institutions. The report then compares and contrasts the characteristics of depository institutions with SSFCs. Next, the report provides a brief analysis of some important differences between the FDIC's conservatorship/receivership authority and that of the Bankruptcy Code. The specific differences discussed are: (1) overall objectives of each regime; (2) insolvency initiation authority and timing; (3) oversight structure and appeal; (4) management, shareholder, and creditor rights; (5) FDIC "superpowers," including contract repudiation versus Bankruptcy's automatic stay; and (6) speed of resolution. This report makes no value judgment as to whether an insolvency regime for SSFCs that is modeled after the FDIC's conservatorship/receivership authority is more appropriate than using (or adapting) the Bankruptcy Code. Rather, it simply points out the similarities and differences between SSFCs and depository institutions, and compares the conservatorship/receivership insolvency regime with the Bankruptcy Code to help the reader develop his/her own opinion.

Chapter 7 – Financial markets continue to experience significant disturbance and the banking sector remains fragile. Efforts to restore confidence have been met with mixed success thus far. This report provides answers to some frequently asked questions concerning ongoing financial disruptions and the Troubled Asset Relief Program (TARP), enacted by Congress in the Emergency Economic Stabilization Act of 2008 (EESA, Division A of H.R. 1424/P.L. 110-343). It also summarizes legislation in the 111th Congress such as H.R. 384, the TARP Reform and Accountability Act of 2009 and H.R. 703, "Promoting Bank Liquidity and Lending Through Deposit Insurance, Hope for Homeowners, and other Enhancements." The report also describes the option of a good-bank, bad-bank split.

Chapter 8 – The current economic slowdown has led to sharply higher estimates of the FY2008 deficit, raising the prospect of another debt limit increase. A debt limit increase was included in the Housing and Economic Recovery Act of 2008 (H.R. 3221) and signed into law (P.L. 110-289) on July 30. The Emergency Economic Stabilization Act of 2008 (H.R. 1424), signed into law on October 3 (P.L. 110-343), raised the debt limit for the second time in. The debt limit was increased for the third time in less than a year with the passage of American Recovery and Reinvestment Act of 2009 on February 13, 2009 (ARRA; H.R. 1). ARRA was signed into law on February 17, 2009 (P.L. 111-5), which raised the debt limit to $12,104 billion, where it now stands. This report will be updated as events warrant.

Chapter 9 – This report first discusses the current state of the economy, including measures that have already been taken by the monetary authorities. The next section reviews the economic stimulus package. The following section assesses the need for, magnitude of, design of, and potential consequences of fiscal stimulus. The final section of the report discusses recent and proposed financial interventions.

Commentary – This section presents the Customer Complaint problem of Product Usage Life cycle(CCPUL). The motivations, scope, goals, contribution and thesis architecture of this research are also discussed in this section.

Versions of these chapters were also published in *Journal of Current Issues in Finance, Business and Economics,* Volume 3, Numbers 1-4, published by Nova Science Publishers, Inc. They were submitted for appropriate modifications in an effort to encourage wider dissemination of research.

In: The Financial Crisis
Editors: Barbara L. Campos and Janet P. Wilkins

ISBN: 978-1-61209-281-2

Chapter 1

CAUSES OF THE FINANCIAL CRISIS

Mark Jickling*
Financial Economics

SUMMARY

The current financial crisis began in August 2007, when financial stability replaced inflation as the Federal Reserve's chief concern. The roots of the crisis go back much further, and there are various views on the fundamental causes.

It is generally accepted that credit standards in U.S. mortgage lending were relaxed in the early 2000s, and that rising rates of delinquency and foreclosures delivered a sharp shock to a range of U.S. financial institutions. Beyond that point of agreement, however, there are many questions that will be debated by policymakers and academics for decades.

Why did the financial shock from the housing market downturn prove so difficult to contain? Why did the tools the Fed used successfully to limit damage to the financial system from previous shocks (the Asian crises of 1997-1998, the stock market crashes of 1987 and 2000-2001, the junk bond debacle in 1989, the savings and loan crisis, 9/11, and so on) fail to work this time? If we accept that the origins are in the United States, why were so many financial systems around the world swept up in the panic?

To what extent were long-term developments in financial markets to blame for the instability? Derivatives markets, for example, were long described as a way to spread financial risk more efficiently, so that market participants could bear only those risks they understood. Did derivatives, and other risk management techniques, actually increase risk and instability under crisis conditions? Was there too much reliance on computer models of market performance? Did those models reflect only the post-WWII period, which may now come to be viewed not as a typical 60-year period, suitable for use as a baseline for financial forecasts, but rather as an unusually favorable period that may not recur?

Did government actions inadvertently create the conditions for crisis? Did regulators fail to use their authority to prevent excessive risk-taking, or was their jurisdiction too limited and/or compartmentalized?

While some may insist that there is a single cause, and thus a simple remedy, the sheer number of causal factors that have been identified tends to suggest that the current financial situation is not yet fully understood in its full complexity. This report consists of a table that summarizes very briefly some of the arguments for particular causes, presents

* E-mail address: mj ickling@crs. loc. gov

equally brief rejoinders, and includes a reference or two for further reading. It will be updated as required by market developments.

INTRODUCTION

The financial crisis that began in 2007 spread and gathered intensity in 2008, despite the efforts of central banks and regulators to restore calm. By early 2009, the financial system and the global economy appeared to be locked in a descending spiral, and the primary focus of policy became the prevention of a prolonged downturn on the order of the Great Depression.

The volume and variety of negative financial news, and the seeming impotence of policy responses, has raised new questions about the origins of financial crises and the market mechanisms by which they are contained or propagated. Just as the economic impact of financial market failures in the 1930s remains an active academic subject, it is likely that the causes of the current crisis will be debated for decades to come.

This report sets out in tabular form a number of the factors that have been identified as causes of the crisis. The left column of Table 1 below summarizes the causal role of each such factor. The next column presents a brief rejoinder to that argument. The right-hand column contains a reference for further reading. Where text is given in quotation marks, the reference in the right column is the source, unless otherwise specified.

Table 1. Causes of the Financial Crisis

Cause	Argument	Rejoinder	Additional Reading
Imprudent Mortgage Lending	Against a backdrop of abundant credit, low interest rates, and rising house prices, lending standards were relaxed to the point that many people were able to buy houses they couldn't afford. When prices began to fall and loans started going bad, there was a severe shock to the financial system.	Imprudent lending certainly played a role, but subprime loans (about $1 – 1 .5 trillion currently outstanding) were a relatively small part of the overall U.S. mortgage market (about $11 trillion) and of total credit market debt outstanding (about $50 trillion).	CRS Report RL33775, Alternative Mortgages: Causes and Policy Implications of Troubled *Mortgage Resets in the Subp rime and Alt-A Markets*, by Edward V. Murphy.
Housing Bubble	With its easy money policies, the Federal Reserve allowed housing prices to rise to unsustainable levels. The crisis was triggered by the bubble bursting, as it was bound to do.	It is difficult to identify a bubble until it bursts, and Fed actions to suppress the bubble may do more damage to the economy than waiting and responding to the effects of the bubble bursting.	CRS Report RL33666, Asset Bubbles: Economic Effects and Policy Options for the Federal Reserve, by Marc Labonte.
Global Imbalances	Global financial flows have been characterized in recent years by an unsustainable pattern: some countries (China, Japan, and Germany) run large surpluses every year, while others (like the U.S and U.K.) run deficits. The U.S. external deficits have been mirrored by internal deficits in the household and government sectors. U.S. borrowing cannot continue in idefinitely; the resulting stress underlies current financial disruptions.	None of the adjustments that would reverse the fundamental imbalances has yet occurred. That is, there has not been a sharp fall in the dollar's exchange value, and U.S. deficits persist.	Lorenzo Bini Smaghi, "The financial crisis and global imbalances – two sides of the same coin," Speech at the Asia Europe Economic Forum, Beijing, Dec. 9, 2008. http://www.bis.org/review/r081212d.pdf

Cause	Argument	Rejoinder	Additional Reading
Securitization	Securitization fostered the "originate-to-distribute" model, which reduced lenders' incentives to be prudent, especially in the face of vast investor demand for subprime loans packaged as AAA bonds. Ownership of mortgage-backed securities was widely dispersed, causing repercussions throughout the global system when subprime loans went bad in 2007.	Mortgage loans that were not securitized, but kept on the originating lender's books, have also done poorly.	Statement of Alan Greenspan before the House Committee on Oversight and Government Reform, October 23, 2008 ("The breakdown has been most apparent in the securitization of home mortgages.")
Lack of Transpareny and Accounta-bility in Mortgage Finance	"Throughout the housing finance value chain, many participants contributed to the creation of bad mortgages and the selling of bad securities, apparently feeling secure that they would not be held accountable for their actions. A lender could sell exotic mortgages to home-owners, apparently without fear of sell toxic mortgages to home-owners, apparently without fear of repercussions if those mortgages failed. Similarly, a trader could sell toxic securities to investors, apparently without fear of personal responsibility if those contracts failed. And so it was for brokers, realtors, individuals in rating agencies, and other market participants, each maximizing his or her own gain and passing problems on down the line until the system itself collapsed. Because of the lack of participant accountability, the originate-todistribute model of mortgage finance, with its once great promise of managing risk, became itself a massive generator of risk."	Many contractual arrangements did provide recourse against sellers or issuers of bad mortgages or related securities. Many non-bank mortgage lenders failed because they were forced to take back loans that defaulted, and many lawsuits have been filed against MBS issuers and others.	Statement of the Honorable John W. Snow before the House Committee on Oversight and Government Reform, October 23, 2008
Rating Agencies	The credit rating agencies gave AAA ratings to numerous issues of subprime mortgage-backed securities, many of which were subsequently downgraded to junk status. Critics cite poor economic models, conflicts of interest, and lack of effective regulation as reasons for the rating agencies' failure. Another factor is the market's excessive reliance on ratings, which has been reinforced by numerous laws and regulations that use ratings as a criterion for permissible investments or as a factor in required capital levels.	All market participants underestimated risk, not just the rating agencies. Purchasers of MBS were mainly should have done their own due diligence sophisticated institutional investors, who investigations into the quality of the instruments.	Securities and Exchang Commission, SEC Approves Measures to Strengthen Oversight of Credit RatingAgencies," press release 2008-284, Dec. 3, 2008.
Mark-to-market Accounting	FASB standards require institutions to report the fair (or current market) value of securities they hold. Critics of the rule argue that this forces banks to recognize losses based on "fire sale" prices that prevail in distressed markets, prices believed to be below long-term fundamental values. Those losses undermine market confidence and exacerbate banking system problems. Some propose suspending mark-to-market; EESA requires a study of its impact.	Many view uncertainty regarding financial institutions' true condition as key to the imperfect—are relaxed, fears that crisis. If accounting standards—however published balance sheets are unreliable will grow.	"Understanding the Mark-to-market Meltdown," Euromoney, Mar. 2008.

Table 1. (Continued)

Cause	Argument	Rejoinder	Additional Reading
Deregulatory Legislation	Laws such as the Gramm-Leach-Bliley Act (GLBA) and the Commodity Futures Modernization Act (CFMA) permitted financial institutions to engage in unregulated risky transactions on a vast scale. The laws were driven by an excessive faith in the robustness of market discipline, or self-regulation.	GLBA and CFMA did not permit the creation of unregulated markets and activities; they simply codified existing markets and practices. ("There is this idea afloat that if you had more regulation you would have fewer mistakes," [Gramm] said. "I don't see any evidence in our history or anybody else's to substantiate it." Eric Lipton and Stephen Labaton, "The Reckoning: Deregulator Looks Back, Unswayed," New York Times, Nov. 16, 2008.)	Anthony Faiola, Ellen Nakashima, and Jill Drew, "What Went Wrong?" Washington Post, Oct. 15, 2008, p. A1.
Shadow Banking System	Risky financial activities once confined to regulated banks (use of leverage, borrowing short-term to lend long,, etc.) migrated outside the explicit government safety net provided by deposit insurance and safety and soundness regulation. Mortgage lending, in particular, moved out of banks into unregulated institutions. This unsupervised risk-taking amounted to a financial house of cards.	Regulated banks—the recipients of most of the $700 billion Treasury TARP program—have not really fared much better than investment banks, hedge funds, OTC derivatives dealers, private equity firms, et al.	Nouriel Roubini, "The Shadow Banking System is Unravelling," Financial Times, Sep. 22, 2008, p. 9.
Non-Bank Runs	As institutions outside the banking system built up financial positions built on borrowing short and lending long, they became vulnerable to liquidity risk in the form of non-bank runs. That is, they could fail if markets lost confidence and refused to extend or roll over short-term credit, as happened to Bear Stearns and others.	Liquidity risk was always present, and recognized, but its appearance at the extreme levels of the current crisis was not foreseeable.	Krishna Guha, "Bundesbank Chief Says Credit Crisis Has Hallmarks of Classic Bank Run," Financial Times, Sep. 3, 2007, p. 1.
Off-Balance Sheet Finance	Many banks established off-the-books special purpose entities (including structured investment vehicles, or SIVs) to engage in risky speculative investments. This allowed banks to make more loans during the expansion, but also created contingent liabilities that, with the onset of the crisis, reduced market confidence in the banks' creditworthiness. At the same time, they had allowed banks to hold less capital against potential losses. Investors had little ability to understand banks' true financial positions.	Beginning in the 1990s, bank supervisors actually encouraged off-balance sheet finance as a legitimate way to manage risk.	Adrian Blundell-Wignall, "Structured Products: Implications for Financial Markets," Financial Market Trends, Nov. 2007, p. 27.
Government-Mandated Subprime Lending	Federal mandates to help low-income borrowers (e.g., the Community Reinvestment Act (CRA) and Fannie Mae and Freddie Mac's affordable housing goals) forced banks to engage in imprudent mortgage lending.	The subprime mortgage boom was led by non-bank lenders (not subject to CRA) and securitized by private investment banks rather than the GSEs.	Lawrence H. White, "How Did We Get into This Financial Mess?" Cato Institute Briefing Paper no. 110, Nov. 18, 2008.

Cause	Argument	Rejoinder	Additional Reading
Failure of Risk Management Systems	Some firms separated analysis of market risk and credit risk. This division did not work for complex structured products, where those risks were indistinguishable. "Collective common sense suffered as a result."	Senior management's responsibility has always been to bridge this kind of gap in risk assessment.	"Confessions of a Risk Manager; A Personal View of the Crisis," The Economist, Aug. 9, 2008.
Financial Innovation	New instruments in structured finance developed so rapidly that market infrastructure and systems were not prepared when those instruments came under stress. Some propose that markets in new instruments should be given time to mature before they are permitted to attain a systemically-significant size. This means giving accountants, regulators, ratings agencies, and settlement systems time to catch up.	In a global marketplace, innovation will continue and national regulators' attempts to restrain it will only put their countries' markets at a competitive disadvantage. Moreover, it is hard to tell in advance whether innovations will stabilize the system or the reverse.	Joseph R. Mason, "The Summer of '07 and the Shortcomings of Financial Innovation," Journal of Applied Finance, vol. 18, Spring 2008, p. 8.
Complexity	The complexity of certain financial instruments at the heart of the crisis had three effects: (1) investors were unable to make independent judgments on the merits of investments, (2) risks of market transactions were obscured, and (3) regulators were baffled.	Standard economic theory assumes that investors act rationally in their own self-interest, which implies that they should only take risks they understand.	Lee Buchheit, "We Made It Too Complicated," International Financial Law Review, Mar. 2008.
Human Frailty	Behavioral finance posits that investors do not always make optimal choices: they suffer from "bounded rationality" and limited self-control. Regulators ought to help people manage complexity through better disclosure and by reinforcing financial prudence.	Since regulators are just as human as investors, how can they consistently recognize that behavior has become suboptimal and that markets are headed for a crash?	Cass Sunstein and Richard Thaler, "Human Frailty Caused This Crisis," Financial Times, Nov. 1 2, 2008.
Bad Computer Models	Expectations of the performance of complex structured products linked to mortgages were based on only a few decades worth of data. In the case of subprime loans, only a few years of data were available. "[C]omplex systems are not confined to historical experience. Events of any size are possible, and limited only by the scale of the system itself."	Blaming models and the "quants" who designed them mistakes a symptom for a cause—"garbage in, garbage out."	James G. Rickards, "A Mountain, Overlooked: How Risk Models Failed Wall St. and Washington, "Washington Post, Oct. 2, 2008, p. A23.
Excessive Leverage	In the post-2000 period of low interest rates and abundant capital, fixed income yields were low. To compensate, many investors used borrowed funds to boost the return on their capital. Excessive leverage magnified the impact of the housing downturn, and deleveraging caused the interbank credit market to tighten.	Leverage is only a symptom of the underlying problem: mispricing of risk and a credit bubble.	Timothy F. Geithner, "Systemic Risk and Financial Markets," Testimony before the House Committee on Financial Services, July 24, 2008.
Relaxed Regulation of Leverage	The SEC liberalized its net capital rule in 2004, allowing investment bank holding companies to attain very high leverage ratios. Its Consolidated Supervised Entities program, which applied to the largest investment banks, was voluntary and ineffective.	The net capital rule applied only to the regulated broker/dealer unit; the SEC never had statutory authority to limit leverage at the holding company level.	Stephen Labaton, "Agency's '04 Rule Let Banks Pile Up New Debt, and Risk," New York Times, Oct. 3, 2008, p. A1, and Testimony of SEC Chairman Christopher Cox, House Oversight and Government Reform Committee, Oct. 23, 2008. (Response to question from Rep. Christopher Shays.)

Table 1. (Continued)

Cause	Argument	Rejoinder	Additional Reading
Credit Default Swaps (CDS)	"An interesting paradox arose, however, as credit derivatives instruments, developed initially for risk management, continued to grow and become more sophisticated with the help of financial engineering, the tail began wagging the dog. In becoming a medium for speculative transactions, credit derivatives increased, rather than alleviated, risk."	Speculation in derivatives generally makes prices of the underlying commodities more stable. We do not know why this relationship sometimes breaks down. Even in CDS, the feared "explosion" of defaults has not happened, albeit the expensive rescue of AIG may have prevented such an event.	Jongho Kim, "From Vanilla Swaps to Exotic Credit Derivatives," Fordham Journal of Corporate & Financial Law, Vol. 1 3, No. 5 (2008), p. 705.
Over-the-Counter Derivatives	Because OTC derivatives (including credit swaps) are largely unregulated, limited information about risk exposures is available to regulators and market participants. This helps explain the Bear Stearns and AIG interventions: in addition to substantial losses to counterparties, a dealer default could trigger panic because of uncertainty about the extent and distribution of those losses.	The largest OTC markets—interest rate and currency swaps—appear to have held up fairly well.	Walter Lukken, "How to Solve the Derivatives Problem," Wall Street Journal, Oct. 10, 2008, p. A1 5.
Fragmented Regulation	U.S. financial regulation is dispersed among many agencies, each with responsibility for a particular class of financial institution. As a result, no agency is well-positioned to monitor emerging system-wide problems.	Countries with unified regulatory structures, such as Japan and the UK, have not avoided the crisis.	U.S. Treasury, Blueprint for a Modernized Financial Regulatory Structure, Apr. 2008.
No Systemic Risk Regulator	No regulator had comprehensive jurisdiction over all systemically-important financial institutions. (The Fed had the role of systemic risk regulator by default, but lacked authority to oversee investment banks, hedge funds, nonbank derivatives dealers, etc.)	Some question whether the problem was lack of authority or failure to use existing regulatory powers effectively.	Henry Kaufman, "Finance's Upper Tier Needs Closer Scrutiny," Financial Times, Apr. 21, 2008, p. 1 3.
Short-term Incentives	Since traders and managers at many financial institutions receive a large part of their compensation in the form of an annual bonus, they lack incentives to avoid risky strategies liable to fail spectacularly every five or ten years. Some propose to link pay to a rolling average of firm profits or to put bonuses into escrow for a certain period, or to impose higher capital charges on banks that maintain current annual bonus practices.	Shareholders already have incentives and authority to monitor corporate compensation structures and levels.	Andrew Ross Sorkin, "Rein in Chief's Pay? It's Doable," New York Times, Nov. 3, 2008.
Tail Risk	Many investors and risk managers sought to boost their returnsby providing insurance or writing options against low-probabilityfinancial events. (Credit default swaps are a good example, but by no means the only one.) These strategies generate a stream of small gains under normal market conditions, but cause large losses during crises. When market participants know that many such potential losses are distributed throughout the system (but do not know exactly where, or how large), uncertainty and fear are exacerbated when markets come under stress.	Dispersal of systematic risk via financialinnovation was believed to make thefinancial system more resilient to shocks.	Raghuram Rajan, "A Tale of TwoLiquidities," Remarks at the Universityof Chicago Graduate School ofBusiness, Dec. 5, 2007, online at http://www.chicagogsb.edu/news/1 2-5 07_Rajan.pdf.

Table 1. (Continued)

Cause	Argument	Rejoinder	Additional Reading
Black Swan Theory	This crisis is a once-in-a-century event, caused by a confluence of factors so rare that it is impractical to think of erectingregulatory barriers against recurrences. According to AlanGreenspan, such regulation would be "so onerous as to basicallysuppress the growth rate of the economy and ... [U.S.] standardsof living." Testimony before the House Oversight and Government Reform Committee, Oct. 23, 2008.	"Some might be tempted to see recentevents in the financial markets as justsuch black swans. But this would be quitewrong, in our view. Many of the flawsthat have led to current turbulentconditions have not ridden on the back of a black swan. Instead, they are the result of weaknesses and failings in the interpretation of risk analysis and the process of oversight." (Booth and Mazzawi)	Geoff Booth and Elias Mazzawi , "BlackSwan or Fat Turkey?" Business StrategyReview, vol. 19, Autumn 2008, p. 34.Also: Michael J. Boskin, "Our NextPresident and the Perfect EconomicStorm," Wall Street Journal, Oct. 23, 2008, p. A17.

Source: Table Compiled by CRS.

Note: Passages in quotation marks are from the source cited in the right-hand column, unless otherwise noted.

In: The Financial Crisis
Editors: Barbara L. Campos and Janet P. Wilkins
ISBN: 978-1-61209-281-2

Chapter 2

GREED WITHOUT TRUST: FINANCIAL CRISIS AND THE BREAK-DOWN IN SPONTANEOUS ORDER

Michael Devaney*
Department of Economics and Finance
Southeast Missouri State University
Cape Girardeau, MO, USA

ABSTRACT

In his *Theory of Moral Sentiments* Adam Smith observed the cupidity of man but never regarded it as something that could be changed. Rather than alter man's nature, he believed greed could be harnessed to create efficient mechanisms for producing desired social behaviors given man's moral limitations. Markets are one method for harnessing greed to create social benefit, but a complex market system can only operate efficiently in the presence of trust. When trust in markets is withdrawn greed alone is not sufficient to maintain "spontaneous order." This paper examines the role of greed and trust enforcement in the context of the financial crisis.

"Bears eat, bulls eat but pigs go hungry."

Anonymous financial market proverb

INTRODUCTION

Greed is often identified as the fuel that powers modern capitalism. The economic benefit of selfishness is one of the central themes of the perennially popular Ayn Rand novel *Atlas Shrugged*. Perhaps the most frequently quoted proponent of the "greed is good" philosophy in popular culture is Gordon Gekko, the unscrupulous financier in the Oliver Stone movie *Wall Street*. The movie was intended as a social critique of the so-called 1980s "age of greed."

* E-mail: mdevaney@semo.edu

More recently large bonuses for Wall Street executives, especially among those working for companies that accepted taxpayer bailouts have ignited public anger.

Despite lavish executive compensation, excess alone may not render greed more distasteful. Someone who withholds a crust of bread from a starving comrade could be regarded as less honorable than the CEO of a bailed-out company who decorated his office with a 19th century commode that cost $32,000. Airmen in WWII bomber squadrons were said to suffer pangs of guilt for unconsciously reacting "better him than me" when another plane was shot from the sky. Such reactions may be forgiven as a genetically coded will to survive but when does Darwinian evolution cease to be justification for craven self-interest?

In his *Theory of Moral Sentiments* Adam Smith probed the distasteful nature of human egocentricity when he asked:

> *"how a man of humanity in Europe would respond to hearing that the great empire of China... was suddenly swallowed up by an earthquake..."? Smith wrote that "If he [this man] was to lose his little finger tomorrow, he would not sleep tonight; but, provided he never saw them [i.e, the people of China], he would snore with the most profound security over the ruin of a hundred million of his brethren, and the destruction of that immense multitude seems plainly an object less interesting to him than this paltry misfortune of his own" (Part III, Chapter 3).*

For those who would *choose* their little finger over the countless multitudes Smith goes on to write that: *"human nature startles with horror at the thought, and the world, in its greatest depravity and corruption, never produced such a villain as could be capable of entertaining it." Of course, we do not get to choose.*

Smith may have lamented the moral limitations of man but he never regarded them as something that could be changed. Instead, he believed human self-interest was a fact of life and that it could be exploited to serve society. In the *Wealth of Nations* Smith described how the economic benefits to society, that were largely unintended, occurred systematically in the marketplace by virtue of competition and the incentive for individual gain. Rather than attempt to change man's moral character so that he places the welfare of others before his own, Smith believed that markets represented the best possible trade-off between social and personal benefit. Smith was not alone in his opinions on man's moral limitations. In politics, Smith's contemporary Edmund Burke (1967) echoed this view when he spoke of a "radical infirmity in all human contrivances."

Unlike Smith who believed that personal incentives were required to evoke desirable behavior, Godwin believed man could be induced to intentionally create social benefits. To Godwin (1969) the *intention* to benefit others was "the essence of virtue" and unintended social benefits were not worthy of notice. When Godwin argued that man was capable of placing the needs of others before his own, he was not describing how people actually behaved but what he regarded as man's underlying potential. The "perfectibility of man" was a common theme among many late 18th century writers and emerged in the 20th century as a new communist archetype. In *Literature and Revolution* Trotsky (1925) wrote:

> "Homo sapiens will once again enter the stage of radical reconstruction and become in his own hands the object of the most complex methods of artificial selection and psychophysical training...man will make it his goal ...to create a higher sociobiological type, a *superman* if you will"

The alternative to markets motivated by individual greed is a centralized economy that depends on planners to direct the means of production. No one articulated their distrust of central planning more convincingly than Friedrich Hayek (1944) author of *The Road to Serfdom*. For Classical economists, the price system was a method for overcoming man's inherent greed. By virtue of the invisible hand, market participants who pursued self-interest were simultaneously maximizing social welfare. Hayek did not see the price system so much as a way to resolve greed but as a means to overcome deficits in the knowledge of market participants.

While Hayek accepted that there were specialists who harbored knowledge in certain fields, he believed that the most important knowledge in society was widely dispersed among the population. Hayek's distrust of experts was not so much that he believed them dishonest, but he thought that a system as complicated as the global economy could only be fully understood by an even more complex system. He believed that much of the most valuable knowledge in society was "tacit knowledge" that could not be easily communicated to others. One can convey a recipe for spaghetti sauce written on a card, but it is difficult to communicate to another the information required to ride a bicycle. Because tacit knowledge is idiosyncratic and hard to classify it is frequently lost in highly centralized systems.

Decentralization exploits tacit knowledge because those who are more autonomous and closer to a problem are better able to utilize all of their skills in finding a solution. Individual knowledge plays a counter-intuitive role in group decisions. Page and Hung (2001) established groups of ten and twenty agents. Each agent was endowed with a different set of skills and asked to solve a relatively sophisticated problem. Some of the agents were individually very good at solving the problem while others did less well. However, when groups with some not so smart agents were mixed with some smart agents, the cognitively diverse groups almost always did better at solving the problem than those comprised of exclusively smart agents. The tacit knowledge of homogenous groups tends to be more redundant than it is for cognitively diverse groups.

At the organization level March (1991) goes so far as to argue that "the development of knowledge may depend on maintaining an influx of the naïve and the ignorant…new recruits are, on average less knowledgeable than the individuals they replace. The gains come from their diversity." March asserts that groups that are too much alike find it harder to keep learning. They spend too much time exploiting and not enough time exploring.

There may also be a tendency for specialists to seek overly complex solutions to problems consistent with their expertise For example, in moving a large substation transformer on a flat bed trailer engineers for an electric utility company encountered a low clearance bridge. Some conferred with the highway patrol on alternate routes while others discussed dismantling the insulators or unloading and reloading the transformer. A small boy standing with his bicycle in a crowd of onlookers suggested deflating the trailer tires and re-inflating them after passing under the bridge which turned out to be the solution used by the engineers. (Union Electric, 1992)

"Group think" is partly a manifestation of homogeneity in tacit knowledge that tends to plague hierarchal organizations that promote like-thinking persons. It can lead to disastrous decisions. In deliberations by the "best and brightest" concerning the Bay of Pigs invasion, historian Arthur Schlesinger Jr. observed: "Our meetings took place in a curious atmosphere of assumed consensus." (Janis, 1982) Kaufman (2004) suggests a similar environment pervaded discussions leading up to the Iraq War.

In his book *The Wisdom of Crowds* Surowiecki (2004) provides numerous examples documenting the superior intelligence of large groups relative to small groups of experts. The success of Wikipedia demonstrates the power of bottom-up, widely dispersed knowledge relative to top-down expert knowledge. Unlike conventional encyclopedias, Wikipedia has been criticized for allowing anyone to edit entries. However, a survey by *Nature* magazine found the error rate in Wikipedia compares favorably with conventional encyclopedias but far exceeds them in scope. The founder, Jimmy Wales, says he thought of Hayek's 1945 article *The Use of Knowledge in Society* when he began reading about the open-source software movement in the early 1990's. (Schiff, 2006)

Hayek believed that all social constructs such as language, the legal system, markets, etc., were evolved processes derived from collective experience in which knowledge is codified into rules of behavior. This collective knowledge is transmitted socially in largely inarticulate form leading to a "spontaneous order." Competition among institutions results in the survival of cultural traits and behaviors that "work" even if the winners or losers never fully understand why they worked. To quote Hayek (1979), there is "more 'intelligence' incurporated in the system of rules of conduct than in man's thoughts about his surroundings."

Despite its benefits, decentralized knowledge can be lost unless there is a mechanism for transmitting it. For Wikipedia the mechanism is open-source software on the Web and for markets it is the price system. Hayek argued that even with the best intentions top-down central planners did not have sufficient knowledge to duplicate the millions of sequential prices necessary to produce an economic outcome superior to the one produced by a bottom-up market system. Despite the frequent undesirable outcome of markets, the inadequate knowledge inherent in planned economies results in an even greater number of undesirable outcomes. Greed motivates the aggregation of knowledge, including the knowledge of the brilliant and the dimwitted, into a price system that cannot be replicated by the technical expertise of Trotsky's supermen.

GREED AND TRUST

Greed may be the organizing principle in markets but their efficient operation is critically dependent on trust. Economists have long observed large variations in trust across nations. Smith (1766) characterized the Dutch as "most faithful to their word" while John Stuart Mill (1848) wrote that a major impediment to commerce in Europe "is the rarity of persons who are supposed fit to be trusted with the receipts and expenditures of large sums of money."

Despite Mills observation on a shortage of trust in 19th century Europe, behavioral experiments reveal a surprising degree of trust in contemporary society. Berg, et. al. (1995) describe anonymous prisoner's dilemma games in which a large percentage of players chose to trust their partners rather than defect to the economically rational Nash equilibrium. Outside the laboratory, trust is evident in the most mundane of economic transactions. When on vacation we eat at the crowded truck stop that we have never frequented nor will again because we trust that the meal will meet minimum standards of hygiene and taste. The same degree of trust is present when we buy milk for our children's breakfast cereal or fill-up the family car with gasoline.

Rules and traditions evolved from human interaction to form the basis for trust. Transactions occur within a social structure that establishes the rewards and penalties for cooperation. Trust is strongest among those most similar (blood relatives) and diminishes as the family tree branches out. Evolutionary biologists refer to this effect as "Hamilton's Rule" which posits that the degree of altruistic or trusting behavior is highest among family members and potentially in-breeding neighbors. Genetic and social ties between dissimilar participants are weaker and the temptation to cheat is stronger. When informal social sanctions fail to discourage cheating, society establishes formal institutions of trust enforcement such as regulators, police and the courts.

In the absence of market generated trust forming systems it is likely that the transaction costs associated with formal enforcement of honest behavior would exceed the benefits for many types of economic exchange. Because trust reduces the cost of transacting, high trust societies produce more output than those with low trust. North (1990) observed that the inability of some societies to create low-cost enforcement of trusting behaviors may be the "most important source of both historical stagnation and contemporary underdevelopment in the Third World." Zak and Knack (2001) find that trusting societies grow faster and that some less developed countries are locked in a "Northian low-trust poverty trap."

Formal trust enforcers in financial markets include the SEC, state and federal financial institution regulators and third party regulators such as debt rating agencies, real estate appraisers and certified public accountants. Informal sanctions are a low-cost substitute for formal institutions and include social ostracism, loss of profit through reputational effects, and guilt associated with the violation of moral norms or religious principle. Formal institutions may be a necessary condition for economic progress within large demographically diverse populations but informal sanctions play an important role in the market for intangible financial assets among developed countries.

If social sanctions impede economic progress in many less developed countries, the excess and failure of formal institutions can retard growth in developed countries. Excess is reflected in overly litigious behavior while regulatory failure derives from inadequate knowledge of expert regulators and the "rule of capture" which is the tendency for regulators to be captured by producers rather than serve consumers. (Stigler, 1971) Third party regulatory agents are typically paid by those they are "rating" leading to moral hazard and adverse selection. Financial regulation is less effective across countries than within borders. This reflects the mobility of international capital, the sovereign status of nations and regulatory arbitrage by investors. International regulation may also be less effective because of Hamilton's Rule.

Regulatory agencies tend to be highly centralized organizations staffed by like thinking persons. Like central planners writ small, regulators experience deficits in knowledge. Harry Markopolos spent nine years trying to convince the SEC to investigate the Madoff Ponzi scheme. In Congressional testimony he blamed the "investigative ineptitude and financial illiteracy" of an SEC staff that is dominated by "securities lawyers." (Bloomberg.com, 2009) In fairness to the SEC, financially literate regulators performed little better.

In early America, government attempts to instill trust via informal reputational effects predate the expansion of formal financial market regulation. During the Revolutionary War many affluent citizens invested in bonds and soldiers were often paid in IOUs that plummeted in price under the confederation. Much of the debt was sold to speculators at large discounts. After the war, some called for redemption at face value to the original holders. Alexander Hamilton understood that "security of transfer" required that government not interfere retroactively in financial transactions even if it meant rewarding greedy speculators and penalizing patriots. To quote Hamilton: "States, like individuals who observe their engagements are respected and trusted, while the reverse is the fate of those who pursue an opposite conduct." Chernow (2004) argues that Hamilton's effort to instill reputational trust laid the foundation for America's future preeminence in finance.

Informal rules that define the boundaries of trust are a key component of tacit knowledge in financial markets. Traders in the futures pit who attempt to renege on money losing trades are quickly ostracized. Commercial bank loan officers are said to place much more trust in the tacit knowledge derived from long-term "lending relationships" than the formal credit reports of rating agencies. The value of intrinsically worthless paper money derives from the collective knowledge and trust in the integrity of the issuing government. In the absence of trust enforcing tacit knowledge the breadth and depth of financial transactions would be substantially reduced.

The Dissipation of Trust and the Break-Down in Spontaneous Order

Under the right circumstances large groups can be profoundly intelligent, however, there are exceptions. History is punctuated by periodic asset bubbles when market participants took leave of their collective senses and embraced the myth of ever-increasing value. The speculative hysteria that characterizes an asset bubble tends to feed on itself. Shiller (2000) describes a "sort of feedback from price increases to increased investor enthusiasm, to increased demand and hence further price increases" a kind of greed gone wild.

In his 1841classic *Extraordinary Popular Delusions and the Madness of Crowds*, Charles MacKay chronicles the Dutch tulip mania of the 17th century. Before the crash in 1637, a few supposedly rare tulip bulbs were so highly valued that some Dutch burghers were reported to have traded the family farm for a single bulb. Asset bubbles are a departure from the "wisdom of crowds." The real estate housing bubble was caused by easy money by the Federal Reserve, lack of due diligence in credit and derivative markets, and a speculative appetite for ever more luxurious homes that one critic christened "housing lust."

Bubbles can cause major economic disruption, but markets have a self-correcting ability to overcome them. However, when assets are highly leveraged with complex decomposition and resale of cash flow, there is the potential for spillover into other credit markets. The Lehman Brothers collapse in the fall of 2008 triggered a run on money market funds. The dissipation of trust caused a paralysis in short-term credit leading to a break-down in the spontaneous order of financial markets. Much of the tacit knowledge that was reliable before the break proved unreliable in the aftermath. The rapid erosion of trust precipitates a flight to presumed "safe havens" such as gold, Treasury bills and government insured bank deposits.

Aghion, et. al., (2008) found that countries with low trust have more regulation suggesting that government attempts to substitute formal enforcement when informal sanctions are lacking. The presumption that the mechanisms of formal and informal trust are good substitutes may be true in the midst of crisis but it is less apparent during recovery. Low trust countries experience slower growth partly because they rely more on the inadequate expert knowledge of high cost formal enforcers rather than the more efficient tacit knowledge reflected in low cost informal sanctions. Because formal enforcement is tied to statutory law it tends to be less adaptive to the kind of technological change that has transformed financial markets over the last twenty years.

There are also social costs associated with the failure of non-regulatory expert knowledge. Cracks in the intellectual edifice of the new science of "financial engineering" first became apparent with the spectacular collapse and government constructed bailout of Long-Term Capital Management (LTCM). Formed in 1994, LTCM utilized the financial expertise of two Nobel economists to post annualized returns of over 40% in the early years before losing $4.6 billion in four months of 1998. If the private sector had been required to work out the problems associated with LTCM, it might have humbled some Wall Street rocket scientists and served as a stop sign on the road to the current mess. Instead, it was little more than a speed bump.

Very few financial experts anticipated the systemic risk that culminated in the financial crisis. Instead, they churned out a plethora of research trumpeting the risk mitigating benefits of "financial innovation." The dissenting opinion that surfaced was overwhelmed by the group-think of assumed consensus. Academics and financial economists in industry and government should accept more collective responsibility for fostering an intellectual climate that ignored institutional imperatives in favor of the false mathematical precision that Hayek (1974) labeled a "pretense of knowledge."

A Zogby Poll found that more than 80% of respondents believe that political corruption was a "major factor" in the financial crisis. There are ongoing investigations of alleged corporate fraud related to the crisis in 38 large companies and the FBI believes the number could eventually exceed 100. (Ryan, 2009) It is likely that there are many thousands of financial service industry employees and home buyers who are ethically if not legally complicit in the crisis. For many of them the penalty for violating public trust is the loss of their job or house. Unfortunately, many more who were *not* complicit will suffer a similar fate.

It took almost 30 years or a generation for the U.S. stock market to recover its 1929 value in real dollars. As of February 15, 2009 the Japanese stock market was at 67% of its 1989 value. Stock ownership today is much more widely dispersed suggesting that trust must be restored across a broader spectrum of the population. Despite the resilience of markets, it will take time to restore public trust. Government attempts to accelerate the process by nationalizing risk could prove counter-productive. Like military action, government enforcement is most effective as a policy of "last resort." When government action proves ineffective the psychological environment can worsen precisely because there is no obvious alternative.

REFERENCES

Aghion, P., Y. Algan, P. Cahuc and A. Shleifer. (2008). "Regulation and Distrust," *National Bureau of Economic Research.* July 3.

Berg, J.J. Dickhaut, and K. McCabe. (1995). "Trust Reciprocity, and Social History, " *Games and Economic Behavior,* 10, 122-42.

Bloomberg.com. (2009). "Madoff Tipster Cites SEC Ineptitude. February, 4. http://www.bloomberg.com/apps/news?pid=newsarchiveandsid=a_UBDG13Gld0.

Burke, E. (1967). *The Correspondence of Edmund Burke*, Chicago; University of Chicago Press, Volume 1. p. 48.

Chernow, R. (2004). *Alexander Hamilton*, The Penguin Press, New York, New York. p.299.

Godwin, W. (1969). *Enquiry Concerning Political Justice*, Toronto: University of Toronto Press, Volume 1. p. 156.

Janis, I. (1982). *Groupthink: Psychological Studies of Policy Decisions and Fiascoes*, Boston: Houghton Mifflin.

March, J. (1991). "Exploration and Exploitation in Organizational Learning," *Organization Science*, 2 , 71-87, 79,86.

Page, S. and L. Hung. (2001). "Problem Solving by Heterogeneous Agents," *Journal of Economic Theory*, 97, 123-163.

Hayek, F. (1944). *The Road to Serfdom*, London: Routledge and Sons; Chicago: University of Chicago Press

Hayek, F. (1945). "The Use of Knowledge in Society," *American Economic Review*, XXXV, 4, 519-530.

Hayek, F. (1974). *The Pretense of Knowledge.* Acceptance Speech for The Sveriges Riksbank Prize in Economic Science in Memory of Alfred Nobel, December 11, 1974.

Hayek, F. (1979). *Law, Legislation and Liberty,* Chicago: University of Chicago Press, Volume 3. p.157

Kaufmann, C. (2004). "Threat Inflation and the Failure of the Marketplace of Ideas: The Selling of the Iraq War," *International Security*, The MIT Press,29, 1, 2004, pp. 5-48.

Mill, J.S. (1848). *Principles of Political Economy*, London: John W. Parker.

North, D. (1990). *Institutions, Institutional Change and Economic Performance,* Cambridge: Cambridge University Press.

Ryan, K. (2009). "Fraud Directly Related to the Financial Crisis Probed," http://www.abcnews.go.com/TheLaw/Economy/story?id=6855179, February 11.

Schiff, S. (2006). "Know it All: Can Wikipedia Conquer Expertise?" *The New Yorker*, July 31, 2006.

Shiller, R. (2000). *Irrational Exuberance*, Princeton New Jersey, Princeton University Press.

Smith, A. (1776). *The Theory of Moral Sentiments*, Indianapolis Liberty Classic

Smith, A. (1937). *An Inquiry into the Nature and Causes of the Wealth of Nations,* New York Modern Library.

Smith, A. (1997/1766). "Lecture on the Influence of Commerce on Manners," Reprinted in D. B. Klein ed. *Reputation: Studies in the Voluntary Elicitation of Good Conduct,* University of Michigan.

Stigler, G. (1971). "The Theory of Economic Regulation," *The Bell Journal of Law, Economics and Management Science*, 2, 1, 243-263.

Surowiecki, J. (2004). *The Wisdom of Crowds*, Doubleday, New York, NY.

Trotsky, L. (1925). *Literature and Revolution,* Published originally by the United Soviet Socialist Republic.

Union Electric Company. (1992). The anecdote was related by an employee of Union Electric now called Ameren UE, St. Louis, Missouri.

Zak, P. and S. Knack. (2001). "Trust and Growth," *The Economic Journal,* 111, April, 295-321.

In: The Financial Crisis
Editors: Barbara L. Campos and Janet P. Wilkins
ISBN: 978-1-61209-281-2

Chapter 3

ELEMENTS FOR AN EFFECTIVE MANAGEMENT OF A BUSINESS CORPORATION CRISIS SITUATION

Jorge Morales Pedraza[1,*]
Charasgasse 3/13, A-1030, Vienna, Austria

ABSTRACT

Obviously, any business corporation hopes not to face, under any circumstance, a situation that could cause an important interruption of its business activities, particularly if this situation could origin an extensive covering of the media and the public anger.

A crisis is an abnormal situation, or even perception, which is beyond the scope of everyday business and represents a real threat to the operation, safety and reputation of any business organization. A crisis situation disrupts the way an organization conducts business and attracts significant new media coverage and/or public scrutiny. Typically, these crises have the capacity to have negative financial, legal, and moral repercussions on the business corporation, especially if they are not dealt with in a prompt and effective manner.

A crisis management is defined as the intervention or co-ordination by individuals or teams before, during or after an event to resolve the crisis, minimize losses or otherwise protect the organization; in other words the way in which a crisis situation is managed during its evolution by the top management of a business corporation. It is considered a process designed to prevent or reduce to the minimum possible the damage a crisis can inflict on a business corporation activity and to its stakeholders. When a crisis occurred there is no other choice that to handle it properly with the purpose to reduce to the minimum the negative impact that it can cause to the business corporation activities.

---

[1] Jorge Morales Pedraza has a University Diploma on Mathematics and on Economic Sciences. He is a former diplomatic at Ambassador level for more than 25 years. He was Ambassador and Permanent Representative to the IAEA and to the OPCW and former Ambassador for non-proliferation, disarmament and arms control. He was also university professor in Mathematics Science and invited professor on post- graduate studies in the field of international relations and tutor of several pre-graduate thesis in this field. He was former IAEA Senior Manager for regional and international cooperation in the nuclear field. He has wrote in the last three years more than 30 articles and several chapters of different books in the fields of energy, nuclear power, tissue banking, non proliferation and disarmament published by different international publishers houses, including the IAEA

* E-mail address: jmorales47@hotmail.com or jmorales547@yahoo.com, Celular phone: +43 676 742 8225.

For the better handling of a crisis situation is better to divided it in different phases. These phases are the following:

1) pre-crisis phase;
2) crisis response phase;
3) post-crisis phase.

The pre-crisis phase is concerned with prevention and preparation of the business corporation to handling a crisis situation in the best way possible. The crisis response phase is the one during which the top management of a business corporation must respond to a crisis situation. The post-crisis phase looks for ways to better prepare the business corporation for the next crisis. In this phase the top managers of a business corporation should fulfills all commitments adopted during the crisis.

Keywords: Crisis, Crisis management; Crisis management team; Crisis management plan; Crisis situation; Risk management.

1. Introduction

Obviously, any business corporation hopes not to face, under any circumstance, a situation that could cause an important interruption of its business activities, particularly if this situation could cause an extensive covering of the media and provoke the public anger. The public scrutiny that comes immediately with the media involvement in a crisis situation will affect, in one way or another, the normal operations of any business corporation, and often have a negative impact in its prestige and a substantial destruction of its values. This is especially true when the crisis is not correctly managed before the public opinion and the media. For this reason, the management of a crisis situation is an extremely important task and responsibility for the top management of any business corporation affected by a crisis, particularly for those in charge of providing the necessary and precise information during its development.

Crisis situations are characterized by rich, rapidly changing information flows and by tremendous uncertainty. People in stressful situations and conditions of information-overload tend to resort to ineffective decision-making strategies. It is important to note that providing access to information is not enough to support decision-makers during a crisis situation. Much more effective systems are required for helping those in charge of a crisis situation to evaluate, filter and integrate the great amount of information that the crisis generates. It is important also to understand that a crisis situation is different from a routine situation, in which the traditional information systems for decision support operate and, for this reason, the amount of information to be processed by persons involved in the crisis is much higher, complex and sensitive.

In principle, the top management of a business corporation is used to manage certain types of crisis situation almost daily. However, their abilities are really proven when they have to manage important crises that have the potential of interrupting the normal process of creation of value by the business corporation, the competitiveness, the business in course and, in specific cases, the own survival of the affected business corporation.

Not all crises situation are equal or have the same impact on the operation of a business corporation. They may involve a sudden financial problem, an environmental accident, a defect in a key product or service, injuries to employees or the public, or a natural disaster. Each event is unique, requiring special tactics for handling it properly with the purpose to avoid, or to reduce to the minimum, any negative impact in the business corporation activities. Still, managing a crisis situation requires the respect of certain specific guidelines that helps the top managers to reduce to the minimum the negative effects of a crisis situation on the business corporation activities.

Once the top management of a business corporation has determined that a particular event is a genuine crisis, it is important to understand the following: everything the top management of a business corporation does in response to the crisis will be judged from the first moment. When the crisis becomes public knowledge, the first actions adopted by the top management will be the ones most closely examined by government regulators or by other competent authorities, customers, the media and the public.

The biggest mistake that the top management of a business corporation affected by a crisis can make is its denial. This is true not only for big business corporations affected by a crisis situation, but to medium and small companies as well.

How to reduce to a minimum the effect of a crisis? There are several advices that need to be taken into consideration by the top management of a business corporation during a crisis situation, with the purpose of reducing to the minimum the negative consequences of the crisis. Some of these advices are mentioned in the following paragraphs.

The first advice is to prepare, in advance, a contingency plan in order to minimize the negative impact of a crisis situation in the normal operations of a business corporation. For this reason, it is extremely important to identify and announce, as soon as possible, and to all necessary persons of the business corporation involved in a crisis situation, which is the person authorized to talk about it to the external world, particularly the public, the media and competent government authorities. The person designated to act as the spokesman should be included in any crisis management team that the business corporation decides to create, in order to deal in a crisis situation with the outside world.

However, too often plans are left collecting dust on a shelf in the CEO's office, rarely revised, let alone tested for practicality and effectiveness, thus leaving companies open to consequences of epic proportions. After something happens, some companies make the disastrous mistake of going into a state of denial, hoping the crisis will disappear on its own. But denial turns to anger and then corporate panic—and that's the point when real mistakes are made and irreparable damage to a company's image can take place. (Lewis, 2002)

The second advice to be given to the top management of a business corporation involved in a crisis situation is the following: One of the first decisions that need to be made by the top management of a business corporation involved in a crisis situation is to move quickly during the first hours after the crisis exploded. This move is an important one, because the journalists often develop the structure of their information based on what happens within these hours. Independently of the magnitude of the crisis, it is important to transmit the exact and correct information to the media, the public and to government authorities, since it is extremely dangerous and harmful for the business corporation to try to manipulate the information associated with the crisis. There should be no doubt that these actions will harm the reputation and seriousness of the business corporation involved in a crisis, if the intention or the real fact to hide or manipulate sensitive information associated with the crisis situation is discovered.

The third advice is the following: The top manager of a business corporation involved in a crisis situation should act promptly and with determination.

The fourth advice that needs to be considered in a crisis situation is the use of external consultants for the management of the crisis, because these persons will give the most objective advice to the top management of the business corporation involved in the crisis.

The fifth advice to be given to the top management of a business corporation involved in a crisis is the following: When deciding on the actions that should be taken during a crisis situation, the top management of a business corporation, should not only consider the losses in the short-term, but rather the long-term effects of the crisis in the future of the business corporation.

Any good strategy adopted by the top manager of a business corporation considers that the success of its works should rely upon the trust, goodwill and the confidence of the public, the media and the government regulatory authorities. These are based upon a positive perception of their contribution to society, its procedures, transparency, good management practice, competence of its top managers and of the professionals staff at all levels, as well as by its ethical code and standards.

The proper use of an information system in a crisis situation is an important tool that facilitates that relevant information could reach the appropriate persons in the most effective and quick manner. The appropriate use of an information system in a crisis situation could supply decision makers at all levels with the information they need, at the time they need it.

Supplying decision makers with information regarding a crisis situation requires a number of capabilities that need to be in place when the crisis starts. First, the appropriate data related with the crisis situation must be collected, either during the preparation or pre-crisis phase or during the crisis-response phase. Crisis responders require retrieval information regarding the evolution of the crisis situation and access mechanisms to allow them to find and reduce to the minimum and to essential items the information they need in order to assess properly the situation. Delivery mechanisms are indispensable tools to send the appropriate information to the right people and at the right time.

2. The Definition of a Crisis

A crisis is a major and unpredictable event that threatens to harm a business corporation and its stakeholders. There are several definitions of the term crisis[1]. According with reference 5 a crisis is defined as any global, regional or local natural or event caused by humans or business interruption which is capable of:

1) escalating in intensity;
2) having an adverse impact on shareholder value or the organization's financial position;
3) causing harm to people or damage to property or the environment;
4) falling under close media or government scrutiny;

---

[1] According with reference 9, a crisis takes place when a serious breakdown occurs in a system's ability to cope with a situation, resulting in further escalation or spread of the negative effects that prompted the initial response. Ian Mitroff states "that a major crisis results when there is a serious breakdown or malfunction between people, organizations, and technologies inasmuch as it invalidates critical assumptions that people, organizations, and societies had been making about people, organizations, and technologies". (Mitroff, 2004)

5) interfering with normal operations and wasting management's time and/or financial resources substantially;
6) demoralizing employees;
7) jeopardizing the organization's reputation, products, services or officers and as a consequence thereof adversely affecting its future or survival. (Moorthy, 2006)

In other words a crisis, whether natural or human-made disasters, are events with dramatic and sometimes catastrophic impact in a business corporation or the society.

Although crises are unpredictable, they are not unexpected events that happen all the time. Crises can affect all segments of society such as businesses, churches, educational institutions, scientific institutions and centers, families, non-profits organizations and the government, among others and are caused by a wide range of reasons.

There are three elements that are common to most of the current definitions of the term crisis. These elements are the following (See Figure 1).

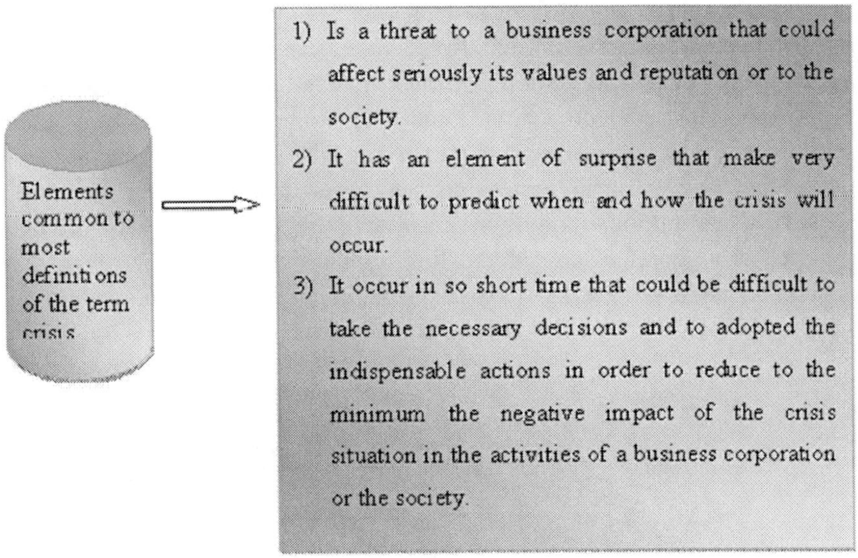

Figure 1.

A crisis in a business corporation can create three related threats:

1) public safety;
2) financial loss;
3) reputation loss.

Some crises, such as industrial accidents and product harm, can result in injuries and even loss of lives. Crises can create financial loss by disrupting operations, creating a loss of market share/purchase intentions, or spawning lawsuits related to the crisis. (Timothy Coombs, 2007)

It is important to understand that independent of the magnitude of a crisis it is easier to manage when the staff of the business corporation feel competent and supported by the top managers.

When dealing with crisis, there is a need for immediate, secondary and follow-up responses. Effective responses not only defuse a particular crisis situation, but also contribute to it control and to reduce to the minimum the negative impact that the crisis could have for the normal operation of a business corporation. For this reason, the top management of a business corporation should be aware of the following: The key to manage a crisis situation successfully is doing as much planning as practical as possible before a crisis starts. The purpose to be achieved is to put the business corporation in the best possible position to respond properly to a crisis situation when it appears and to mitigate such a critical situation as soon as possible in order to reduce to the minimum the negative effect of the crisis.

3. Types of Crises

There are several different types of crises that could occur to a business corporation or the society. These crises can be divided in two big groups (See Figures 2, 3 and 4).

Natural disasters have ranged from sudden cataclysmic weather phenomena—tornados, hurricanes, earthquakes, tsunamis and wildfires—to extremes of temperature and rainfall with resulting droughts or floods. *Man-made disasters* include human conflict up to and including full-scale war, industrial accidents, or widespread environmental destruction. The disruption of the normal lives of an affected population measures the true impact disaster. Infrastructure may be totally disrupted, requiring extensive time to re-establish normal function. Recovery efforts may last years, and local conditions may never be restored to their pre-disaster state. Because disasters are generally considered low probability/high impact events, responsible authorities sometimes defer funding for disaster planning efforts in lieu of current tasks and projects that seem to justify immediate action and attention. (Thompson , 2006)

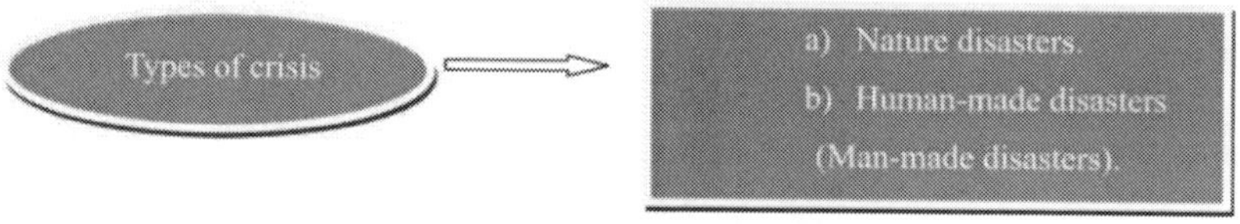

Figure 2.

Figure 3. Nature disaster (Hurricane).

Figure 4. Human-made disaster (Chernobyl accident).

4. Crisis Management

Crisis management can be defined as a systematic attempt by organizational members with external stakcholders to avert crises or to effectively manage those that do occur. (Pearson, 1998) Some others experts define crisis management as a process by which a business corporation involved in a crisis manages a wider impact, such as media relations, and enables it to commence recovery as soon as possible.

Typically, crises have the capacity to have negative financial, legal, and moral repercussions on the business corporation, especially if they are not dealt with in a prompt and effective manner. Over the past several years, high-profile public relations disasters, such as the Firestone tire problems on Ford sport utility vehicles, various product recalls, disturbing product tampering incidents, among others, have thrown an intense spotlight on the issue of crisis management. Indeed, as business corporations have witnessed the damage that poor crisis management can have on business activities, a growing percentage of business corporations and firms have intensified their efforts to put effective crisis management strategies in place.

For this reason, it is important to note that crisis management is not a single event but a process of strategic planning or negative turning point, a process that removes some of the risk and uncertainty from the negative occurrence and thereby allows the organization to be in greater control of its own destiny. A turning point is the moment in time where a crucial decision must be made. Such decisions may include immediate response steps, measures to collect additional information about the scope of an incident, notification of other agencies and authorities who may need to be involved in preventing enlargement of the crisis, and communication with the public about steps to take to protect from further harm. (Thompson, 2006)

Good crisis management gives a business corporation competitive advantage. But protecting the business corporation's reputation, environment, key business assets, employees and other stakeholders is an ongoing challenge, especially in the face of such extreme, complex and constantly changing risks.

A crisis management can be divided in different phases, all of them connected among themselves, conforming a cycle. The crisis management cycle is shown in the following figure (See Figure 5).

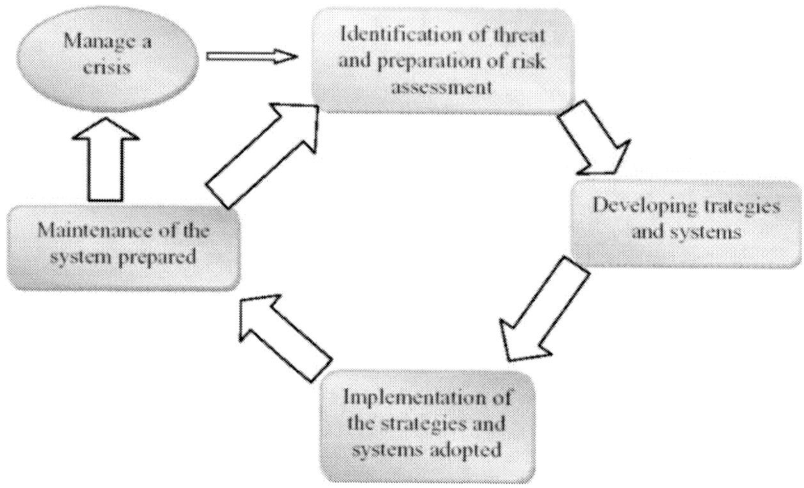

Figure 5. Crisis management cycle.

Crisis management presents problems of large scale and high complexity measurable in numbers of people, amount and diversity of data to be collected, databases and applications involved. Crisis management includes methods to respond to both the reality and perception of the crises.

Lastly, it is important to understand how a crisis situation should be managed and the relative importance of the different components in which the crisis could be divided. Effective crisis management handles the threats sequentially. The primary concern in a crisis has to be public safety. A failure to address public safety intensifies the damage from a crisis. Reputation and financial concerns are considered after public safety has been remedied. Ultimately, crisis management is designed to protect an organization and its stakeholders from threats and/or reduce the impact felt by threats. (Timothy Coombs 2007)

5. Crisis Management Principles

Crisis management is not a fixed process. Every crisis situation is unique and must be managed accordingly. Any set of rules or tools tailored too narrowly in order to deal with a hypothetical crisis situation would be too confining to be of practical value in a real crisis. With the purpose to deal properly with a crisis situation it is indispensable to develop an appropriate strategy prepared on the basis of certain set of principles. There are several principles that should be follows to response, in the most effective manner, to a crisis situation. These principles are the following:

1. Understand Media Interest in a Crisis Situation and How They are Going to Handle It

The media are the prime driver of most crises. It is important to understand that the media wants to know three things about a crisis situation: a) what happened? b) why did it happen? and c) what are you going to do to make sure that it never happens again? If the top manager of a business corporation understands the media's psyche, then he/she will be in the best position to find a solution to the crisis situation that reduce to the minimum possible the negative impact of the crisis in the business corporation activities. They are very much accustomed to the crisis environment in a way that most of the top managers of a business corporation are not. In fact, many reporters are used to work in the crisis environment in a way that most top managers are not very familiar with. For this reason, it is important to understand the media interest, much the way top managers understand customers and competitors.

2. Define the Problem That Cause the Crisis Situation and Determine the Best Strategy to Follow in Order to Reduce to the Minimum the Negative Impact in the Business Corporation Activities

The top managers of a business corporation must be sure that the staff in charge of a crisis situation is addressing the core problem that is affecting the work of the business corporation in the most effective manner. Once the top manager of a business corporation has defined the problem, he/she can best determine the goals of the crisis management process and the strategy to be applied in order to deal with it in the most effective manner. The chosen strategy must be flexible and tailored to the specific crisis situation affecting the business corporation that is trying to solve, rather than be an artificially imposed standard of "good" or "bad" crisis management.

3. Ensure Compliance with All Legal and Regulatory Matters Established by the Competent Government Authorities

The appropriate response by the top managers of a business corporation to a crisis situation should take care of the rules and/or guidelines set by regulatory bodies established by the government to deal with this type of situation. For this reason, top managers should seek for in-house or external expertise on legal/regulatory matters in order to take into account their recommendations to be followed during a crisis response.

4. Manage the Flow of Information Associated with the Crisis

The media often spread information regarding a crisis situation that could be sometimes correct and sometimes vague or even totally or partially incorrect. In case the media spread incorrect information regarding a crisis situation affecting a business corporation, such information can flow back unchecked to internal audiences and distort internal perceptions and proper corporate decision-making. Therefore, top managers should manage, through the crisis management team and in the most appropriate manner, the full flow of information associated with the crisis situation with the purpose to avoid confusion and panic.

5. Assume That the Worst Scenario Will Appears and That the Situation Will Escalate and Get Worse Before It Get Better

Start with the understanding that the crisis situation is likely to get worse before it gets better. Be careful not to be very optimistic or make categorical statements minimizing the negative impact and the consequences of the crisis situation for the business corporation operation in the early stages of a crisis, because this could not reflect properly the real situation of the impact of the crisis in these stages.

6. Remember All Constituencies When Dealing with a Crisis Situation

Use the best technology available within the business corporation in order to communicate directly and effectively to all constituencies. Caught in the pressure of a real crisis situation, business corporations often overlook direct communications to affect constituencies, such as employees and advisory boards, among others.

7. Measure Results Achieve in Managing the Crisis in Real Time

Crises are a dynamic process always moving from one phase to another, if actions are not taken to stop this process. For this reason, it is imperative that top managers of a business corporation affected by a crisis should continually measure the effectiveness of the actions adopted by the crisis management team, with the purpose to adopt any additional measures that are required in order to reduce to the minimum the negative impact of the crisis situation.

8. Identify the Facts That Need to Be Measured

It is important that all facts that need to be measured associated with the evolution of a crisis situation be identified as soon as possible, but in any case before the crisis start to affect the business corporation operations.

9. Avoid Looking or Sounding too Defensive and Resist Being Drawn into a Situation That Could Weakness the Position of the Business Corporation during the Crisis Situation

Always remember that the general approach and attitude adopted by the top manager in front of a crisis situation is as important as any other matter associated or related with the operation of a business corporation.

10. Speedy Communication Is Essential, Especially with the Media and the Public

It is extremely important to designate, as soon as the crisis starts, a spokesman as the unique, main and authoritative source of information regarding the crisis situation, particularly to the external world.

For the correct handling of a specific crisis situation it is important to follows some other principles and standards of behavior. Some of these additional principles are the following (See Figure 6):

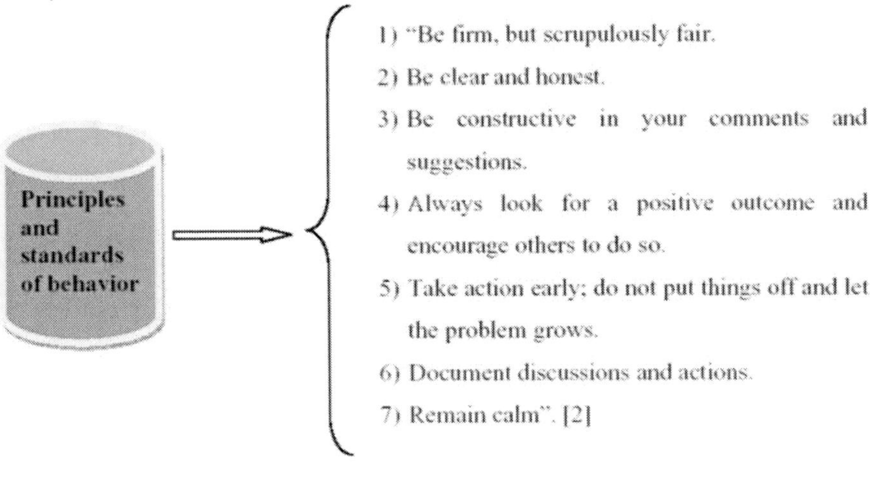

Figure 6.

6. Assemble a Crisis Management Team

A key element of getting a business corporation in the best position to react to, and recover from a crisis situation, is the creation of a crisis management team that is ready to quickly come together to help to find a way out of the crisis. Unless extremely care is taken the crisis situation will take over the entire business corporation operations affecting negatively the day to day activities. A crisis management team must be assigned to handle the crisis situation while others get on with the day to day job of running things in the most efficiency manner and avoiding any new incident that could further affect the business corporation operations.

The crisis management team will be responsible for all aspects related with the crisis and will be in charge of the control and of all communications regarding it. At the same time, the crisis management team will gathering as much information as possible, in order to allow top manager to be well informed about the develop of the crisis and how effective were the actions adopted and implemented by the team. The main purpose of these actions is to reduce to the minimum the negative impact of the crisis in the business corporation activities. It is important to single out that a crisis management team composed of members with prior interactions in previous crisis situation may be more likely to generate and share ideas with one another than a crisis management team composes by members who know less about one another.

During a crisis situation the crisis team manager will serve as key liaison between the top management of the business corporation and the crisis management team. It is important to be aware that crises are not the time for democratic decision making; they are not also the time for autocracy. The crisis team manager and the top management of a business corporation affected by a crisis situation will need to hear the advice of their crisis management team and make decisions in light of — but not necessarily deferring to — those recommendations.

It is important to single out that small business enterprises or companies, who do not necessarily have the resources or personnel to form a crisis management team, can still utilize this process to prepare for a crisis situation. The owner(s) can be their own team, following the same review and issue identification process listed above. It would be suggested that a list of advisors or professionals – such as attorneys, insurance agents, etc. – be made. These people can be called on for their particular expertise not only during the planning stage but also during the development of a crisis. [1]

7. Crisis Management Team Operational Principles

The following are a set of operational principles that should be followed by a crisis management team during the development of a crisis situation:

1) members of the crisis management team must be recruited based on their potential personal contributions and capabilities of operating effectively under extreme circumstances and stress, which is the normal situation that the team will face during a crisis;
2) the crisis management team should be the highest level decision-making authority during a crisis situation and should act as a coordination body within the business corporation. The crisis management team should adopt all possible decisions related with the crisis situation by consensus. However, if the crisis management team should adopt a decision by voting, then each member of the team should have one vote;
3) all information regarding the crisis management team such as its structure, responsibilities, membership and role should be public information and should be considered within the business corporation as a necessary and vital process during a crisis situation. All information regarding the crisis management team should be updated on a regular basis;

4) crisis management team should take decisions bearing in mind the best interests of the business corporation and of all stakeholders and should replace any policy or standard operating procedure in force within the business corporation, as necessary:
5) members of the crisis management team and, particularly their crisis team manager, must be aware that in a crisis situation participation on the activities of the team is their maximum priority;
6) in a crisis situation, the crisis management team should be the only business corporation representative to all internal corporation units and in front of any external organizations affected or impacted by the crisis;
7) the crisis management team must possess all necessary capabilities and capacities to maintain a stable and periodic communication to all external stakeholders requiring information about the evolution and impact of the crisis;
8) the crisis management team must possess or have immediate access to all available information that could be extremely useful to face the crisis and should have the capability to adopt critical time-sensitive decisions related on any issue that may float up from any crisis situation. These include the capacity to evaluate all possible threats to the day to day operations to the business corporation, the risks that should be faced by the business corporation and to establish the probabilities of the impact of a crisis in the business corporation activities;
9) crisis management team should not replace or modify the mandate or responsibility of any other corporation utility groups, which should continue operating as usual. The crisis management team should not change either any existing standard emergency response processes or plans adopted to support the stated mandate and role of those utility groups;
10) crisis management team policies, rules, guidelines and principles must be clear and should not be open to different interpretation. However, these policies, guidelines and principles should be as flexible as necessary in order to respond to any changing corporation needs in a crisis situation;
11) crisis management team must be viewed as an indispensable mechanism to face a crisis situation affecting business corporation activities and should be understood and supported by it top management.

In all crisis situation, it is extremely important to provide up-to-date information to large segments of the public, the media and government authorities, because it permits them to take appropriate actions in helping people to prevent panic, to speed remediation efforts and to prevent new crises or that the current crisis get out of control or provoke public anger or unrest. The following are a group of principles that the spokesman or crisis team manager should follows in a crisis situation:

1) the crisis team manager should be the sole contact point for the media, constituents and for anyone else who needs information from the business corporations regarding the evolution of the crisis situation;
2) the information to be provided to all parties involved or affected by a crisis situation about its evolution should be clear, factual, non-emotional and consistent with law enforcement requirements;

3) the crisis team manager should not have other duties to attend during a crisis situation;
4) the media may be interested in the crisis situation and, for this reason, they may be the most effective way to communicate important information to the outside world;
5) the crisis team manager should talk to the media in a clear, direct and honest manner;
6) the message that the crisis team manager wish to deliver to the media should be drafted and revised before delivered. It is important to identify two or three key points in the message to be delivered to the media and stick to them during the presentation or interviewed.

The crisis team manager is under no obligation to answer specific media questions, particularly if these questions are going to affect the day to day operations of a business corporation in a crisis situation. However, in this case the crisis team manager should be aware that if a story is to run, then he/she may wish to contribute to the story presenting the point of view of the business corporation.

8. The Ten Most Common Mistakes Made in a Crisis Situation

The following is a list of things not to do in case of a crisis situation, according with Robert D. Ramsey[2]. These things, considered as the ten most common mistakes made in a crisis situation, are the following:

1) do not fall apart. Unraveling is no way to hold things together. If you become a basket case, everyone else will, too;
2) do not freeze or become immobilized. Crisis management requires actions, not paralysis;
3) do not run away - physically, mentally or emotionally. The first keys to recovery from mishap are presence and visibility;
4) do not ignore the problem. Pretending bad things did not happen won't make them go away. It will only make you look like a fool on top of everything else;
5) do not deny the obvious. Denial is a form of lying;
6) do not attempt a cover-up. It usually makes things worse;
7) avoid blaming and finger-pointing. These are excuses, not solutions;
8) do not procrastinate. Delaying actions only adds to the problem;
9) do not just keep on doing what you have been doing. When something goes wrong, more of the same is not an antidote;
10) do not give up. Once you surrender, there is no possibility for triumph. During the dark hours, avoiding costly mistakes can give you a leg up on out-lasting disaster. (Ramsey, 2002)

[2] For additional information see reference 7.

9. Crisis Management Plan

The adoption of a crisis management plan is an indispensable tool in the hands of the top managers of a business corporation. The plan will allow top managers to deal properly with a future crisis situation affecting the day to day business corporation operations. A crisis should not catch the top manager of a business corporation unprepared. Almost all eventualities should and can be anticipated and planned for.

There are a number of steps that need to be considered for the preparation of a crisis management plan. The first step is establishing contact. If there are institutions or individuals that are not supportive of the activities of the business corporation involved in the crisis, then it is indispensable for the top manager or the crisis team manager to talk to them and explain what is happening, the possible negative consequences of the crisis, what has been done to reduce to the minimum these negative consequences and why. They might never be convinced but understanding might prevent them from moving from being an informed audience to an active audience in a crisis situation.

The second step is anticipation. Decide as soon as possible what defines a crisis situation for the business corporation in order to react accordingly with this situation occurs. There are always a handful of things that are likely to cause problems or a crisis situation to a particular business corporation. Identify which are these handfuls of things and what are the problems that could cause them. In order to facilitate this task it is important that the following questions:

a) what might go wrong?
b) what outside events might affect the business corporation?
c) what response should be made in each case?

A crisis management plan should be part of an overall safety and emergency preparedness plan and a standard part of the overall strategic planning process adopted by a business corporation. As important as dealing with any emergency situation is dealing with perceptions – what the public thinks happened. This should be planned in the same way you would plan for damage to property or injuries to people. Planning for perception will also protect your company's image/credibility and its ability to recover after a crisis. Too often, companies make the mistake of waiting until a crisis occurs to plan a reaction. This gives the company the smallest chance of surviving the crisis without damage. Be prepared ahead of time and your company has the greatest chance to weather the crisis unharmed. [1]

The crisis management plan should contain, among others, the following elements (See Figure 7).

Crisis management plan should identify what scenarios constitute a real crisis situation and for this reason should consequently trigger the necessary response mechanisms in force within a business corporation. The purpose of these actions is to reduce to the minimum the negative impact of the crisis on the daily operation of a business corporation.

Crisis management plan should not deals exclusively with the immediate response to a crisis, but should ensure that business corporation can continue implementing their main activities in the most effective manner in order to avoid that the crisis stops all business corporation activities.

Summing up can be stated the following: The benefits of managing effectively a crisis situation are numerous and inmediate. They include, among others, the following (See Figure 9).

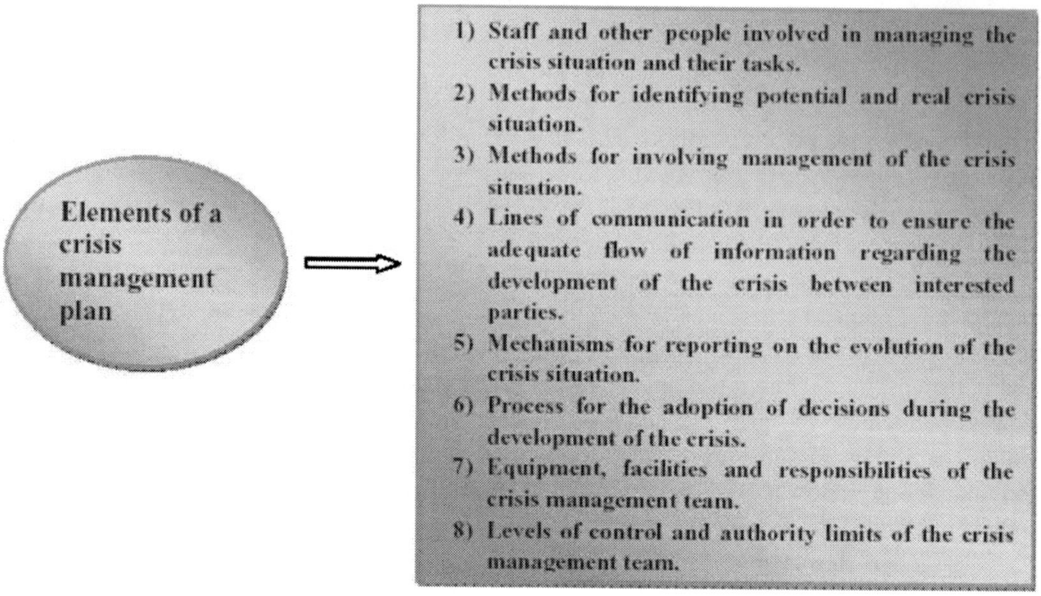

Figure 7.

9.1. Common Weaknesses in Crisis Management Planning

The most common weaknesses in crisis management planning are the following (See Figure 8):

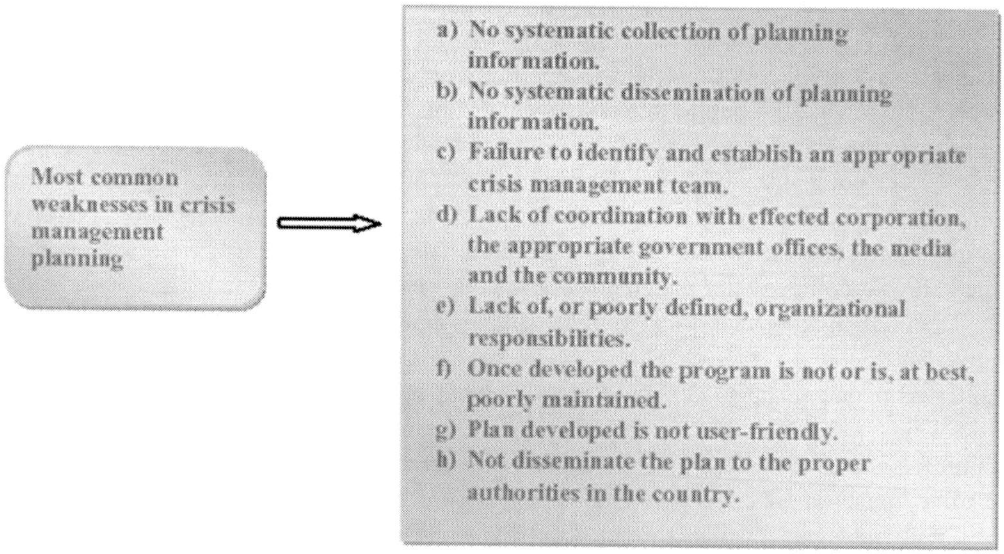

Figure 8.

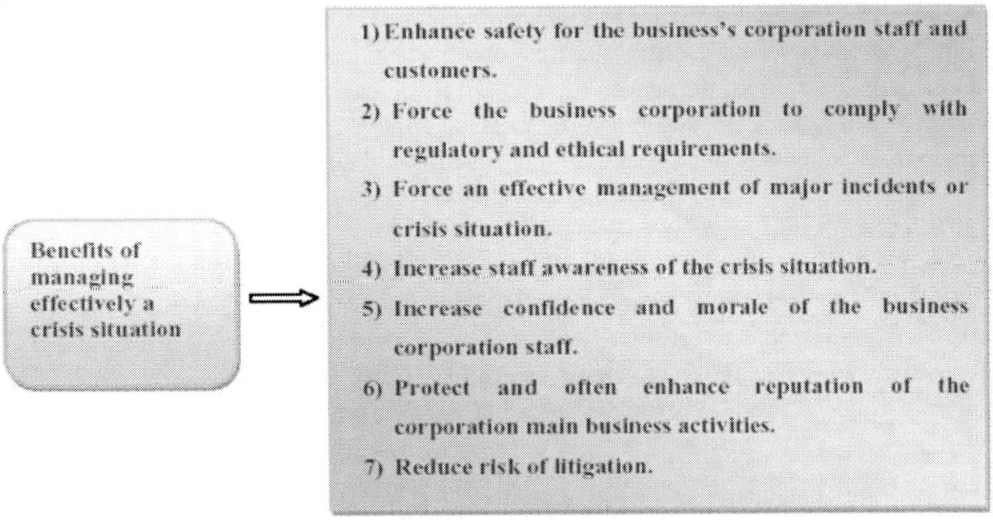

Figure 9.

9.2. Crisis Communication Plan

One of the most important parts of the crisis management plan has to be the crisis communications plan. The top manager of a business corporation hope that if a crisis occurs that no one will notice and he/she will be able to just deal with the issues and fix the problem. Sometimes that happens. Other times the crisis situation reaches the media and the public and suddenly it seems like the entire world knows about the situation facing the business corporation. It is this later case the top manager of a business corporation must be prepared to handle it in order to minimize the negative impact of the crisis.

There is a huge range of different types of communications available in today's world, along with a variety of techniques and means that can be used within a crisis situation. A responsible top manager of a business corporation must learn how to use them, particularly in a crisis situation. In this specific situation the business corporation involved, particularly the staff in charge of communications, should know how to deliver the right message, to the right audiences, in the right way and at the right time.

Communication is so closely tied to whatever action is being taken, that communicators must sit at the table with the crisis response team. Furthermore, communication must be twofold—communicating within the organization to make sure the well being of employees is being addressed, then communicating to outsiders, including the community, suppliers, customers, government authorities and the media. The latter must be used as conduit for getting valid information out to those that are affected. But remind the basic rule in dealing with the press never, never lie and whatever is said must be based on fact. However, apply the rule with a degree of judgment. (Lewis, 2002) The following are the most relevant methods of communication in a crisis situation.

9.2.1. The Spoken Word

Direct speech to the different audiences in case of a crisis situation is not only the most extensively method of communications used, but it is also the most potent one, if use adequately. The reason is very simple. The spoken word combine personality and words and both are essential in case of a crisis situation, but must be used properly.

During the delivery of the speech be sure that it is clear, precise, unhurried, confident and straightforward, in order to transmit to the audience the assurance that the crisis situation is under control and that the negative consequences of it will be minimal.

9.2.2. Written Communications

In case of a crisis situation it is extremely important to write down the message to be delivered in order to be clear, precise and straightforward. In a written communications be sure to clarify your objectives, thoughts and facts before putting them down on paper or on screen and always check the final version carefully. (Heller, 2002)

Before a document is written, be sure that the answers of the following questions are known:

a) why the document should be written?
b) what should be the main content of the document and which is the main message that the document is going to deliver?
c) who are going to read the document?
d) what kinds of actions or reactions are expected from the persons that are going to read the document?

9.2.3. Visual Images

In case that the top manager of a business corporation or a crisis team manager in a crisis situation decides to use visual images to provide information to the audience, be sure to chose well designed images with the purpose to convey powerful meanings. Appropriated pictures speak louder than word and help listeners and readers to retain the message that you would like to delivery.

During the presentation of the images the following steps are important to be followed: First, be sure to make a good introduction of the existing crisis situation, summarizing the main points of the presentation that is going to be delivered to the audience. Second, divide the main points of the presentation in order to single out the main elements of the messages that want to be delivered related with the crisis situation. Third, close the presentation with a summary of what have been said to the audience regarding the crisis situation.

It is extremely important that during the presentation the existing crisis situation is presented to the audience in the clearest way, with the purpose to ensure that the message delivered is well-received by the audience.

9.2.4. Mixed Methods

The combination of the different method of communications mentioned above could be extremely useful in specific crisis situation. However, if one of more of the methods of communication mentioned above is, or is going to be used, then it is important to ensure that all of them are used equally well. The purpose of communication is shown in the following figure (See Figure 10):

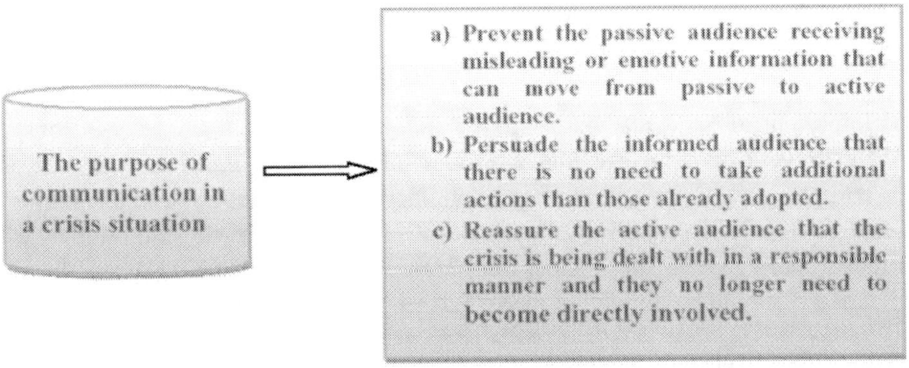

Figure 10.

The credibility of a written document can be destroyed if the material is not well written. A confusing graphic can weaken an important presentation. An organization may create a separate web site to provide relevant information regarding the evolution of the crisis, or designate a section of its current web site for this purpose. The web site should be designed prior to the crisis. This requires the crisis management team to anticipate the types of crises a business corporation could face in the future and the types of information needed for the web site

9.2.5. Internet and Intranet

Of course not placing information on the web site can be strategic in a crisis situation. A business corporation may not want to publicize the crisis by placing information about it on the web site, particularly when the crisis is very small and that stakeholders are unlikely to hear about it from another source. In this case, Intranet sites can be very useful. The reason is very simple. Intranet sites limit access, typically to employees only, though some could include suppliers and customers. Intranet sites provide direct access to specific stakeholders so long as those stakeholders have access to the Intranet.

The communication value of an Intranet site is increased when used in conjunction with mass notification systems designed to reach employees and other key stakeholders. With a mass notification system, contact information (phones numbers, e-mail, etc.) are programmed prior to a crisis. Contacts can be any group that can be affected by the crisis including employees, customers and community members living near a facility. Crisis managers can enter short messages into the system, then tell the mass notification system who should receive which messages and which channel or channels to use for the delivery. The mass notification system provides a mechanism for people to respond to messages as well. The response feature is critical when crisis managers want to verify that the target has received the message. (Timothy Coombs, 2007)

10. PHASES OF A CRISIS MANAGEMENT

Is a crisis an inevitable event or can be avoided by the adoption of specific preventive measures? “A crisis is inevitable in one form or another,” says S. Fink, CEO of Lexicon Communications Corp. But a crisis is not necessarily bad. We view it as a turning point for better or worse—depending on how things are handled. Many have come through a crisis stronger and more highly regarded among employees, shareholders and customers. (Lewis, 2002)

It is important to be aware that a crisis management is not a single event but a process designed to prevent or reduce to the minimum possible the damage a crisis can inflict on business corporation activities and to its stakeholders. When a crisis occurred there is no other choice that to handle it properly with the purpose to reduce to the minimum the negative impact that it can cause to the business corporation activities. For the better handling of a crisis situation it should be divided in three different phases. These phases are the following:

1) pre-crisis phase;
2) crisis-response phase;
3) post-crisis phase.

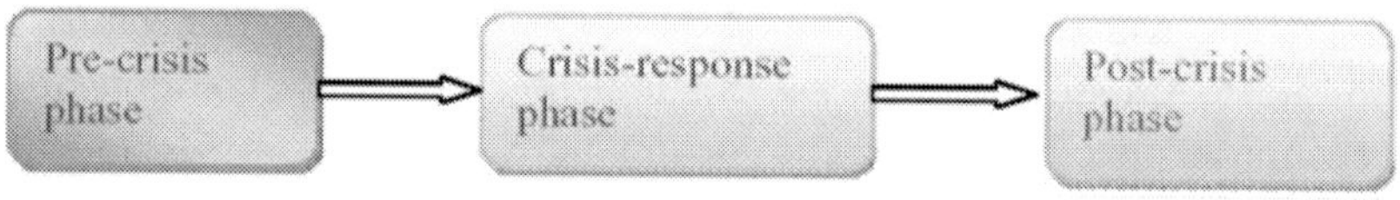

Figure 11.

10.1. Pre-crisis Phase

The pre-crisis phase is concerned with prevention and preparation of the business corporation to handling a crisis situation in the best way possible. The crisis-response phase is the one during which the top management of a business corporation must respond to a crisis situation. This phase include response and mitigation actions. The post-crisis phase looks for ways to better prepare the business corporation for the next crisis. In this phase the top manager of a business corporation should fulfills all commitments adopted during the crisis. This phase include follow-up information and recovery actions.

It is important to single out that all phases of a crisis management are characterized to be an information and communication intensive activity that imposes demanding and precise requirements on the information system and technology to be applied during the crisis. The purpose is to provide the accurate and precise information that is needed by the top managers in charge of the crisis management or by the crisis team manager to take the right and appropriate decisions.

10.1.1. Prevention and Preparation

The pre-crisis is the phase of a crisis management during which the business corporation is put in the best position to react to, and recover from, a crisis situation that could affect it in the future. This phase cover two sub-phases: Prevention and preparation. Prevention involves seeking to reduce all known risks that the business corporation could face that lead it to a crisis. This is part of a business corporation's risk management programme. Preparation involves creating the crisis management plan, selecting and training the crisis management team, and conducting exercises to test the crisis management plan and crisis management team. (Timothy Coombs, 2007)

A business corporation are better prepare to handle crises when they have a crisis management plan that is updated periodically, have a designated crisis management team ready to be called in short notice, conduct periodically exercises to test the crisis management plan and the crisis management team, and pre-draft some crisis messages to be delivery to the press and to the public affected by the crisis situation.

A lot can be done before anything ever goes wrong. All too often top manager of a business corporation believe they can fix a mess affecting the corporation without having a plan to do this, and in some cases this might be true. However, good planning in advance can make even major crises manageable.

Three actions should be implemented in order to minimize the negative impact of a crisis. These are the following (See Figure 12):

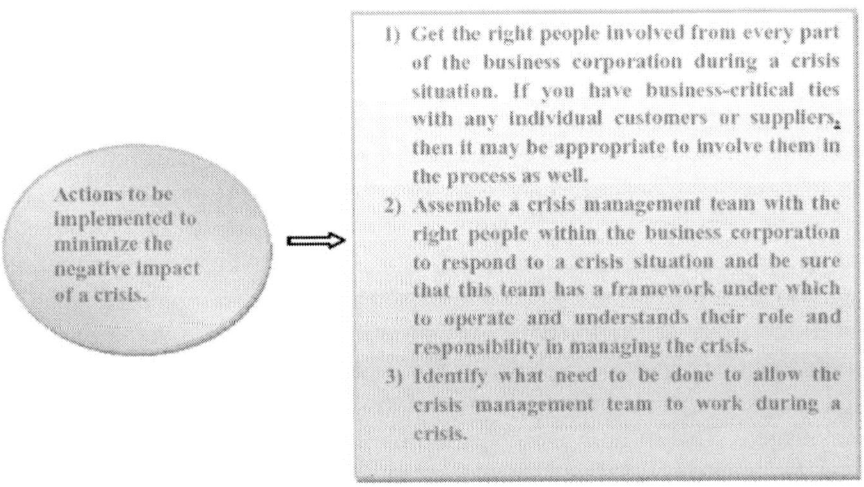

Figure 12.

Before the crisis starts, it is important to build good will and good relations on a daily basis with the media, the public, government regulatory authorities, other business corporations and companies, among others. The way a top manager of a business corporation affected by a crisis situation are treated by the media and the public will be determined in part by what they think of the top manager at the beginning of the crisis situation.

The other vital component of crisis management preparation is the creation of an intelligent and forceful strategy for dealing with various crises, if they do occur at the same time. Many top managers believe that a crisis is something that happens to other top managers but not to them. For these top managers a crisis is a rare and distant even that can quickly be relegated to the back of the mind, and replace it by concern on profit and productivity of the business corporation. But business owners and managers who choose to put off assembling a crisis management preparation do so at significant risk. Indeed, the hours and days immediately following the eruption of a crisis situation are often the most important in shaping public perception of the crisis. A business corporation that has a good crisis management preparation is far more likely to make good use of this time than one that is forced into a pattern of response by on-the-spot improvisation, or one that offers little response at all in the hopes that the whole mess will just go away.

There are two main elements that should be considered during the pre-crisis phase that are unique in order to manage properly a crisis situation. The goal to be achieved is to have employees who know when to report problems to the top managers and a team of senior employees who are ready to react to them. These two elements are the following:

a) creating escalation rules for your employees;
b) creating a crisis management team.

One of the essential elements of a pre-crisis situation is the creation of escalation rules for the business corporation employees in order to allow them to report to the top management of a business corporation any event that could be critical. This is an essential element in crisis prevention, detection and control. Top manager of a business corporation should train their employees in order to bring matters to the attention of senior managers for their analysis and handling as soon as possible, preferably before they become critical. It means not only setting clear rules for when an employee must notify senior managers of a problem detected by him or her, but also empowering staff to feel comfortable reporting concerns to senior managers. It is important to stress that without such rules, a developing crisis situation may go unnoticed by the top manager of a business corporation until it develops, appears in the press and/or turns into a disaster for the business corporation activities.

Planning for possible disasters or crisis situation helps business corporation head off crises altogether with the minimum possible damage[3]. In the worst scenario, planning a crisis will provides the necessary framework for controlling the damage and the negative impact that the crisis situation could has to the normal business cooperation operations involved.

A good image is a terrible thing to lose and this is something that should be in the mind of all top managers. This truth is especially evident among small businesses corporation that are affected by a crisis situation, since they are less likely to have necessary financial resources to weather unpleasant public relations developments. After all, business corporation crises often throw multiple financial blows to the corporation. One of the most widely recognized blows are diminished sales as a result of unfavorable publicity, boycotts, etc. However, this no mean that other blows can have a significant cumulative negative impact in the activities of a business corporation as well. Added expenses often come knocking in the areas of increased insurance premiums, recall/collection programmes, reimbursements, attorneys' fees, and the need to retrieve lost customers through additional advertising.

The pre-crisis phase also includes day-to-day training and exercises activities as part the preparation of the business corporation to successful overcome a future crisis situation. This phase includes the development and revision of plans elaborated to guide the response and to increase available resources indispensable to successful handling a crisis situation. The preparation of a business corporation is enhanced by training crisis responders who may be called into action in a crisis situation.

Emergency preparedness exercises and other planning activities are critically important and could help to mitigate some of the problems that a business corporation involved in a crisis situation could be facing, particularly during the communications and coordination

[3] However, according to the American Management Association, a survey on Crisis Management and Security carried out after the terrorist attack on 11 September 2001 showed "that 51% of the organizations do not have a crisis management in place and 59% to not have written policies and procedures for crisis management". [1]

efforts that might be needed to be carried out in order to reduce to the minimum the negative impact of the crisis. However, in many cases these efforts are not enough. It should be possible to do a better job by learning from past events of similar characteristics. The learning process could take several forms, including post-crisis analysis, in which all relevant personnel of the business corporation involved in the crisis should actively participate.

The following conditions should be used as a guide in order to develop a prioritized list of the worst things that could happen to a business corporation in a crisis situation (See Figure 13):

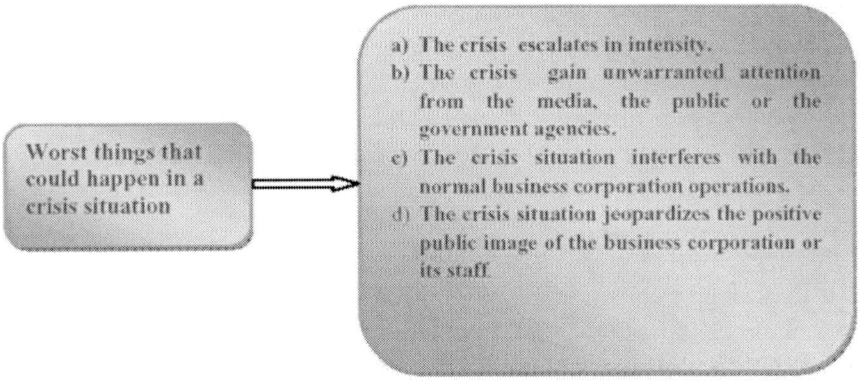

Figure 13.

10.2. Crisis-Response

Crisis-response is the phase of a crisis management in which immediate actions for the protection of life and property are implemented. It requires not only urgent actions in order to reduce to the minimum the negative effect of a crisis situation in the activities of a business corporation, but the coordination in the application of resources, facilities and efforts beyond those regularly available to handle routine problems faced by a business corporation during its normal activities. The crisis-response phase includes actions taken in response to the immediate impact of a crisis as well as actions taken during the buildup of a crisis situation, with the purpose to increase the business corporation's ability to respond effectively to the crisis.

10.2.1. Detection

The first step for the properly managing of any type of crisis situation is detection. It is impossible to react to a crisis situation, if it is not detected by the top management of a business corporation.

The detection includes identifying opportunities for early warning of developing threats that can discriminate between normal background variability and a potential cluster of cases, identifying or developing a reporting mechanism of essential data elements, determining thresholds for actively collecting additional information, and utilizing opportunities to automate surveillance and early warning systems as much as is technologically feasible. (Thompson, 2006)

Crisis responders need to get information regarding a crisis situation as clear, precise, quick and flexible as possible. Information presentation must also be flexible. People need to extract relevant information on a crisis situation rapidly, in order to identify which information is relevant and which information are not, because this type of information varies across individuals and at different phases of a crisis management.

It is important to stress that not all the data collected during a crisis situation needs to be disseminated to all staff involved in it, particularly to all top management of the business corporation. However, what is extremely important is to collect all the information related with the evolution and impact of a crisis situation because this may be invaluable data for an extensive and deep analysis of the development of the crisis situation and the impact in the day to day operations of the business corporation and for training purposes. Some of the staff involved in a crisis situation need to have a general picture of the crisis situation, others need to receive a summary of the information related with the crisis situation, while the rest need to have access to all necessary details related with the evolution and impact of the crisis situation in the business corporation activities.

10.2.2. Mitigation

Mitigation is the second step within the crisis-response in which actions are taken in order to reduce to the minimum possible the negative impact of the crisis on the normal operation of the business corporation, people and property. Mitigation can be a slow and time-consuming process, is administratively intensive and can involve countless situation and location-specific details.

One of the main activities that should be carried during the mitigation process is the education of the community. This type of education, as part of the mitigation efforts, is an important activity because ,in general, people are not familiar with crisis situation, they do not know how to handle it properly and which are the risks involved in this type of situation. For these and another reasons, people tend to believe that a potential disaster, if happens, are not going to affect them. The purpose of the education activities is to educate and prepare people on mitigation measures that should be taken by them in the future under specific circumstances and in order to overcome the difficulties associated with a crisis situation in which these peoples could be involved (See Figure 14).

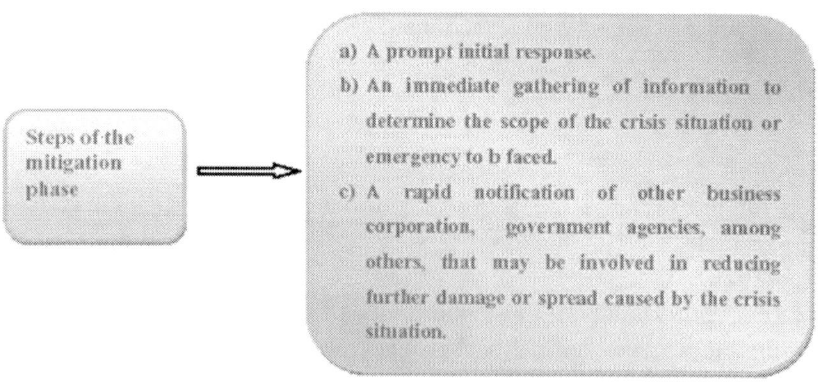

Figure 14.

The implementation of these steps require that all agencies, authorities and governments understand the first few steps that must be taken by each in response to an emergency and that all be prepared to respond immediately, especially in the face of incomplete information about the incident. It is also necessary to have considered the methods by which a rapid assessment may be performed so time will be devoted to collecting only the most essential data. Finally, this phase calls for immediate notifications to be made so that other agencies may prepare to respond if their assistance or resources are needed. (Thompson, 2006)

11. POST-CRISIS PHASE[4]

The crisis management process does not end once a crisis situation has over. Each crisis situation should be carefully evaluated by the top management of a business corporation when it has ended. It is important to look at the media coverage received, the resulting image of your business corporation, short- and long-term programmes to be adopted in order to rebuild image and review position statements for relevance and necessary revisions.

The post-crisis is the phase of a crisis management encompasses short and long-term activities intended, in the first case, to return the business corporation to normal operation and, in the second, to return infrastructure systems to pre-crisis conditions. The post-crisis phase is much slower than the crisis-response phase and involves a substantial administrative work.

The following are some measures that could be taken by the top managers of a business corporation in order to speed the process of recovering from a crisis (See Figure 15):

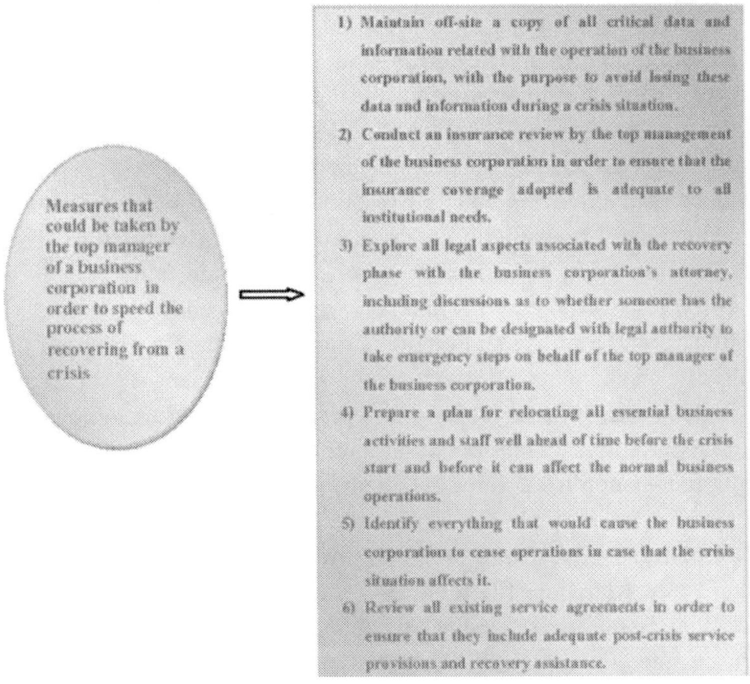

Figure 15.

[4] This phase is also called "Recovery phase".

11.1. Business Recovery Plan

When it comes to turnaround a business recovery plan should be prepared and adopted by the top management of the business corporation. The purpose of the Business Recovery Plan is to effectively execute turnaround crisis management. A business recovery plan must contain, among other elements, the following major areas of information (See Figure 16):

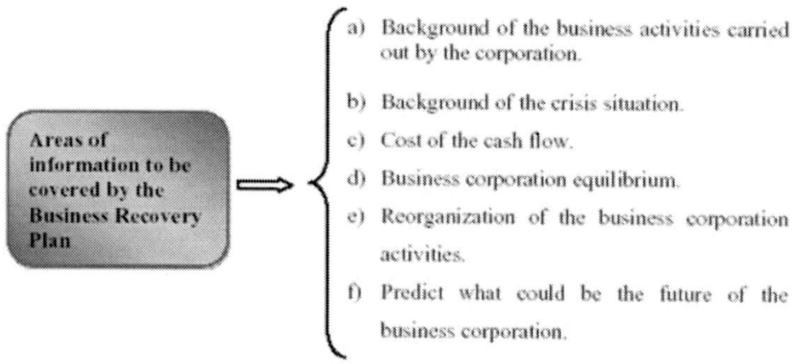

Figure 16.

The Business Recovery Plan should be used primarily by business corporations, advisors and board members, bankers and certain creditors and stakeholders to overcome the negative impact that in the business operations provoke the crisis. It can also be shared with the corporation employees, particularly with those that are in direct relation with the crisis management team. This plan needs to be prepared as soon as possible after the top managers commit to execute a turnaround. The turnaround crisis management strategy adopted by the top management of a business corporation will depend on the quality and on how well the Business Recovery Plan is prepared.

In the particular case of the post-crisis phase associated with a nature disaster, the Business Recovery Plan should include all resources necessary to meet emergency needs for food, water, medical care, housing and restoring damaged infrastructure. This often requires extensive consideration of surge capacity—how to obtain additional supplies and equipment and hospital bed space to replace whatever was damaged in a natural disaster, locate additional healthcare workers to manage the additional injured or diseased persons, and find alternative delivery mechanisms of food, water and equipment, if the usual transportation infrastructure is damaged. In a large-scale disaster, many additional experts in public safety, engineering, transportation, communication and mass care may be needed, as well as specialized equipment, supplies and food. (Thompson, 2006)

In the post-crisis phase, the business corporation should return to their normal activities. However, it is important to be aware of the following: The crisis is no longer the focal point of management's attention but still requires some attention. There is important follow-up communication that is required. First, crisis managers often promise to provide additional information during the development of the crisis situation. The crisis managers must deliver on those informational promises or risk losing the trust of publics wanting the information. Second, the organization needs to release updates on the recovery process, corrective actions adopted, and/or investigations of the origin of the crisis. The amount of follow-up communication required depends on the amount of information promised during the crisis and the length of time it takes to complete the recovery process. If you promised a reporter damage estimate, for example, be sure to deliver that estimate when it is ready. Crisis managers agree that a crisis should be a learning experience. The crisis management effort needs to be evaluated to see what is working and what needs improvement. The same holds true for exercises. The organization should seek ways to improve prevention, preparation and/or the response. .(Timothy Coombs, 2007)

12. Risk Management

One of the main tasks of the top managers of a business corporation is to lead the process of identifying and assessing all potential risks associated to the activities carried out by the business corporation. The objective to be achieved is the reduction of the negative impact of a crisis in case that this situation affects the day to day operation of the corporation.

Risk management is the process of identifying risk, assessing risk and taking steps to reduce risk to an acceptable level. (Stoneburner, Goguen, Feringa, 2002)

Risk management is a management responsibility and encompasses three processes (See Figure 17):

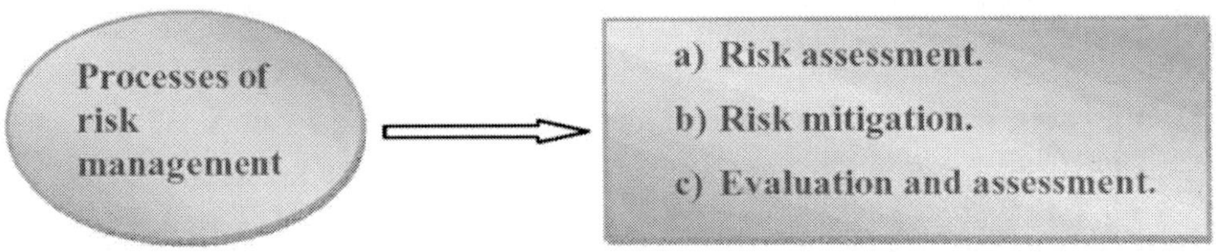

Figure 17.

Risk assessment is the first process in the risk management methodology. Business corporation use risk assessment to determine the extent of the potential threat and the risk associated to specific crisis situation that could affect the day to day operation of the business corporation. The output of this process helps to identify appropriate controls for reducing or eliminating risk during the risk mitigation process. (Stoneburner, Goguen, Feringa, 2002)

The risk assessment must address the following outcomes or consequences associated to a crisis situation:

a) the impact on people;
b) the probability of the crisis event;
c) can mitigation measures prevent or minimize the impact?
d) is the policy defendable and able to withstand public scrutiny?
e) availability and adequacy of resources for risk mitigation;
f) organization's commitment and willingness to mitigate the incident;
g) what would be the effect of failure to act? (Moorthy, 2006)

Risk mitigation is the second process in the risk management methodology. This process involves prioritizing, evaluating and implementing the appropriate risk-reducing controls recommended from the risk assessment process. Because the elimination of all risk is usually impractical or close to impossible, it is the responsibility of senior management and functional and business managers to use the least-cost approach and implement the most appropriate controls to decrease mission risk to an acceptable level, with minimal adverse impact on the organization's resources and mission. (Stoneburner, Goguen, Feringa, 2002)

Risk mitigation is used by senior management of a business corporation with the purpose to reduce all potential risks that can affect the day to day operations of the corporation. This can be achieved through any of the following risk mitigation options:

1) **Risk assumption.** To accept the potential risk or to implement controls to lower the risk to an acceptable level;

2) **Risk avoidance.** To avoid the risk by eliminating the risk cause and/or consequence;

3) **Risk limitation.** To limit the risk by implementing controls that minimize the adverse impact of a threat's exercising vulnerability (e.g. use of supporting, preventive, or detective controls);

4) **Risk planning.** To manage risk by developing a risk mitigation plan that prioritizes, implements and maintains controls;

5) **Research and acknowledgment.** To lower the risk of loss by acknowledging the vulnerability or flaw and researching controls to correct the vulnerability;

6) **Risk transference.** To transfer the risk by using other options to compensate for the loss, such as purchasing insurance. (Stoneburner, Goguen, Feringa, 2002)

The goals and mission of a business corporation should be considered in selecting any of these risk mitigation options. It may not be practical to address all identified risks, so priority should be given to the threat and vulnerability pairs that have the potential to cause significant impact or harm to the activities of the business corporation.

In most business corporation there is a tendency to expand, as much as possible, their operations and business activities. For this reason, business activities will be changed, replaced or updated with newer activities from time to time. In addition, during the life of a business corporation staff changes will occur at all levels and security policies are likely to change from time to time in order to takes into account the new situation that could emerge. All of these changes mean that new risks will float up and risks previously mitigated may again become a concern.

The principal goal of a business's corporation risk management process should be to protect the organization and its ability to perform their mission during any crisis situation that affects the day to day operation of the corporation. For this reason, the risk management process should not be considered as a technical function but as an indispensable management function of the top manager of a business corporation.

13. Actors Involved in a Crisis Management Situation

There are several actors that normally are involved in a crisis management situation. Crisis response requires effective delivery to and use of information by many different actors. The following are actors that normally are involved in a crisis situation[5] (See Figure 18):

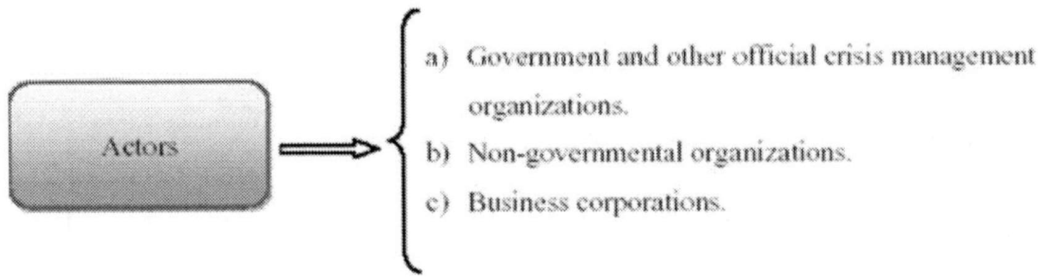

Figure 18.

13.1. Government and Other Official Crisis Management Organizations

Government at all levels may be involved in responding to a crisis situation, particularly in the case of a nature disaster, providing the primary response to most emergencies. The main objectives of the participation of governments organizations in this type of crisis is to provide the resources that are considered necessary to meet the immediately and most urgent needs of the people affected by a nature disaster, as well as to maintain continuity of government activities. In case of human-made disasters, the aim of the involvement of government officials is to ensure to the public that the crisis is under the control of the responsible business corporation staff and that all necessary measures have been adopted in order to reduce to the minimum the negative consequences of the crisis.

13.2. Non-governmental Organizations

Non-governmental organizations might also play a significant role in a crisis response, particularly in the case of nature disasters. After the occurrence of this type of disaster, non-governmental organizations will provide the most urgent and immediately services for the people affected by this crisis situation, as well as to governmental agencies that needs their unique services, if necessary. Frequently, these organizations are pre-identified and are trained to maximize their efficiency and ability to assist in a crisis situation and to be integrated into response-and-relief efforts.

[5] This crisis situation could be produced by a natural disaster or by a disaster produced by human beings.

13.3. Business Corporation

Business corporations can also play an important role in crisis-response phase, as a consequence of a nature or human-made disasters, due to both self-interest and the significant resources they can bring to help under a crisis situation. Business and industry leaders recognize that mitigation and preparedness measures can make a difference in terms of a company surviving a crisis situation, including nature disasters.

14. Other Elements That Characterize a Crisis Situation

There are some additional elements that characterize a crisis situation. These elements are the following:

1) features of a crisis;
2) usual reaction;
3) handle the crisis.

14.1. Features of a Crisis

Three main characteristics are associated to a crisis situation. These are the following:

14.1.1. Someone Is to Blame

A crisis situation that could not have been anticipated but is the result of natural forces could not usually cause a crisis to a business corporation.

However, if the event is the result of someone's negligence, then the business corporation involved could become the focus of the government, media and public attentions and, perhaps public anger. Under this situation the presence of the media is assured and its presence could significantly complicate the management of the crisis.

14.1.2. Something Is at Stake

There is no crisis if there is nothing that can be damaged by the public anger, media exposure or government intervention. For this reason, in the presence of specific situation that could be transformed in a real crisis, the top management of a business corporation involved in it should do what are necessary to avoid any significant damage to the public that can be transformed in anger and social unrest. In this case, it will be almost impossible to avoid the presence of the media and the impact of its presence in the crisis situation.

14.1.3. Someone Finds Out

A crisis only begins when it becomes public. For this reason, the most important responsibility of the top management of a business corporation is to avoid the public knowledge of a situation affecting the business corporation operations. However, in some cases the public knowledge of a crisis situation cannot be avoided. In this case, the top management should take all necessary measures to avoid that the crisis get out of control and be transformed in public anger, or in social unrest affecting the future of the business corporation.

14.2. Usual Reaction

There are two possible public reactions in case of a crisis situation. These reactions are the following (Figure 19):

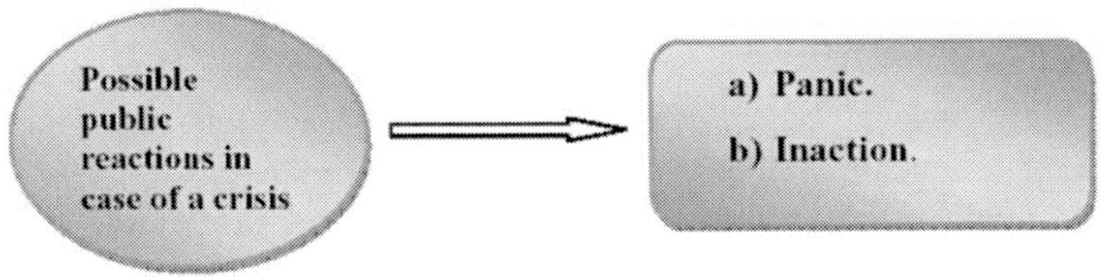

Figure 19.

In the first case, the impact of the crisis could be very negative for the survival of the business corporation affected by the crisis, and the public and the media will react in a very negative manner during the whole development of the crisis. This situation could become a nightmare for the top manager of a business corporation, if the crisis is not well managed by the people in charge of it. In the second case, the consequences of any inaction by the top manager of a business corporation could be the following:

a) public anger grows;
b) rumor replaces facts;
c) government officials, politicians and regulatory and other competent authorities become deeply involved;
d) confidence collapses and crisis spirals out of control.

There should be no doubt that, in this specific case, the survival of the business corporation involved in the crisis will depend on how deep is the damage to the reputation produced by the crisis, its specific characteristics, the public anger and the position adopted by the media and the governments agencies.

14.3. Handle the Crisis

If a crisis becomes inevitable, then the following actions should be taken by the top manager of a business corporation affected by the crisis, in order to avoid unnecessary damage.

14.3.1. Stop Whatever Is Causing the Problem

This might be costly and inconvenient but it removes the cause of the emotion and shows the good will and the sensitive of the top managers of the business corporation and its responsibilities in front of the public. It can also demonstrate a commitment to transparency, good management practice, responsibilities, safety, quality, or whatever else it represents. It is important to trace the main causes of the incident back to their roots. The only way that the problem that caused the crisis situation to a business corporation can be eliminated is by finding and removing that cause.

14.3.2. Put Out Holding Statement

Say something to show that the problem has been identified, it is being dealt with responsibility, there is no cause for public alarm and, most importantly, that the business corporation crisis management team is a reliable source of information on the subject and has the crisis situation under control. This will allow rumors to be stopped before they get into the media or into the knowledge of the public. If the rumors reach this stage, then the incident that caused the crisis situation will be more difficult to be eliminated.

In any case, think very carefully what are going to be said before actions are taken. It is important to understand that responding quickly is not the same thing as being rash or giving in to panic. When the top manager of a business corporation first see a crisis breaking, it is extremely important that he/she take a few moments to collect their thoughts. After collecting their thoughts, the top manager must decide what messages have to be prepared and determine how and where to present them most effectively. It is important that the top manager of a business corporation affected by a crisis situation act in a rapid manner to let the public know that he is in charge and that the crisis management process – and the business corporation—has the crisis situation firmly under control.

14.3.3. Decide on Audiences

Decide in advance who should be informed in a crisis situation. The information to be provided on a crisis situation will depends on the audience. For specific audiences the top manager of a business corporation, or a crisis team manager, should provide the specific information that they need to know. In general, the audiences might be the general public, politicians, parliamentarians, medical and other professionals and businessmen, people close related with the activities of a business corporation, as well as professional bodies and associations, among others. It is also extremely important not to forget to inform the staff of the business corporation what is happening. They are an audience too.

14.3.4. Decide What Will Be Said

Separate messages will probably be needed for different audiences. The audiences will fall into one or more of the following three groups (See Figure 20):

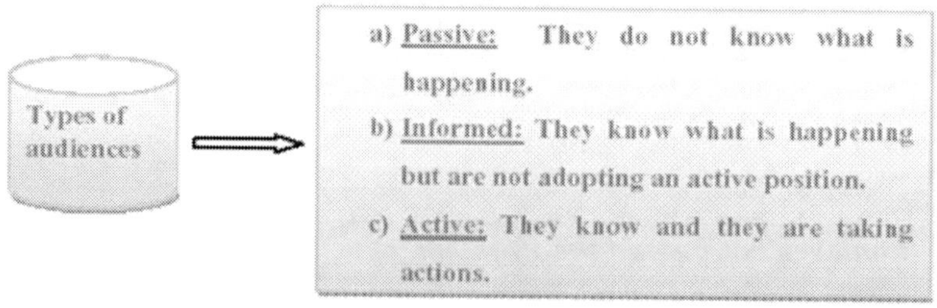

Figure 20.

It is important to single out that the top manager of a business corporation or a crisis team manager can choose how, where and what information regarding a crisis situation will be communicated, but not to whom. For this reason, in any specific crisis situation top manager of a business corporation or a crisis team manager should be prepared to face different kind of audiences in any setting.

15. A Case to Be Studied

The following could be considered as a case study in which some of the above features can be found. Medic Alert is a charity organization that was founded by a parent whose child almost died of an allergic reaction to a food while at a playgroup. The child's allergy had been explained but the information was not passed on. Consequently, when the child became unconscious no one recognized the cause and it was only by chance that it was saved. Medic Alert provides a database of the medical conditions and current treatment for hundreds of thousands of people. People at risk wear a disc bearing a personal identification number and a 24-hour emergency telephone number. It ensures that if that person is taken ill or is injured or cannot provide information about it illness, then vital information can be given through a disc in their possession, which might save their lives. Since the use of this disc hundreds of lives have been saved.

Obviously, the more people who know about it the more can benefit. The charity organization decided that television was the ideal media for spreading the message in order to reach as much people as possible. They approached the producers of several popular television drama series with true stories of people who would have been unwittingly killed by routine treatment when they were unconscious but at the last minute someone noticed the badge and called the emergency number. They stressed the dramatic nature of this moment away from death.

The result of the different actions adopted was that Medic Alert was featured in three television series - a hospital drama and two police dramas all with an audience of several million. The advantage of using fictional television or radio series is not only publicity but, in cases where there are ethical or religious objections, the argument itself can become part of the program story line.

Conclusion

It is obvious that any business corporation hopes not to face, under any circumstance, a situation that could cause an important interruption of its normal operation, particularly if this situation could provoke an extensive covering of the media and public anger. The public scrutiny that come immediately of the media involvement in a crisis situation will affects, in one way or another, the normal operation of the business corporation, and often has a negative impact in its prestige and a substantial destruction of values, especially when the crisis situation is not correctly managed before the public opinion and the media.

If a crisis situation become inevitable, then it is extremely important to understand that everything that the top manager of a business corporation does in response to the crisis will be judged from the first moment. When the crisis situation becomes public, the first actions adopted by the top management will be the ones most closely examined by government regulators, customers, the media and the public. For this reason, the preparation in advantage of a contingency plan could helps to minimize the negative impact of a crisis situation to the business corporation operations.

Identify and announce, as soon as possible, and to all necessary staff of the business corporation involved in a crisis situation, which is the person authorized to talk about the crisis to the external world, particularly to the public, to the media and to competent government authorities. At the same time, constitute a crisis management team to handle the crisis. If necessary, use external consultants for the management of the crisis, because these persons will give the most objective and impartial advice to the top management of the business corporation involved in the crisis, as well as to the crisis team manager.

When a crisis occurred then it must be handled properly with the purpose to reduce to the minimum the negative impact that it can cause to the business activities of the corporation involved. For the better handling of a crisis situation it should be divided in different phases: a) pre-crisis phase; b) crisis-response phase; and c) post-crisis phase. The top manager of a business corporation involved in a crisis situation should ensure that all of these phases are well prepared and understood by all staff involved, with the purpose to reduce to the minimum the negative impact of the crisis in the future of the business corporation.

Acknowledgment

I would like to thanks the contribution made by the Master Lisette Morales Meoqui, from Dialog & Konzept Financial Services, Austria, for her support in the preparation of this paper, to Magister Jorge Morales Meoqui, currently carrying out Doctorate studies in the field of economics in the Vienna University of Economics and Business Administration, Institute for International Economics and Development for his comments on the first draft and to Master Juan Carlos Portal, from Ceiba Investment Ltd, U.K., for his assistance in the selection of the bibliography and on his comments to the first draft.

References

A Guide to Developing Crisis Management Plans; NTA's Market Development Council; March 2000 (Updated January 2003).

Heller, R.; *Manager's Handbook*, Dorling Kindersley Limited, London, 2002.

Lewis, L.; *Courting Disaster*; California Grocer; August 2002.

Mitroff, Ian, I.; *Crisis Leadership: Planning for the Unthinkable,* Hoboken, NJ: John Wiley and Sons, Inc.; 2004.

Moorthy, A. K.; *Dynamic Business Continuity Planning for Enhanced Loss Prevention,* ASIS International; 2006.

Pearson, C. M. and Clair; J. A. *Reframing Crisis Management*, Academy of Management Review 23, 1998.

Ramsey, R. D.; *Top-10 CM mistakes*; Supervision, Vol. 65, Issue 10, October 2004.

Stoneburner, G.; Goguen, A.; Feringa, A.; *Risk Management Guide for Information Technology Systems*; Recommendations of the National Institute of Standards and Technology; 2002.

Thompson, D. F. and Louie, R. P.; *Cooperative Crisis Management and Avian Influenza. A Risk Assessment Guide for International Contagious Disease Prevention and Risk Mitigation;* Center for Technology and National Security Policy; March 2006.

Timothy Coombs, W.; *Crisis Management and Communications*; Institute for Public Relations; October 30, 2007.

In: The Financial Crisis
Editors: Barbara L. Campos and Janet P. Wilkins
ISBN: 978-1-61209-281-2

Chapter 4

A CONTRIBUTION TO THE POSITIVE THEORY OF THE PUBLIC DEBT

Emanuele Canegrati *
Catholic University of Milan, Italy

ABSTRACT

Are social security transfers associated with public debt? In this paper I discuss a probabilistic voting model, where two office- motivated candidates must choose a debt issuance policy in order to win the election. Under the assumption that the political power of a cohort depends positively on the level of leisure, I demonstrate that, in equilibrium, the burden of debt, represented by the taxes levied to repay it, is borne by the younger cohort. Furthermore, the tax system induces the old to retire and allows them to receive a positive social transfer, paid by the young.

Keywords: public debt, probabilistic voting theory, overlapping generations model.

1. INTRODUCTION

Is the burden of public debt equally borne by all the cohorts? This paper discusses an overlapping generations model, where two political candidates have to choose a debt issuance policy in order to maximise the probability of winning the election. The structure of the model is based on the Probabilistic Voting Theory (Coughlin, 1992, Lindbeck and Weibull, 1987), but it assumes that the density function, which describes the distribution of the political preferences of voters, is a function of leisure, following the Single-mindedness idea proposed by Mulligan and Sala-i-Martin, 1999 and Profeta, 2002. I demonstrate that, in equilibrium, the government chooses the effective marginal tax rates on labour in order to satisfy the most powerful, or single-minded, cohort. This policy generates distorting effects on the labour supply and the burden of public debt, represented by the taxes levied by the government to repay the debt, is not equally borne by all the cohorts. Therefore, the need to

* E-mail address: emanuele.canegrati@unicatt.it. (Corresponding author)

levy taxes to repay the debt has redistributive effects, and I demonstrate that the old, being the most powerful group, receive a positive social security transfer, while the young must borne the entire burden of taxation. Summarizing, the debt issuance has real economic consequences on cohorts' welfare, both in terms of efficiency and equity.

The paper is organized as follows: section two discusses the literature on public debt, section three introduces the basic version of the model, section four illustrates the results of numerical simulations and section five concludes.

2. Public Debt Issuance and Ricardian Equivalence

The Ricardian Equivalence is one of the most debated theory in the history of Economics. Originally proposed, to be rejected later, by the 19-th century English economist David Ricardo, 1951, the theory achieved its peak of fame with Robert Barro's works, 1974, 1979. It was Barro himself who, in his On the Determination of the Public Debt, described the Ricardian equivalence theorem as

> the proposition that shifts between debt and tax finance for a given amount of public expenditure would have no first-order effect on the real interest rate, volume of private investment, etc.

Furthermore, in his famous paper Are Government Bonds Net Wealth? he wrote in his conclusions

> The basic conclusion is that there is no persuasive theoretical case for treating government debt, at the margin, as a net component of perceived household wealth

and that

> in the case where the marginal net-wealth effect of government bonds is close to zero (...) fiscal effects involving changes in the relative amounts of tax and debt finance for a given amount of public expenditure would have no effect on aggregate demand, interest rates, and capital formation.

This last conclusion is a negation of the Keynesian theory, which states that fiscal policies have real effects on the economy, according to the Keynesian multiplier mechanism. Furthermore, Barro's theory contradicts the theory of public debt which was developing in the 70's by prominent economists such as Buchanan, Modigliani and Diamond. Other economists, who were working on the theory of social security systems, such as Feldstein felt criticized. In 1976 Feldstein demonstrated that, even in the presence of an economy characterized by the existence of bequests, the government debt reduces private savings and the equilibrium rate of capital to labour if, unlike Barro's assumptions, the economy has not a constant population and the growth of rate is different from zero. If the rate of interest on public debt is lower than the growth of rate, Feldstein argued, then the first generation do not increase the amount of bequest, knowing that no future generation must borne the burden of the debt. But, what if the rate of interest on public debt exceeds the rate of growth of the economy? Even in this case, when the difference between the two greatnesses is small,

Feldstein demonstrated that the first generation increases its bequest by less than the value of the debt. Another critique to Barro's theory came from Buchanan, 1976, who accused Barro to have misread Ricardo's original statement and, even though he was himself accused by O'Driscoll, 1977, not to have understood that the actual Ricardo's position, was against rather than proRicardian equivalence. At the beginning of the '80s first econometric studies, aiming to discover whether the Ricardian Equivalence actually held, was conducted by Feldstein, 1982,, who concluded that changes in government spending or taxes do have substantial effects on the aggregate demand, denying Barro's equivalence. Instead, the Monetarist Theory spoused the Ricardian Equivalence; McCallum, 1984, validated the monetarist hypothesis according to which a constant, positive budget deficit can be maintained permanently and without inflation, if it is financed by government bonds rather than taxation. Nevertheless, as himself recognized, uncertainty, distribution effects and multiple interest rates are ignored by Barro's theory but, in his opinion, this did not represent a problem since "the same is true of most policy-oriented theoretical analyses of macroeconomic phenomena ", then "there is no apparent reason why the issue at hand requires a different type of treatment "and "it would seem satisfactory to neglect them there, as elsewhere". Some years later, Feldstein, 1988, demonstrated that Barro's theory did not hold even in the presence of non-negative bequests, considering individuals who are uncertain about their future incomes and, as a consequence, modify their consumption path, raising consumption at present time as a consequence, for instance, of a tax cut. Hence, the reaction to a change in fiscal policies is non-neutral but consumption modifies according to the sign of the policy.

3. The Basic Model

I consider an overlapping generations model, where each generation lives only for two periods, the youth and old age. Generations are unlinked, meaning that there is no possibility to leave bequests. Individuals consume all the available income earned at a given period of time. It is not possible neither to save nor to borrow money.

Then, at time t, let a population of size one be partitioned into two generations of workers, the young, representing the generation born at time t and denoted by i-, and the old, representing the generation born at time t - 1 and who denoted by i--1. I use capital letters to indicate a cohort and small letters to indicate single individuals belonging to that cohort. The size of a cohort does not change over time. Each worker has to decide how to divide his endowment of time t between labour and leisure, denoted by l.

Furthermore, I assume that the old and the young are identical in every respect except two:

Axiom 1 *the weight that the old workers attach to leisure,* $\psi^{\tau-1}$*, is greater than the weight that the young workers attach,* $\psi^{\tau-1}$*. That is,* $\psi^{\tau-1} > \psi^{\tau-1} >$ *_1.*

This axiom states that the old desire to supply less labour than the young, for example because time endowments reduces with age, due to health considerations (Profeta, 2002).

Axiom 2 *the wage of the old is higher than the wage of the young. That is:* $w^{\tau-1} > w^{\tau}$*. The wage rate does not change over time.*

These assumptions are supported by a robust empirical evidence. For a complete discussion on the differences in preferences for leisure and wages, see Canegrati, 2008, Mulligan and Sala-i-Martin, 1999 and Gruber and Wise, 1999.

3.1. Timing of the Game

The game takes place on a time horizon which runs from time $t - 1$ to time $t + 2$. At every period two political candidates, A and B, run for the election. Candidates aim to maximize the probability of winning, or, equivalently, the number of votes[1]. Both of them have an ideological label (e.g. "Democrats" or "Republicans"), exogenously given.

In the first stage of the electoral game, the candidates, simultaneously and independently, announce (and commit to) a policy vector, q^A and q^B.

In the second stage the election takes place. A candidate wins if and only if it obtains the simple majority of votes; in case of a tie a coin is tossed, in order to decree the winner.

Finally, in the third stage, workers choose their amount of leisure, given the policies chosen by candidates.

3.2. Utility Functions and Budget Constraints

A representative worker of generation τ - 2 at time t - 1 has the following lifetime quasi-linear utility function[2]:

$$U^{\tau-2} = c_{t-1}^{\tau-2} + \psi^{\tau-2} \log l_{t-1}^{\tau-2} \tag{1}$$

where $c_{t-1}^{\tau-2}$ denotes the consumption at time $t - 1$, $l_{t-1}^{\tau-2}$ leisure at time $t - 1$ and $\psi^{\tau-2}$ is a parameter representing the preference of the worker for leisure, $\psi^{\tau-2} \in (0, 1)$.

The worker consumes all his labour income:

$$c_{t-1}^{\tau-2} = \left(w^{\tau-2}(1-\tau) + a_{t-1}^{\tau-2}\tau\right)\left(\bar{t} - l_{t-1}^{\tau-2}\right) \tag{2}$$

where ω^{T-2} is the unitary wage per hour worked, T the tax rate on labour income (equal for every group and constant over time) and $a_{t-1}^{\tau-2}$ the tax credit.

Similarly, a representative worker of generation 7 – 1 at time t – 1 has the following lifetime utility function:

[1] Lindbeck and Weibull,1987 and Dixit and Londregan, 1996, demonstrate that the Nash equilibrium obtained if candidates maximize their vote share is identical to that obtained when candidates maximize their probability of winning.

[2] A quasi-linear utility function entails the non existence of the income effect.

$$U^{\tau-1} = c_{t-1}^{\tau-1} + \psi^{\tau-1} \log l_{t-1}^{\tau-1} + \beta(c_t^{\tau-1} + \psi^{\tau-2} \log l_t^{\tau-1}) \tag{3}$$

Since at time $t-1$ a worker of generation τ–1 knows that at time t will be old, their utility function includes the leisure of the next period, weighted by a discount factor $\beta \in (0, 1)$.

The worker's inter temporal budget constraint is given by:

$$\begin{aligned} c_{t-1}^{\tau-1} + \beta c_t^{\tau-1} &= (w_{t-1}^{\tau-1}(1-\tau) + a_{t-1}^{\tau-1}\tau)(\overline{t} - l_{t-1}^{\tau-1}) \\ &+\beta((w_t^{\tau-1}(1-\tau) + a_t^{\tau-1}\tau)(\overline{t} - l_t^{\tau-1}) - b_t) \end{aligned} \tag{4}$$

where b_t represents the per capita share of public debt.

A representative worker of generation τ at time t has the following utility function:

$$U^{\tau} = c_t^{\tau} + \psi^{\tau} \log l_t^{\tau} + \beta(c_{t+1}^{\tau} + \psi^{\tau} \log l_{t+1}^{\tau}) \tag{5}$$

under the budget constraint

$$\begin{aligned} c_t^{\tau} + \beta c_{t+1}^{\tau} &= (w_t^{\tau}(1-\tau_L) + a_t^{\tau}\tau)(\overline{t} - l_t^{\tau} - b_t) \\ &+\beta((w_{t+1}^{\tau}(1-\tau_L) + a_{t+1}^{\tau}\tau_L)(\overline{t} - l_{t+1}^{\tau}) + (1+r)b_t) \end{aligned} \tag{6}$$

where r represents the interest rate paid on public debt.

Finally, a representative worker of generation $\tau + 1$ at time $t + 1$ has the following utility function:

$$U^{\tau+1} = c_{t+1}^{\tau+1} + \psi^{\tau+1} \log l_{t+1}^{\tau+1} + \beta(c_{t+2}^{\tau+1} + \psi^{\tau+1} \log l_{t+2}^{\tau+1}) \tag{7}$$

under the budget constraint

$$\begin{aligned} c_{t+1}^{\tau+1} + \beta c_{t+2}^{\tau+1} &= (w_{t+1}^{\tau+1}(1-\tau) + a_{t+1}^{\tau+1}\tau)(\overline{t} - l_{t+1}^{\tau+1}) \\ &+\beta((w_{t+2}^{\tau+1}(1-\tau) + a_{t+2}^{\tau+1}\tau)(\overline{t} - l_{t+2}^{\tau+1})) \end{aligned} \tag{8}$$

3.3. The Government

The macroeconomic literature on public debt has almost always considered the existence of a benevolent government, which aims to maximize a Social Utility Function by choosing the optimal tax rate on labour, subject to a budget constraint where the public expenditure is financed either by current taxation or the issue of public debt. For instance, Barro, 1979, uses a budget equation where, in each period, interest payments during period t are assumed to apply to the stock of debt outstanding at the beginning of the period (*see equation 1*).

Furthermore, Barro considers an overall budget constraint where the present value of government expenditure, aside from interest payments, added to the initial amount of debt is equated to the present value of taxes over an infinite horizon of time (*see equation 2*). Barro's idea to consider an infinitely living government which chooses tax rates at every period is unrealistic and at odds with reality, where, instead, governments are short-lived and remain in charge only for few years. Reality gets even worse if we consider that governments are often office-seekers, rather than benevolent. Under these assumptions, the results achieved by Barro's theory are no longer ensured. To demonstrate the limits of Barro's theory I use the Probabilistic Voting Theory, considering a model where candidates act in order to maximize the probability of being elected. The policy vector they have to choose is written as follows:

$$\mathbf{q} = (a_{t-1}^{T-2}, a_{t-1}^{T-1}, a_t^{T-1}, a_t^{T}, a_{t+1}^{T}, a_{t+1}^{T+1})$$

encompassing tax credits a at time t –1, just before the debt issuance, at time t, when the debt is issued, and at time t + 1 when the debt is paid back. I assume that from period t + 2 on, tax credits are the same as at t – 1.

Hence, I introduce government's budget equations for every period of time.

3.3.1. At Time t – 1

$$n^{T-2}\tau(\bar{t} - l_{t-1}^{T-2})(w_{t-1}^{T-2} - a_{t-1}^{T-2}) + n^{T-1}\tau(\bar{t} - l_{t-1}^{T-1})(w_{t-1}^{T-1} - a_{t-1}^{T-1}) = 0 \quad (9)$$

where $n^{T-2}\tau(\bar{t} - l_{t-1}^{T-2})(w_{t-1}^{T-2} - a_{t-1}^{T-2})$ represents the total revenues generated by the taxation of generation $T-2$ at time t–1 and $n^{T-1}\tau(\bar{t} - l_{t-1}^{T-1})(w_{t-1}^{T-1} - a_{t-1}^{T-1})$ the total revenues generated by the taxation of generation $T-1$.

Since revenues are proportional to the amount of labour, the taxation generates inefficiencies, since it distorts workers' decisions on the amount of labour to supply. I also assume that the contingent budget surplus is entirely used to pay a public transfer scheme, e.g. pensions to the retirees.

3.3.2. At time t

At time *t,* the government issues an amount of debt equal to *Bt*, seen as an one-period, single-coupon bonds and issued at par, allocated among voters who get exactly the same share of debt, bt. The government's budget equation is:

$$n^{T-1}\tau(\bar{t} - l_t^{T-1})(w_t^{T-1} - a_t^{T-1}) + n^{T}\tau(\bar{t} - l_t^{T})(w_t^{T} - a_t^{T}) + B_t = 0 \quad (10)$$

3.3.3. At time t + 1

At time t + 1 the government repay the real interests on debt, *rBt*, and the principal. The budget equation may be written as:

$$n^{\tau}\tau(\bar{t}-l^{\tau}_{t+1})(w^{\tau}_{t+1}-a^{\tau}_{t+1})+n^{\tau+1}\tau(\bar{t}-l^{\tau+1}_{t+1})(w^{\tau+1}_{t+1}-a^{\tau+1}_{t+1})=(1+r)B_t \tag{11}$$

3.4. EQUILIBRIUM

I solve the competition game, starting from period t –1, where a representative worker of generation $T-2$ solves the following optimization problem:

$$\max_{\{l^{\tau-2}_{t-1}\}} U^{\tau-2}=c^{\tau-2}_{t-1}+\psi^{\tau-2}\log l^{\tau-2}_{t-1}$$

$$s.t.\ c^{\tau-2}_{t-1}=w^{\tau-2}((1-\tau)+a^{\tau-2}_{t-1}\tau)(\bar{t}-l^{\tau-2}_{t-1})$$

Solving with respect to lt $l^{\tau-2}_{t-1}$ obtain the optimal amount of leisure:

$$l^{\tau-2*}_{t-1}=\frac{\psi^{\tau-2}}{w^{\tau-2}((1-\tau)+a^{\tau-2}_{t-1}\tau)} \tag{12}$$

Substituting 11 into 1 I obtain the Indirect Utility Function:

$$V^{\tau-2}=\bar{t}w^{\tau-2}((1-\tau)+a^{\tau-2}_{t-1}\tau)-\psi^{\tau-2}+\psi^{\tau-2}\log\psi^{\tau-2}-\psi^{\tau-2}\log(w^{\tau-2}((1-\tau)+a^{\tau-2}_{t-1}\tau)) \tag{13}$$

I do the same for a representative worker of generation $\tau-1$:

$$\max_{\{l^{\tau-1}_{t-1},l^{\tau-1}_{t}\}} U^{\tau-1}=c^{\tau-1}_{t-1}+\psi^{\tau-1}\log l^{\tau-1}_{t-1}+\beta(c^{\tau-1}_{t}+\psi^{\tau-2}\log l^{\tau-1}_{t})$$

$$s.t.\ c^{\tau-1}_{t-1}+\beta c^{\tau-1}_{t}=w^{\tau-1}((1-\tau)+a^{\tau-1}_{t-1}\tau)(\bar{t}-l^{\tau-1}_{t-1})+\beta((\bar{t}-l^{\tau-1}_{t})w^{\tau-1}((1-\tau)+a^{\tau-1}_{t}\tau)-b_t)$$

$$l^{\tau-1*}_{t-1}=\frac{\psi^{\tau-1}}{w^{\tau-1}((1-\tau)+a^{\tau-1}_{t-1}\tau)} \tag{14}$$

$$l^{\tau-1*}_{t}=\frac{\psi^{\tau-1}}{w^{\tau-1}((1-\tau)+a^{\tau-1}_{t}\tau)} \tag{15}$$

$$V^{\tau-1}=\bar{t}w^{\tau-1}((1-\tau)+a^{\tau-1}_{t-1}\tau)-\psi^{\tau-1}+\psi^{\tau-1}\log\psi^{\tau-1}-\psi^{\tau-1}\log w^{\tau-1}(((1-\tau)+a^{\tau-1}_{t-1}\tau))$$
$$+a^{\tau-1}_{t-1}\tau)+\beta\bar{t}((1-\tau)+a^{\tau-1}_{t}\tau)+\beta\psi^{\tau-2}(\log\psi^{\tau-1})-\psi^{\tau-1}\log(w^{\tau-1}((1-\tau)+a^{\tau-1}_{t}\tau)-b_t) \tag{16}$$

The same for a representative worker of generation τ

$$\max_{\{l_t^{\tau-1}, l_{t+1}^{\tau-1}\}} = c_t^{\tau} + \psi^{\tau} \log l_t^{\tau} + \beta(c_{t+1}^{\tau} + \psi^{\tau-1} \log l_{t+1}^{\tau})$$

$$s.t.\ c_t^{\tau} + \beta c_{t+1}^{\tau} = w^{\tau}((1-\tau)+a_t^{\tau}\tau)(\overline{t}-l_t^{\tau}) - b_t + \beta((\overline{t}-l_{t+1}^{\tau})w^{\tau}((1-\tau)+a_{t+1}^{\tau}\tau)+rb_t)$$

$$l_t^{\tau *} = \frac{\psi^{\tau}}{w^{\tau}((1-\tau)+a_t^{\tau}\tau)} \tag{17}$$

$$l_t^{\tau *} = \frac{\psi^{\tau}}{w^{\tau}((1-\tau)+a_t^{\tau}\tau)} \tag{18}$$

$$\begin{aligned} V^{\tau} &= \overline{t}w^{\tau}((1-\tau)+a_t^{\tau}\tau) - \psi^{\tau} + \psi^{\tau}\log\psi^{\tau} - \psi^{\tau}\log w^{\tau}(((1-\tau)+a_t^{\tau}\tau)) \\ &+a_t^{\tau}\tau) - b_t + \beta\overline{t}((1-\tau)+a_{t+1}^{\tau}\tau) + \beta\psi^{\tau}(\log\psi^{\tau}) - \psi^{\tau}\log(w^{\tau}((1-\tau)+a_{t+1}^{\tau}\tau)+rb_t) \end{aligned} \tag{19}$$

and for a representative worker of generation $\tau + 1$

$$\max\ U^{\tau+1} = c_{t+1}^{\tau+1} + \psi^{\tau+1}\log l_{t+1}^{\tau+1} + \beta(c_{t+2}^{\tau+1} + \psi^{\tau+1}\log l_{t+2}^{\tau+1})$$

$$s.t.\ c_t^{\tau+1} + \beta c_{t+2}^{\tau+1} = w^{\tau+1}((1-\tau)+a_{t+1}^{\tau+1}\tau)(\overline{t}-l_{t+1}^{\tau+1}) + \beta((\overline{t}-l_{t+2}^{\tau+1})w^{\tau+1}((1-\tau)+a_{t+2}^{\tau+1}\tau)+rb_{t+1})$$

$$l_{t+1}^{\tau+1*} = \frac{\psi^{\tau+1}}{w^{\tau+1}((1-\tau)+a_{t+1}^{\tau+1}\tau)} \tag{20}$$

$$l_{t+2}^{\tau+1*} = \frac{\psi^{\tau+1}}{w^{\tau+1}((1-\tau)+a_{t+2}^{\tau+1}\tau)} \tag{21}$$

$$\begin{aligned} V^{\tau} &= \overline{t}w^{\tau+1}((1-\tau)+a_{t+1}^{\tau+1}\tau) - \psi^{\tau+1} + \psi^{\tau+1}\log\psi^{\tau+1} - \psi^{\tau+1}\log w^{\tau+1}(((1-\tau)+a_{t+1}^{\tau+1}\tau)) \\ &+a_{t+1}^{\tau+1}\tau) + \beta\overline{t}((1-\tau)+a_{t+2}^{\tau+1}\tau) + \beta\psi^{\tau}(\log\psi^{\tau+1}) - \psi^{\tau+1}\log(w^{\tau+1}((1-\tau)+a_{t+2}^{\tau+1}\tau) \end{aligned} \tag{22}$$

In the second stage the election takes place. It is easy to verify that the election's outcome is a tie. The proof arises as an obvious consequence of the resolution of the first stage, where it is demonstrated that, in equilibrium, both parties choose an identical policy vector. They face exactly the same optimization problem and maximize their share of votes or, equivalently, the probability of winning. The resolution is made for candidate *A*, but it also holds for candidate *B*.

$$\max\ \pi^A = \frac{1}{2} + \frac{h}{s} \sum_{I=\{T-1,T\}} n^I s^I \left(V^i(\vec{q}^A) - V^i(\vec{q}^B)\right)$$

$$n^{\tau-1}\tau(\overline{t} - l_t^{\tau-1})(w_t^{\tau-1} - a_t^{\tau-1}) + n^{\tau}\tau(\overline{t} - l_t^{\tau})(w_t^{\tau} - a_t^{\tau}) = 0$$

For the resolution of the game it is useful to remind that

Definition 3. generation A is said to be more politically powerful than generation B if its density is higher than B's. That is if $s^A > s^B$.

In the Probabilistic Voting Theory, the political power of a group is definable as its ability to influence candidates' choices, when they have to take decisions about the policy vector. In traditional probabilistic voting models this power is expressed by the density function which captures the distribution of the political preferences of the constituency (Persson and Tabellini, 2000).

Furthermore, I assume that

Axiom 4. the density function of a generation is monotonically increasing in the consumption of leisure. That is $s^l = s(l)$, with $\frac{\partial s}{\partial l} > 0$.

This axiom affirms that the degree of ideological homogeneity of the cohort's members, which influences its political power, depends on the consumption of leisure. This idea was originally formulated by Mulligan and Sala-i-Martin, 1999, and suggests *that the old turn out to be more politically successful, because they are focused on a single issue,* such as the social transfers they get if they retire.

For the resolution of the game I follow the methodology used by Profeta, 2002 and Canegrati, 2008.

Proposition 5. The utility levels reached by workers are the same; that is: $V^{iA} = V^{iB}$.
Proof. See Appendix.

Proposition 6. *The tax credit is more beneficial for the old.*
Proof. Obtained via numerical simulations. See Appendix.

Proposition 7. *Optimal tax credits are a function of the numerosity and density of both groups, of the marginal tax rate, of the total endowment of time and of the parameters representing preferences of cohorts for leisure.*

Proof. See Appendix.

These results suggest that effective tax rates are differentiated across cohorts, as Proposition 2 states. Therefore, if a traditional normative model concludes that a benevolent governments *should tax* less the poorest social groups, this political economy model suggests that vote-seeker governments actually tax cohorts according to their ability to threat the candidates during the electoral competition.

Proposition 8. In equilibrium, the amount of leisure for the old is higher than the amount of leisure for the young.
Proof. See Appendix.

Proposition 9. Tax revenues collected via labour taxation on the young are positive; tax revenues generated via the labour taxation on labour taxation on the old are negative.
Proof. It derives from Proposition 2 and 4.

Thus, the fiscal system described by this model is compatible with the decision of the old to retire early. As a consequence, revenues collected through the taxation of the young are positive and equal to the amount of social security transfers that the old receive. The fact that tax revenues are negative for the old and positive for the young means that the old get a net transfer financed by the taxes paid by the young.

Proposition 10. The old are more single-minded than the young. That is: $s^{T-1} > s^{T}$.
Proof. The result originates from the assumption that the density function is monotonically increasing in leisure (remind that $s = s(l)$). Since the old choose more leisure in equilibrium, the density of the old is higher and, by definition, the group is more single-minded with respect to leisure.

4. Numerical Simulations

Numerical simulations are necessary because an analytical solution for the sys¬tem is difficult to compute. Indeed, to get the optimal policy vector we have to solve several systems of three equations with three unknowns (the two tax credits and the Lagrange multiplier). Nevertheless, also this process suffers from some problems. First of all, the *simultaneity*. We have assumed that the density function is endogenous in leisure; this implies that we are able to know the value of the density only after having calculated the optimal level of leisure which depends on the level of taxation but which is exactly what we want to evaluate! A possible way out for this problem is to guess a numerical value for the density function and verify afterwords that the level of leisure calculated is compatible with the initial guess; in other words, if we assume that the density is monoton ically increasing in leisure, we should expect to find higher levels of leisure for the group of the old for which we have guessed an higher density. Should not this happen, it would mean that our guess is wrong and the assumption fails. Furthermore, we also know that in equilibrium optimal leisure is an increasing function of ψ As a consequence, the density function should be an increasing function ψ of as well. This is why I will use a Logit Density Function of ψ as a proxy for the actual Logit Density Function of leisure.

Finally, the Lagrange multiplier has a political meaning: it represents the increase in the probability of winning for a candidate, if it had an additional dollar available to spend on redistribution.

4.1. Main Findings

Main results are reported in Appendix, tables 1-3. Tables 1.a, 2.a and 3.a report the matrix of inputs, while tables 1.b, 2.b and 3.b the matrix of outcomes. Tables 1.a and 1.b refer to period t - 1, tables 2.a and 2.b refer to period t and table 3.a and 3.b refer to period t + 1. We may observe some interesting results.

Remark 11. *Tax credits granted to the old are systematically higher than those granted to the young. This happens at every period of time.*

Remark 12. *The tax credits follow a different trend among cohorts over time. In fact, the trend of tax credits for the old is increasing over time, while that one of the young increases only from period t - 1 to time t, and it dramatically decreases from period t to time t + 1.*

Table l.a. Results of the numerical simulations with Mathematica 5.2 - Input Matrix - Period *t* - 1

$n^{\tau-2}$	$n^{\tau-1}$	τ	$\bar{t}$	$\psi^{\tau-2}$	$\psi^{\tau-1}$	$s^{\tau-2}$	$s^{\tau-1}$	ω	r	B
0:5	0:5	0:3	0:9	0:8	0:2	0:689	0:549	2	0:1	0:5
0:5	0:5	0:4	0:9	0:8	0:2	0:689	0:549	2	0:1	0:5
0:5	0:5	0:6	0:9	0:8	0:2	0:689	0:549	2	0:1	0:5
0:5	0:5	0:4	0:9	0:8	0:2	0:689	0:549	2	0:06	0:3
0:5	0:5	0:4	0:9	0:8	0:2	0:689	0:549	2	0:14	0:7

Table l.b. Results of the numerical simulations with Mathematica 5.2 - Output Matrix - Period *t* - 1

$a_t^{\tau-2}$	$a_t^{\tau-1}$	$\bar{t}-l_{t-1}^{\tau-2}$	$\bar{t}-l_{t-1}^{\tau-1}$	$T_{t-1}^{\tau-2}$	$T_{t-1}^{\tau-1}$	L_{t-1}	Y_{t-1}
1:478	0:169	0:550	0:633	-0:078	0:078	1:183	9:146
1:358	0:377	0:550	0:633	-0:078	0:078	1:183	9:146
1:239	0:584	0:550	0:633	-0:078	0:078	1:183	9:146
1:358	0:377	0:550	0:633	-0:078	0:078	1:183	9:146
1:239	0:584	0:550	0:633	-0:078	0:078	1:183	9:146

Table 2.a. Results of the numerical simulations with Mathematica 5.2 - Input Matrix - Period *t*

$n^{\tau-1}$	n^{τ}	τ	$\bar{t}$	$\psi^{\tau-1}$	ψ^{τ}	$s^{\tau-1}$	s^{τ}	ω	r	B
0:5	0:5	0:3	0:9	0:8	0:2	0:689	0:549	2	0:1	0:5
0:5	0:5	0:4	0:9	0:8	0:2	0:689	0:549	2	0:1	0:5
0:5	0:5	0:6	0:9	0:8	0:2	0:689	0:549	2	0:1	0:5
0:5	0:5	0:4	0:9	0:8	0:2	0:689	0:549	2	0:06	0:3
0:5	0:5	0:4	0:9	0:8	0:2	0:689	0:549	2	0:14	0:7

Looking at these two results, a first conclusion may be drawn: at time when debt is issued, both groups gain from a reduction in the effective marginal tax rate: the debt acts as a substitute of taxation. Otherwise, at time when the debt is paid off, we realize that the burden is borne only by the young, while the old get an even greater reduction in the effective marginal tax rate.

Table 2.b. Results of the numerical simulations with Mathematica 5.2 - Output Matrix - Period *t*

$a_t^{\tau-1}$	a_t^{τ}	$\bar{t}-l_{t-1}^{\tau-1}$	$\bar{t}-l_{t-1}^{\tau}$	$T_{t-1}^{\tau-1}$	T_{t-1}^{τ}	L_{t-1}	Y_{t-1}
3:748	0:373	0:68	0:653	-0:561	0:061	1:334	8:536
4:924	4:484	0:744	0:816	-1:168	-0:569	1:560	6:713
2:374	0:686	0:68	0:653	-0:561	0:061	1:334	8:536
2:406	0:523	0:643	0:652	-0:362	0:062	1:296	8:847
-0:459	-1:287	-	-	0	0	0	0

Table 3.a. Results of the numerical simulations with Mathematica 5.2 - Input Matrix - Period t + 1

n^{τ}	$n^{\tau+1}$	τ	$\bar{t}$	ψ^{τ}	$\psi^{\tau+1}$	s^{τ}	$s^{\tau+1}$	w	r	B
0.5	0.5	0.3	0.9	0.8	0.2	0.689	0.549	2	0.1	0.5
0.5	0.5	0.4	0.9	0.8	0.2	0.689	0.549	2	0.1	0.5
0.5	0.5	0.6	0.9	0.8	0.2	0.689	0.549	2	0.1	0.5
0.5	0.5	0.4	0.9	0.8	0.2	0.689	0.549	2	0.06	0.3
0.5	0.5	0.4	0.9	0.8	0.2	0.689	0.549	2	0.14	0.7

Table 3.b. Results of the numerical simulations with Mathematica 5.2 - Output Matrix - Period t + 1

a_t^{τ}	$a_t^{\tau+1}$	$\bar{t}-l_{t-1}^{\tau}$	$\bar{t}-l_{t-1}^{\tau+1}$	T_{t-1}^{τ}	$T_{t-1}^{\tau+1}$	L_{t-1}	Y_{t-1}
6.426	-11.449	0.747	0.9	-1.217	1.680	1.647	11.849
5.069	-8.337	0.747	0.9	-1.217	1.680	1.647	11.849
3.713	-5.22	0.747	0.9	-1.217	1.680	1.647	11.849
-0.04	-0.510	0.212	0.394	0.088	0.119	0.607	7.388
4.508	-8.635	0.733	0.9	-1.029	1.869	1.703	12.295

Another interesting result refers to the labour supply; we may note that the elder generation tends to work (rest) less (more) than the younger, with only one exception at time $t + 1$ for simulations obtained with a nominal tax rate equal to 0.3 and 0.6. Nevertheless, notice that tax credits granted to the two cohorts are nearly the same. Furthermore, the labour supply increases over the three periods for both cohorts. As a consequence, also the total labour supply increases steadily over time. Tax revenues are always positive for the young and always negative for the old, meaning that the former is a net taker, while the second is a net payer. Notice also that the tax benefit for the old tends to increase over time and that tax revenues for the young decreases when the debt is issued, but dramatically increases once the debt is repaid. This again highlights the asymmetry in the allocation of the burden of debt: the young borne the cost of the repayment.

The last result refers to the production level. For numerical simulations I used a production function equal to $Y = 10\sqrt{L} - w^{\tau-1}(1-(1-a^{\tau-1}\tau)(\bar{t}-l^{\tau-1}) + w^{\tau}(1-(1-a^{\tau}\tau)(\bar{t}-l^{\tau})$, where $L = \bar{t}-l^{\tau-1}+\bar{t}-l^{\tau}$. It can be observed that at the period when the debt is issued the production decreases, while it achieves its highest level at time when the debt is paid off.

Conclusion

In this paper I explained the political interaction between taxation, social security transfers and public debt policies. I demonstrated why the old have an incentive to consume more leisure than the young and why, in equilibrium, they receive a positive social security transfer. As I explained, the issuance of public debt as negative effects on the young cohort, which has to borne the entire burden of public debt. The model explains why the public debt is a policy instruments which can generate harmful effects on intergenerational wealth and on the labour supply of the old workers.

ACKNOWLEDGMENTS

I am particularly grateful to Massimo Bordignon, Federico Etro, Torsten Persson, Ronnie Razin, Jorgen Weibull, Micael Castanheira and Rachel Ngai for the very helpful comments and Santino Piazza; to all the participants at the WISER Conference in Warsaw, in particular to Maksymilian Kwiek and Anna Ruzik; to the Catholic University of Milan and to the London School of Economics where this paper was written. All errors are mine.

APPENDIX

In this Appendix I provide a complete resolution to the candidates' optimization problem. The two candidates solve exactly the same problem; they maximize their share of votes or, equivalently, the probability of winning. The resolution is made for candidate A, but it also holds for candidate B.

$$\max \ \pi^A = \frac{1}{2} + \frac{h}{s} \sum_{I=\{T-1,T\}} n^I s^I \left(V^i(\overline{q}^A) - V^i(\overline{q}^B)\right)$$

$$T_1 := n^{\tau-2}\tau(\bar{t} - l_t^{\tau-2})(1 - a_t^{\tau-2}) + n^{\tau-1}\tau(\bar{t} - l_t^{\tau-1})(1 - a_t^{\tau-1}) = 0$$

at time $t-1$

$$T_1 bis := n^{\tau-1}\tau(\bar{t} - l_t^{\tau-1})(1 - a_t^{\tau-1}) + n^{\tau}\tau(\bar{t} - l_t^{\tau})(1 - a_t^{\tau}) + B_t = 0$$

at time t

$$T_1 tris := n^{\tau}\tau(\bar{t} - l_t^{\tau})(1 - a_t^{\tau}) + n^{\tau+1}\tau(\bar{t} - l_t^{\tau+1})(1 - a_t^{\tau+1}) = (1+r)B_t$$

at time $t+1$

I write the Lagrangian function for a given budget constraint BC:

$$\mathcal{L} = \frac{1}{2} + \frac{h}{s} \sum_{I=\{T-1,T\}} n^I s^I [V^i(\overline{q}^A) - V^i(\overline{q}^B)] + \lambda(BC)$$

I obtain the following first order conditions which may be seen as a modified version of the original Lindbeck and Weibull, 1987, first order conditions, at time t:

(1) $\frac{\partial \mathcal{L}}{\partial a_t^{\tau-1}} = n^{\tau-1} \frac{\partial s^{\tau-1}}{\partial l_t^{\tau-1}} \frac{\partial l_t^{\tau-1}}{\partial a_t^{\tau-1}} (V^{\tau-1A} - V^{\tau-1B}) + n^{\tau-1} s^{\tau-1} (\frac{\partial V^{\tau-1}}{\partial a_t^{\tau-1}}) = \lambda \frac{\partial T(1)}{\partial a_t^{\tau-1}}$

(2) $\frac{\partial \mathcal{L}}{\partial a_t^{\tau}} = n^{\tau} \frac{\partial s^{\tau}}{\partial l_t^{\tau}} \frac{\partial l_t^{\tau}}{\partial a_t^{\tau}} (V^{\tau A} - V^{\tau B}) + n^{\tau} s^{\tau} (\frac{\partial V^{\tau}}{\partial a_t^{\tau}}) = \lambda \frac{\partial T(1)}{\partial a_t^{\tau}}$

(3) $BC = 0$

According to the result stated in Corollary 1, first order conditions can be rewritten in the following manner:

$$(1)\quad \frac{\partial \mathcal{L}}{\partial a_t^{\tau-1}} = n^{\tau-1}s^{\tau-1}\left(\frac{\partial V^{\tau-1}}{\partial a_t^{\tau-1}}\right) = \lambda\frac{\partial T(1)}{\partial a_t^{\tau-1}}$$

$$(2)\quad \frac{\partial \mathcal{L}}{\partial a_t^{\tau}} = n^{\tau}s^{\tau}\left(\frac{\partial V^{\tau}}{\partial a_t^{\tau}}\right) = \lambda\frac{\partial T(1)}{\partial a_t^{\tau}}$$

$$(3)\quad BC = 0$$

and after some easy calculations, I obtain:

$$(1)\quad n^{\tau-1}s^{\tau-1}\left(\bar{t}\tau + \frac{\psi^{\tau-1}\tau_L}{1-(1-a_t^{\tau-1})\tau}\right) - \lambda\left(\frac{(1-a_t^{\tau-1})\tau_L^2\psi^{\tau-1}n^{\tau-1}}{\left(1-(1-a_t^{\tau-1})\tau\right)^2} - n^{\tau-1}\tau\left(\bar{t} - \frac{\psi^{\tau-1}}{1-(1-a_t^{\tau-1})\tau}\right)\right) = 0$$

$$(2)\quad n^{\tau}s^{\tau}\left(\bar{t}\tau + \frac{\psi^{\tau}\tau_L}{1-(1-a_t^{\tau})\tau}\right) - \lambda\left(\frac{(1-a_t^{\tau})\tau^2\psi^{\tau}n^{\tau}}{(1-(1-a_t^{\tau})\tau)^2} - n^{\tau}\tau\left(\bar{t} - \frac{\psi^{\tau}}{(1-(1-a_t^{\tau})\tau_L)}\right)\right) = 0$$

$$(3)\quad BC = 0$$

From (1) and (2) obtain:

$$\lambda = \frac{n^{\tau-1}s^{\tau-1}\left(\bar{t} + \frac{\psi^{\tau-1}}{1-(1-a_t^{\tau-1})}\right)}{\frac{(1-a_t^{\tau-1})\tau\psi^{\tau-1}n^{\tau-1}}{\left(1-(1-a_t^{\tau-1})\tau\right)^2} - n^{\tau-1}\left(\bar{t} - \frac{\psi^{\tau-1}}{1-(1-a_t^{\tau-1})\tau}\right)} = \frac{n^{\tau}s^{\tau}\left(\bar{t} + \frac{\psi^{\tau}}{1-(1-a_t^{\tau})}\right)}{\frac{(1-a_t^{\tau})\tau\psi^{\tau}n^{\tau}}{(1-(1-a_t^{\tau})\tau)^2} - n^{\tau}\left(\bar{t} - \frac{\psi^{\tau}}{1-(1-a_t^{\tau})\tau}\right)}$$

Solving this system of equations analytically is a very difficult task. This is why I perform some numerical simulations instead. In the following tables the main results are reported.

References

Barro, R. (1974) Are Government Bonds Net Wealth? *Journal of Political Economy,* 82(6) pp. 1095-1117

Barro, R. (1979) On the Determination of the Public Debt, *Journal of Political Economy,* 87(5) pp. 940-971

Brennan, G. and Buchanan, J. M (1980) *The Power to Tax: Analytical Foundations of a Fiscal Constitution Cambridge*: Cambridge University Press

Buchanan, J. M. (1976) Barro on the Ricardian equivalence theorem, *Journal of Political Economy*, 84, pp. 337–342

Canegrati, E. (2008) The Single Mindedness Theory Micro-foundation and Application to Labor Market, *Ekonomia*, vol. 20

Coughlin, P. (1992) *Probabilistic Voting Theory*, Cambridge University Press

Diamond P. and Gruber J. (1997) Social Security and Retirement in the U.S., *NBER Working Paper* 6097

Diamond P. (1965): National Debt in a Neoclassical Growth Theory, *American Economic Review*, 60, pp.1126-50

Dixit, A. and Londregan J. (1994) *Redistributive Politics and Economic Efficiency, NBER Working Papers* 1056

Feldstein, M. (1976) Perceived Wealth in Bonds and Social Security: A Comment, *Journal of Political Economy*, 84 (2), pp. 331-336

Feldstein, M. (1982) Government deficits and aggregate demand, *Journal of Monetary Economics*, 9, pp. 1-20.

Feldstein, M. (1988) The Effects of Fiscal Policies When Incomes Are Uncertain: A Contradiction to Ricardian Equivalence, *American Economic Review*, 78(1), pp. 14-23.

Greenwood, J. and Vandenbroucke, G. (2005): Hours Worked: Long-run Trends, *NBER Working Paper* 11629

Gruber, J. and Wise, D. A. (1999): *Social Security and Retirement Around the World*, Chicago University Press

Hershey D., Henkens K. and Van Dalen H. (2006): *Mapping the Minds of Retirement Planners: A Cross-cultural Perspective*, mimeo

Hinich M.J. (1977): Equilibrium in Spatial Voting: The Median Voter Theorem is an Artifact, *Journal of Economic Theory*, 16, pp. 208-219

Ihori, T. (1996): *Public Finance in an Overlapping Generations Economy*, MacMillan Press

Ihori, T. and Tachibanaki, T. (2002): *Social Security Reforms in Advanced Countries*, Routledge

Lindbeck A. and Weibull J. W. (1987): Balanced-Budget Redistribution as the Outcome of Political Competition, *Public Choice* 52, pp. 273-297

McCallum, B. (1984): Are Bond-financed Deficits Inflationary? A Ricardian Analysis, *The Journal of Political Economy*, 92(1), pp. 123-135.

Mulligan C. B. and Sala-i-Martin (1999): Gerontocracy, Retirement and Social Security, *NBER Working Paper* 7117

Mulligan C. B. and Sala-i-Martin (1999): Social Security in Theory and Practice (I): Facts and Political Theories, *NBER Working Paper* 7118

Mulligan C. B. and Sala-i-Martin (1999): Social Security in Theory and Practice (II): Efficiency Theories, Narrative Theories and Implications for Reforms, *NBER Working Paper* 7119

Mulligan C. B. and Sala-i-Martin (1999): Social Security, Retirement and the Single-Mindness of the Electorate, *NBER Working Paper* 9691

O'Driscoll, G. P. (1977): The Ricardian Nonequivalence Theorem,*The Journal of Political Economy*, 85, pp.207-210

Profeta, P. (2002) Retirement and Social Security in a Probabilistic Voting Model, *International Tax and Public Finance*, 9, pp. 331-348

Persson T. and Tabellini G. (2000): *Political Economics: Explaining the Economic Policy*, MIT Press

Ricardo, D (1951) On the Principles of Political Economy and Taxation, *The Works and Correspondence of David Ricardo*, edited by P.Sraffa. Vol.1 Cambridge, Cambridge University Press

The Financial Crisis
Editors: Barbara L. Campos and Janet P. Wilkins
ISBN: 978-1-61209-281-2

Chapter 5

An Analysis of the Determinants of Credit Default Swap Spread Changes Before and During the Subprime Financial Turmoil

Antonio Di Cesare [1,*] ***and Giovanni Guazzarotti*** [2,†]
[1]Bank of Italy
Economic Outlook and Monetary Policy Department
Via Nazionale, 91, 00184 Roma, Italy
[2]Bank of Italy
Structural Economic Analysis Department
Via Nazionale, 91, 00184 Roma, Italy

Abstract

This paper analyzes the determinants of credit default swap spread changes for a large sample of US non-financial companies over the period between January 2002 and March 2009. In our analysis we use variables that the literature has found have an impact on CDS spreads and, in order to account for possible non-linear effects, the theoretical CDS spreads predicted by the Merton model. We show that our set of variables is able to explain more than 50% of CDS spread variations both before and after July 2007, when the current financial turmoil began. We also document that since the onset of the crisis CDS spreads have become much more sensitive to the level of leverage while volatility has lost its importance. Using a principal component analysis we also show that since the beginning of the crisis CDS spread changes have been increasingly driven by a common factor, which cannot be explained by indicators of economic activity, uncertainty, and risk aversion.

Keywords: Credit default swaps, bond spreads, credit risk, Merton model.

JEL Subject Classification: G12, G13.

---

*E-mail address: antonio.dicesare@bancaditalia.it
†E-mail address: giovanni.guazzarotti@bancaditalia.it

The views expressed in the article are those of the authors and do not involve the responsibility of the Bank of Italy. We would like to thank Giuseppe Cappelletti, Giuseppe Grande and Marcello Pericoli for their helpful comments and suggestions. All remaining errors are our own. The original version of this paper focused on CDSs denominated in euro; an electronic copy is currently available at http://www.greta.it/credit/credit2005/Friday/Poster/05_DiCesare_Guazzarotti.pdf.

1. Introduction

Empirical work on the determinants of credit risk – the risk of default of borrowers – has traditionally looked at corporate spreads, that is spreads between corporate and government bonds. [1] The common finding has been that only a small share of observed spreads can be actually considered as a compensation for the risk of default of borrowers, whereas the greatest share can be traced back to taxes and liquidity issues, and to the presence of other systematic risk factors (e.g. Elton et al., 2001, Amato and Remolona, 2005, and Driessen, 2005).

Although the bond market has traditionally been regarded as the best place in which the creditworthiness of a borrower can be evaluated, in recent years there has been a huge development of financial instruments, called credit derivatives, that are specifically designed to make credit risk easily tradable.[2] Among these innovative instruments, credit default swaps (CDSs) have proved particularly successful. Essentially, a CDS works like an insurance contract: the policy holder (i.e. the buyer of protection) pays a premium to the insurer (i.e. the seller of protection) in order to receive compensation if a particular event occurs. In the case of CDSs this event, called a credit event, usually includes bankruptcy, failure to pay and restructuring and, for sovereign issuers, repudiation and moratoria. Generally speaking all these events are subsumed in the term "default". The main difference between a CDS and an insurance contract is that, while in the case of insurance the policy holder gets a reimbursement only for the actual damages suffered, with a CDS it is possible to buy or sell protection against credit events independently from the real exposure to the risk of default of the reference entity. A CDS can thus be used not only for hedging credit risk but also for taking pure speculative positions, as with forward and futures contracts. This aspect clearly distinguishes the CDS market from the bond market. While the short selling of bonds, i.e. of credit risk, is usually limited by the low level of liquidity of the repo market, especially for high-yield bonds, and by the short maturity of repo contracts, CDSs allow investors to short sell credit risk easily. Thanks to this characteristic, the CDS market has been growing dramatically during the last few years. According to the International Swap and Derivatives Association (ISDA) the notional value of outstanding CDSs has increased from 1 to 62 trillion USD between 2001 and 2007. The notional amount of outstanding CDSs was so large that it turned out to be a serious potential source of instability during the financial turmoil triggered by the subprime crisis in the United States because of the corresponding counterparty risks. In order to reduce these risks, CDS market dealers started entering multilateral netting of CDS contracts, thus reducing the notional amount of outstanding CDS to 39 trillion by the end of 2008 (see European Central Bank, 2009a). According to Fitch Ratings (2006) CDSs represent more than a half of the whole credit derivatives market.[3]

Because of its particular features, the CDS market is potentially much more efficient than the bond market in signaling the creditworthiness of borrowers. The relationship between bond and CDS markets has been the subject of several academic papers. Blanco et al.

[1] We use the terms "credit spreads" and "credit premia" as synonyms of "corporate spreads" and "CDS spreads". By "corporate spreads" or "bond spreads" we mean the differential between the yields of bonds issued by private companies and the yields of government bonds with similar characteristics. We also use the term "risk-free yields" as a synonym of "government bond yields".

[2] See the Committee on the Global Financial System (2003).

[3] More detailed information about the CDS market can be found in European Central Bank, 2009b.

(2005) find that CDS and bond markets reflect firm-specific characteristics equally in the long run, while in the short run CDS prices appear to be more efficient than bond spreads in the price discovery process. Zhu (2004) confirms that credit risk tends to be priced equally in the two markets in the long run and that the derivatives market seems to lead the cash market in anticipating rating events and in price adjustments. Other literature (Hull et al., 2004, Norden and Weber, 2004, Di Cesare, 2005) which analyzes the relationship between CDS spreads and credit ratings show that the CDS market is usually very effective in anticipating rating changes.

The development of the CDS market has also attracted researchers' interest in analyzing whether factors that determine corporate spreads are also relevant for CDS spreads. As said before, the nature of CDSs is such that this question does not have an obvious answer. The aim of this paper is to contribute to this literature by analyzing how the recent financial turmoil has changed the way that credit risk is priced in the CDS market. Most of existing literature use data from the early stage of the CDS market only, thus not taking into account more recent developments. To the best of our knowledge, only Annaert et al. (2009) and Raunig and Scheicher (2009) analyze the period following the onset of the current financial turmoil in July 2007, but they focus on the banking sector. Moreover, with the exception of Alexander and Kaeck (2008) and Pires et al. (2009), no other paper takes into account the non-linear relationship between CDS spreads and default factors. In this paper we use a large data set of CDS quotes on US non-financial companies from January 2002 to March 2009 that allow us to analyze the effects of the recent financial turmoil on the determinants of CDS spread changes. We also take into account the issue of non-linearity by explicitly using a theoretical CDS spread calculated using the Merton model in our regressions. In this respect, our paper is similar in spirit to Byström (2006) which uses the CreditGrades model to calculate theoretical CDS spreads and compare these with empirically observed spreads for CDS indices (iTraxx) covering Europe. Byström (2006) finds that theoretical and empirical spread changes are significantly correlated. Given that the specific functional form provided by a theoretical model could misspecify the true relationship between CDS spreads and default factors, we also add in our regressions the single default factors separately as well as other factors that theory and empirical evidence found to be significant in explaining credit spreads.

Our main results are: i) the inclusion of a theoretical CDS spread in our regressions improves the explanatory power of the fundamental variables. Our extended model is able to explain 54% of the variations in CDS spreads in the pre-crisis period (from January 2002 to June 2007) and 51% in the crisis period (from July 2007 to March 2009), which is higher than previous findings of studies on corporate bond and CDS spread changes; ii) when the theoretical spread calculated from the Merton model is introduced in the regressions, the coefficient of equity volatility decreases significantly; that of leverage, on the contrary, maintains its usefulness in explaining CDS spread changes; iii) the contribution of leverage to the explanation of CDS spread changes is much higher during the crisis than before, as investors appear to have become more aware of individual risk factors; at the same time, the impact of equity volatility substantially decreases, possibly because the large swings in implied volatility that have characterized the crisis period have made this indicator a poor proxy for long-term asset volatility; iv) the overall capacity of the model to explain CDS changes is almost the same before and during the turmoil, thus highlighting that the underlying risk factors identified by the literature as relevant for the pricing of the credit risk have maintained their explanatory power also in a period of remarkable stress for the CDS market; v) during the crisis CDS spreads appear to have been moving increasingly together, driven by a common factor that our model was able to explain only in part.

The following section surveys the literature on the determinants of credit spreads and on previous empirical studies. In Section 3. we describe the model introduced by Merton (1974) and the way in which it can be used to estimate model-based CDS spreads. In Section 4. we describe the dataset and the statistical methodology used in the paper to look for the determinants of CDS spread movements. Our results are reported in Section 5. and Section 6. concludes.

2. A Review of the Literature on Credit Spreads

This section briefly reviews the main contributions to the literature on the determinants of credit spreads. Early research on this topic has focused on assessing how much of observed bond spreads can be explained by structural default factors, that is by factors that theoretical models of default suggest are linked to credit risk. Then, having observed that bond spreads predicted by theoretical models are generally much lower than observed spreads, the academic research has turned its attention to investigating the origins of such unexplained extra yields, testing for alternative hypotheses.

2.1. Main Determinants of Credit Spreads

Credit risk models are usually divided into structural and reduced-form models. [4] Under the first approach the liabilities of a firm are seen as a contingent claim on the assets of the firm itself and default occurs when the market value of the assets, which is modeled as a stochastic process, reaches some limit. The reduced-form approach, instead, postulates that default occurs randomly, due to some exogenous factor(s) whose probability of occurring, dubbed the "intensity", is modeled and calibrated using market data. Models belonging to this latter class are also called intensity-based models. Reduced-form models have been praised by practitioners because of their capacity, by construction, to fit market data, but structural models have been usually seen by academics as better suited to analyzing the determinants of credit risk. Although the capacity of individual structural models to describe the actual behavior of credit risk is still a matter of debate (e.g. Anderson and Sundaresan, 2000, Eom et al., 2004, Tarashev, 2005, and Ericsson et al., 2007), during the last few years there has been a new strand of literature that, departing from any specific model, aimed at measuring the explanatory power for observed credit spreads of the variables that structural models predict are theoretically linked to credit risk.

The first structural model on credit risk was introduced by Merton (1974) and because of its importance is described in detail in the next section. For the moment it will suffice to say that in the Merton model a default occurs when the market value of the firm, which is assumed to be described by a random process, is below the face value of the outstanding

[4] Giesecke (2004) provides an interesting survey of both approaches. He also introduces the incomplete information approach that, strictly speaking, can be seen as an extension of the structural approach.

debt at the maturity of the debt itself. In that case the shareholders give the assets of the firm up to the bondholders. Merton's intuition was that a bond subject to credit risk can be seen as a combination of a long position in a risk-free bond and short position in a European put option sold to the shareholders with a strike price equal to the face value of the risky bond. In this setting, the price of the risky bond can be determined through standard option pricing methods which link its value to the parameters of the stochastic process driving the firm value and to the level of outstanding debt. The prediction of the Merton model is that credit spreads should be a function of the following variables:

i) *risk-free interest rate*: the risk-free interest rate represents the drift of the process describing the value of the assets of the firm under the risk-neutral measure. Higher interest rates increase the future expected value of the assets, thus reducing credit spreads;

ii) *nominal outstanding amount of debt*: the nominal value of the debt represents the threshold at which default is triggered. A higher amount of debt makes default more likely so that higher credit spreads are expected;

iii) *firm value*: higher values for the assets of the firm make the regular payment of the debt more likely and credit spreads are expected to be lower;

iv) *asset volatility*: higher asset volatility increases the value of the put option granted to the shareholders, thus increasing the compensation required by the bondholders through higher credit spreads.

The aim of the Merton model and other structural models is to explain the share of the bond spreads which arises from credit risk using a small number of factors such as those just described. However, there are other factors not linked to credit risk that have been shown to be a non-negligible part of bond spreads. These include:

i) *taxes*, to the extent that credit instruments and government bonds are subject to different tax rates;

ii) *liquidity*, as risky credit instruments have lower volumes and higher transaction costs than government bonds;

iii) *supply and demand shocks*, which can affect both corporate and government bond markets;

iv) *systematic risk factors*, such as those prevailing in the equity and in the corporate bond markets (e.g. Elton et al., 2001).

During the last few years these additional factors have led to a growing empirical literature on credit spreads that has used the CDS market as its object of research. Working on CDS quotes has at least three advantages with respect to using bond spreads. First, the CDS market already quotes in terms of a "spread", so that it is not necessary to introduce another market in the analysis, like that of government bonds, which can be subject to its own specific factors. Second, CDS contracts are rather standardized, while bonds are characterized by non-homogeneity in terms of coupons, maturities, outstanding amounts, embedded options, and so on, which make comparisons difficult. Finally, because of the nature of CDSs as derivatives contracts, CDS quotes should be less prone to supply and demand effects than the bond market, which is constrained by the physical nature of bonds.

2.2. Empirical Studies

Given the relatively recent development of the CDS market, empirical work on the determinants of credit risk has traditionally looked at corporate spreads. A first group of empirical studies identifies factors that can explain why corporate spreads are much larger than what would be predicted by historical rates of default and recovery rates (the so-called "credit spread puzzle"). Elton et al. (2001) identify the expected default loss, a tax premium, and a risk premium for the systematic, and thus not diversifiable, part of the risk on corporate bonds, as the main components of credit spreads. Following the same line of research, Driessen (2005) shows that risk premia for liquidity and jump-to-default risks are also important components of bond spreads. Amato and Remolona (2005) propose an alternative explanation for the "credit spread puzzle" arguing that, while previous studies mostly focused on the expected loss component of credit risk, extra spreads may actually compensate for non-diversifiable credit risk. Their argument is that the high degree of skewness in bond returns makes diversification more difficult: the size of the portfolio required to reduce the probability of extreme losses by diversification is actually very large and thus difficult to attain in practice. Due to this difficulty investors in corporate bonds would require additional premia in the form of higher spreads.

A second group of studies on corporate spreads departs from trying to reconcile historical default losses with observed credit premia and instead aims at explaining credit spreads in a purely statistical way by regressing (changes in) observed spreads on (changes in) factors that theoretical models suggest are relevant in determining both default and non-default components of credit spreads. The advantage of this approach is that it allows the impact of any single fundamental factor on credit spreads to be estimated directly. Collin-Dufresne et al. (2001) initiate this strand of research by showing how factors that should represent the main explanatory variables for credit spreads, according to structural default models, actually explain only 25% of observed bond spread changes. They also show that the missing component is represented by a common risk factor which is independent of equity, swap and Treasury returns. They conclude that bond spread changes are mostly driven by supply and demand shocks which are specific to the corporate bond market and independent of both default and liquidity factors. Campbell and Taksler (2003) focus on the effect of equity volatility on corporate bond yields. They show that idiosyncratic firm-level volatility can explain as much cross-sectional variation in yields as can credit ratings. In the same vein, Guazzarotti (2004) investigates the determinants of changes in individual credit spreads of non-financial European corporate bonds by looking at the relevance of both structural default factors (like leverage, asset volatility, and the level and slope of the risk-free yield curve) and of some non credit-risk factors (e.g. market liquidity and market risk). He finds that: i) default risk factors account for less than 20% of total variation of credit spreads; ii) liquidity risk and aggregate market risk factors, although significant, explain only an additional 10%; iii) the remaining part of credit spread changes remains unexplained. More recently, Avramov et al. (2007) analyze the capacity of structural models to explain changes in corporate credit risk using a set of common factors and company-level fundamentals. They are able to explain more than 54% (67%) of the variation in credit spread changes for medium-grade (low-grade) bonds with no clearly dominant latent factor left in the unexplained variation. Cremers et al. (2008) introduce measures of volatility and jump risks that are based on individual stock options to explain bond spreads. They show that implied volatilities of individual options contain useful information for credit spreads and improve on historical volatilities when explaining the cross-sectional and time-series variations in a panel of corporate bond spreads.

Turning to the empirical analysis on CDS spreads, one of the first papers on the topic is that by Aunon-Nerin et al. (2002). As the credit derivatives market was still in its infancy when that paper was written, the sample of CDSs which has been used is rather small and with a predominance of financial companies. Moreover, the analysis is conducted on the levels of the variables thus leaving the door open to econometric problems related to the non-stationary nature of the data. [5] Greatrex (2008) digs deeper into the relevance of these econometric issues for the study of the determinants of CDS spreads and shows that variables commonly used for this kind of analysis are usually non-stationary in levels but stationary in first differences; running regressions on non-stationary variables could result in high values for the R^2 statistics but also in inefficient coefficient estimates, sub-optimal forecasts, and invalid significance tests (Granger and Newbold, 1974). Ericsson et al. (2009), in a paper circulating since 2004, use data for the period 1999-2002 and show that estimated coefficients of a limited number of theoretical determinants of default risk are consistent with the theory. Among these factors, volatility and leverage have substantial explanatory power. Moreover, a principal component analysis of spreads and residuals indicates limited evidence for a residual common factor, confirming that the variables explain a significant amount of the variation in the data. Zhang et al. (2005) focus on information arising from the equity market. They show that volatility and jump risk measures derived from the equity market using high frequency data, together with credit ratings, macroeconomic conditions, and firms' balance sheet information, can explain up to 77% of the total variation of CDS spreads. However, their results are obtained using variables in levels and are subject to the same econometric problems mentioned above. More recently, some works have focussed on CDSs on banks and on the differences between the periods before and after the recent financial crisis. Annaert et al. (2009) show that: i) the determinants of changes in bank CDS spreads exhibit significant time variation; ii) variables suggested by structural credit risk models are not significant in explaining bank CDS spread changes, either in the period prior to the crisis or in the crisis period itself; iii) some of the variables used as proxies of the general economic conditions are significant, but the magnitude of the coefficient estimates and their sign have changed over time. Raunig and Scheicher (2009) also find the crisis had an impact on the pricing of CDSs on banks. In particular, they show that the perception of bank credit risk by market participants approaches the level of the most risky non-bank companies.

---

[5] More recently, Abid and Naifar (2006) performed an analysis on CDS spread levels.

3. Merton Model

As we already mentioned, Merton (1974) introduces the first model of credit risk based on the structural approach. Merton assumes that the whole debt of a firm is represented by a zero-coupon bond maturing at time T, with face value D. Moreover, the market value of the firm's assets V_t between 0 and T follows a geometric Brownian motion given by

$$dV_t = rV_t dt + \sigma V_t dW_t \tag{1}$$

where r and σ are constants representing, respectively, the risk-free interest rate and the volatility of the process. Merton assumes that a default occurs if the value of the firm at time T is lower than D. In that case the ownership of the firm is transferred from the shareholders to the creditors. In this framework the creditors of the firm can be seen as holding a long position in a risk-free zero-coupon bond and a short position in a European put option granted to the shareholders. The underlying of the option is represented by the assets of the firm, the strike price is equal to D and the maturity is T. The spread between corporate and government yields is the compensation required by creditors for selling the put option.

Similarly, the equity value can be seen as the value of a European call on the assets of the firm, with the strike price equal to D and maturity T. The value of equity at time T, denoted E_T, is thus given by $\max(0, V_T - D)$. Using standard option valuation tools (Black and Scholes, 1973), one obtains

$$E_t = V_t N(d_1) - e^{-r(T-t)} DN(d_2) \tag{2}$$

at time $t < T$, where

$$d_1 = \frac{\log(V_t/D) + (r + \sigma^2/2)(T-t)}{\sigma\sqrt{T-t}}$$

$$d_2 = d_1 - \sigma\sqrt{T-t}$$

and $N(x)$ is the standard normal cumulative distribution function evaluated at x. The value of the debt at time t, which we denote with D_t, is thus equal to $V_t - E_t$. It is also possible to recover the expected costs of default C_t as the difference between the face value of the debt, discounted at the risk-free rate, and the actual value of the debt, that is

$$C_t = e^{-r(T-t)} D - D_t$$

In this simple framework, in which the default can occur only at the maturity of the debt, the annual spread s_t of a CDS with quarterly payments and T years to maturity is such that it makes C_t equal to

$$D\frac{s_t}{4}\sum_{n=1}^{4T} \exp\left(-r\frac{n}{4}\right),$$

that is

$$s_t = \frac{4C_t/D}{\sum_{n=1}^{4T} \exp\left(-r\frac{n}{4}\right)}$$

In order to use the Merton model to estimate the CDS spread it is thus necessary to have four ingredients: the level of the risk-free interest rate, the face value of the firm's total debt, its market value and the volatility of its assets. Although the last two variables are not directly observable, for listed firms it is nonetheless possible to observe the market value of equity and to estimate the historical volatility. In the case in which there are options written on the shares of the firm it is also possible to have a forward-looking measure of the equity volatility, which is the volatility implied by stock option prices. Equity value and equity volatility can therefore be used directly as proxies for asset value and asset volatility. However, they can also be used to obtain estimates of asset value and asset volatility. In fact, applying Ito's lemma the dynamics of E_t is given by a geometric Brownian motion with diffusion coefficient equal to $\sigma V_t \frac{dE_t}{dV_t}$, where the last term is the derivative of the equity with respect to the value of the assets (a quantity commonly called "the delta"), and is equal to $N(d_1)$. Under the further assumption that the dynamics of the equity can be described by a geometric Brownian motion with diffusion coefficient $\sigma_E E_t$, one has that

$$E_t = V_t N(d_1) \frac{\sigma}{\sigma_E}. \tag{3}$$

Given the other observable variables, it is thus possible to solve using numerical methods the system of non-linear equations (2) and (3) for the values of the two unknown variables V_t and σ.

Figure 1 shows the theoretical spread s_t on a 5-year CDS obtained using the Merton model as a function of the volatility of the equity (Panel A), for three different levels of the ratio of total assets ($A_t = D + E_t$) to equity (E_t) – the definition of leverage we adopt throughout the paper – and as a function of the leverage (Panel B), for three different levels of volatility. The risk-free interest rate is assumed to be fixed at 4%. All values are in percentages except for the CDS spread which is in basis points. As made clear by the figure, the main driver of the CDS spread in the Merton model is the level of volatility. When the volatility of the equity falls below 30, the CDS spread is almost negligible, no matter what the leverage is. In fact, for $\sigma_E = 30$ the theoretical CDS spread is still below 10 basis points even when the amount of debt is twice the value of equity (leverage=300). As the level of equity volatility increases, the theoretical CDS spread surges sharply and the relative (absolute) difference among firms with different leverages decreases (increases). If Panel A shows that the relationship between the theoretical CDS spread and the volatility of the equity is non-linear, an even stronger non-linearity arises when the theoretical CDS spread is expressed as a function of the leverage. Panel B, in fact, not only confirms the relevance of the equity volatility for the level of the theoretical spread but also shows a non-monotone relationship between the CDS spread and the leverage of the firm. This pattern arises from the fact that, when numerically solving equations (2) and (3), it turns out that higher levels of debt are associated with lower levels of asset volatility. This is because the higher the leverage the lower the weight the equity volatility receives as an estimator of the volatility of the whole value of the firm. Hence, at some point the negative impact that the higher debt has on the credit risk of the firm starts to be more than compensated by the positive impact of a decreasing asset volatility.

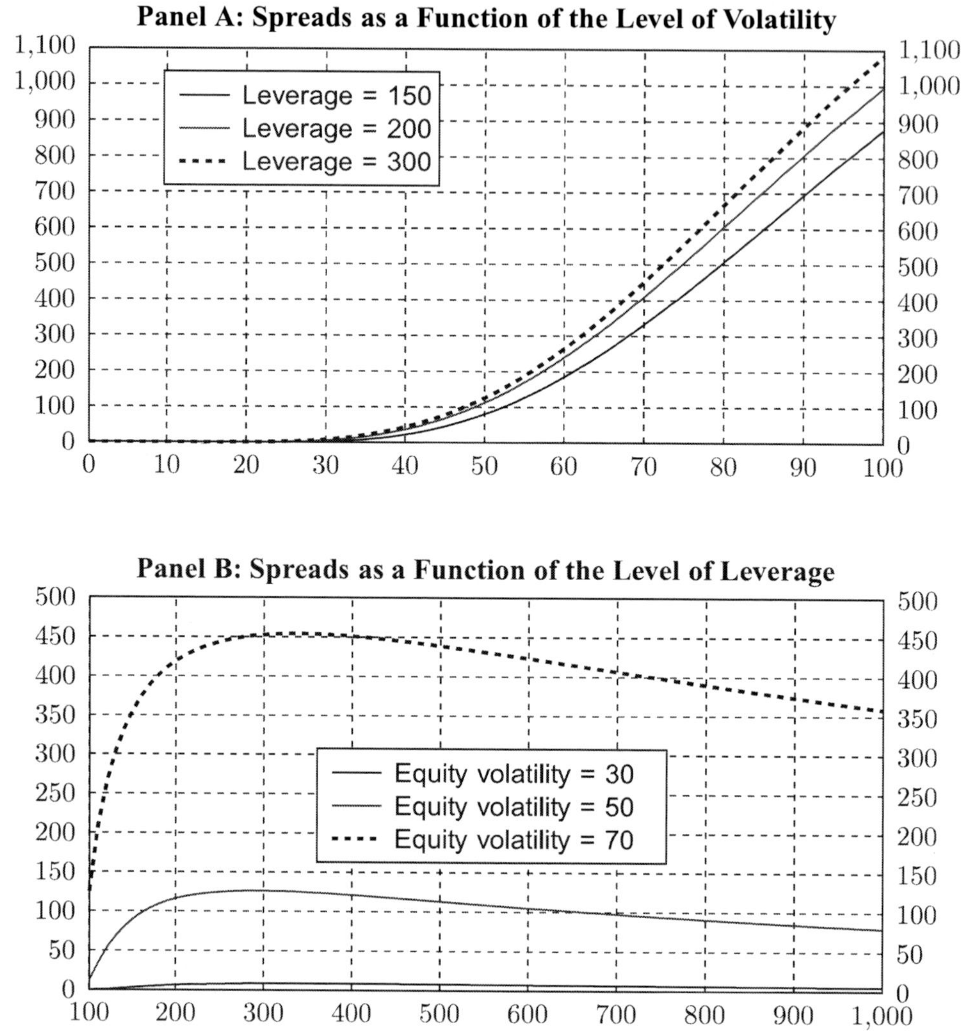

Figure 1. **Theoretical CDS Spreads Generated by the Merton Model.** Theoretical CDS spreads on the debt of firms with different leverage (or equity volatility) calculated using the Merton model, as a function of equity volatility (or leverage). The spreads are supposed to be paid with a quarterly frequency, the risk-free interest rate is constant and equal to 4% and the maturity of the debt is 5 years. Leverage is defined as the ratio of total assets (total liabilities plus market capitalization) to market capitalization. Theoretical CDS spreads are in basis points; equity volatility and leverage are in percentages.

The Merton model, due to its simplicity, provides a nice tool for understanding how fundamental variables, such as leverage and asset volatility, affect credit spreads. However, there are several features of real financial markets that are not taken into account by the model and that have led to many other extensions.[6] The three main drawbacks of the model are:

[6]For several extensions of the Merton model, see Cossin and Pirotte (2001) and references therein.

1. *There is only one kind of debt securities*. In the Merton model only the case of a single zero-coupon bond is considered. Not only do most corporate bonds pay coupons but firms usually issue several kinds of bonds with different characteristics;

2. *Default occurs only at the maturity of the debt and if and only if the value of the assets is below the face value of the debt*. In the real world default can occur at any time before the maturity of the debt if the firm fails to meet any kind of obligation, such as the payment of coupons. Moreover, bankruptcy is a process that usually involves several forms of cost which can result in models with default barriers different from the face value of the debt (e.g. Leland and Toft, 1996);

3. *Volatility is assumed to be constant for all maturities*. Empirical work on option pricing shows that implied volatility is not constant, neither for different strikes nor for different maturities. This means that volatility implied by equity options, which have maturity usually up to one year, could be a biased estimator of the volatility of equity over longer horizons.

All these caveats have to be borne in mind when evaluating the results of any empirical application of the Merton model like the one we describe in the next section.

4. Methodology

In this section we describe the data, the model and the statistical methodology used in our analysis.

4.1. Data Description

We started by selecting all CDS contracts in US dollars available through Bloomberg with maturity equal to 5 years (which are usually the most liquid contracts), written on the senior debt of US non-financial firms. We used end-of-day mid quotes for CDSs. In order to have data on market capitalization we restricted our sample to listed firms. For each company we gathered quarterly data on current liabilities, non-current liabilities, and cash and equivalents, from Bloomberg for the period between January 2002 and March 2009. We also collected daily data on companies' market capitalization, stock returns, and implied volatility derived from equity options. We then selected those contracts for which we could recover all data for at least 3 years, ending up with a sample of 167 companies. As a proxy of the risk-free interest rate curve we used the zero-coupon curve calculated by Datastream on US government bonds. We also collected daily data on the average levels of credit spreads for AA and BBB-rated US industrial companies (the option-adjusted spreads for the Merrill Lynch corporate industrial indices for US companies with AA and BBB ratings), a broad US equity market index (the S&P Composite index), and a broad index of US market implied volatility (the VIX index). In our regressions we use monthly average data for CDS spreads and for all other daily financial indicators. Quarterly balance sheet data were linearly interpolated. In order to control for the quality of CDS data we dropped daily observations whenever equal to the value of the previous day; we also dropped those monthly observations based on less than 5 daily data. Our final dataset, after dropping any

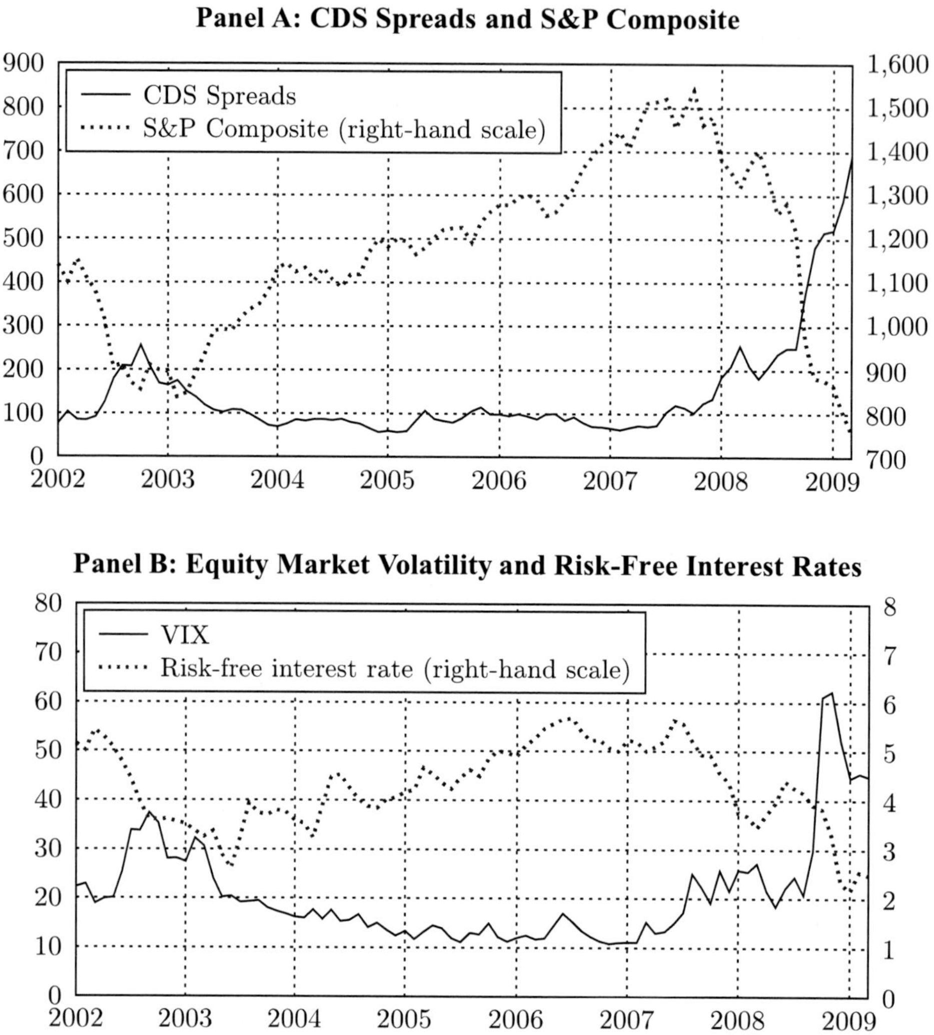

Figure 2. **Historical Behavior of CDS Spreads and Other Financial Series.** Monthly averages. CDS spreads are in basis points; the risk-free interest rate is in percentages and is the zero-coupon 5-year rate on US Government bonds.

firm-month observation with one or more missing values, includes 11,084 firm-month observations: 8,140 in the pre-crisis period (from January 2002 to June 2007) and 2,944 in the crisis period (from July 2007 to March 2009).

Table 1. Descriptive Statistics of the Data Set

	Mean	Median	Standard deviation	Min	Max
		Whole period (January 2002 – March 2009)			
CDS Spreads	116	54	221	6	7,995
Theoretical Spreads	71	3	213	0	1,862
Leverage	219	175	190	94	6,044
Volatility	35	30	19	7	369
Market Capitalization	25,939	13,616	39,549	58	420,623
		Pre-crisis period (January 2002 – June 2007)			
CDS Spreads	87	47	122	6	2,811
Theoretical Spreads	31	1	108	0	1,793
Leverage	214	174	162	94	4,420
Volatility	31	28	13	7	369
Market Capitalization	25,951	13,555	39,810	481	386,416
		Crisis period (July 2007 – March 2009)			
CDS Spreads	199	89	366	10	7,995
Theoretical Spreads	184	23	348	0	1,862
Leverage	234	179	252	104	6,044
Volatility	47	39	25	7	223
Market Capitalization	25,906	14,086	38,824	58	420,623

CDS spreads are end-of-day mid quotes. The theoretical spread is the spread calculated using the Merton model. Leverage is defined as the ratio of total assets (total liabilities plus market capitalization) to market capitalization. Volatility is the mean of implied volatilities on call and put stock options. CDS spreads and theoretical spreads are in basis points; leverage and volatility are in percentages; market capitalization is in millions of US dollars.

Table 2. Descriptive statistics of the Firms: Breakdown by Leverage

Leverage quartiles	Number of observations	CDS spreads	Theoretical spreads	Leverage	Volatility	Market capitalization
Whole period (Jan. 02 - Mar. 09)	11,084	116	71	219	35	25,939
108-148	2,789	59	27	132	32	43,972
148-186	2,809	82	62	166	33	24,719
186-242	2,894	101	71	210	35	18,069
242-1,527	2,592	233	128	380	40	16,643
Pre-crisis period (Jan. 02 - June 07)	8,140	87	31	214	31	25,950
108-148	2,009	45	7	131	28	44,197
148-186	2,023	59	26	161	29	24,752
186-242	2,174	77	25	206	31	17,764
242-1,527	1,934	170	66	364	35	17,451
Crisis period (July 07 - Mar. 09)	2,944	199	184	234	47	25,906
108-148	780	96	79	135	41	43,391
148-186	786	142	156	180	44	24,635
186-242	720	172	213	223	49	18,990
242-1,527	658	416	311	428	55	14,265

The breakdown refers to the average leverage of the firms in the whole period. Number of observations and mean values of the indicated variables. CDS spreads are end-of-day mid quotes. The theoretical spread is the spread calculated using the Merton model. Leverage is defined as the ratio of total assets (total liabilities plus market capitalization) to market capitalization. Volatility is the mean of implied volatilities on call and put stock options. CDS spreads and theoretical spreads are in basis points; leverage and volatility are in percentages; market capitalization is in millions of US dollars.

Table 3. Descriptive statistics of the Firms: Breakdown by Sector

	Number of observations	CDS spreads	Theoretical spreads	Leverage	Volatility	Market capitalization
Whole period (Jan. 02 - Mar. 09)	11,084	116	71	219	35	25,939
Industry	1,984	83	69	206	34	27,991
Communications/Technology	1,738	118	66	178	35	41,476
Basic materials/Energy	1,973	76	57	186	35	20,086
Consumer cyclical	2,752	204	127	279	42	18,746
Consumer non-cyclical	1,752	74	31	185	29	31,790
Utilities	885	88	24	285	27	14,656
Pre-crisis period (Jan. 02 - June 07)	8,140	87	31	214	31	25,951
Industry	1,416	65	36	202	30	28,025
Communications/Technology	1,328	93	42	170	32	41,661
Basic materials/Energy	1,432	57	14	186	30	18,475
Consumer cyclical	2,026	137	48	268	35	19,098
Consumer non-cyclical	1,285	61	11	177	26	32,529
Utilities	653	80	18	292	25	14,212
Crisis period (July 07 - Mar. 09)	2,944	199	184	234	47	25,906
Industry	568	127	152	214	45	27,905
Communications/Technology	410	200	144	205	43	40,879
Basic materials/Energy	541	127	171	184	48	24,352
Consumer cyclical	726	392	349	309	60	17,764
Consumer non-cyclical	467	110	87	208	38	29,756
Utilities	232	111	41	266	32	15,904

Number of observations and mean values of the indicated variables. CDS spreads are end-of-day mid quotes. The theoretical spread is the spread calculated using the Merton model. Leverage is defined as the ratio of total assets (total liabilities plus market capitalization) to market capitalization. Volatility is the mean of implied volatilities on call and put stock options. CDS spreads and theoretical spreads are in basis points; leverage and volatility are in percentages; market capitalization is in millions of US dollars.

The historical behavior of a few of our variables is shown in Figure 2. The plot shows the huge increase of CDS spreads after the onset of the financial crisis. It also makes apparent the negative relationships of CDS spreads with stock returns and government bond yields as well as the positive relationship with the level of volatility. All these facts are coherent with the theory underlying the Merton model. Some descriptive statistics of our dataset are reported in tables 1 to 2. As mentioned earlier, average CDS spreads increase sharply in the crisis period, from 87 to 199 basis points (Table 1). As expected, average CDS spreads increase with leverage (Table 2). They are much higher for firms in the Consumer cyclical and the Communication/Technology sectors (respectively, 137 and 93 basis points before the crisis and 392 and 200 basis points in the crisis period; Table 3). The theoretical spreads derived from the Merton model are consistently much lower than the observed ones (the average values in the whole sample period are 71 and 116, respectively); however, they appear to replicate spread variations through sectors and leverage classes rather well. Leverage and implied volatility also rise drastically during the crisis. Leverage is highest in the Utilities and Consumer cyclical sectors, lowest in Communication/Technology. Volatility is highest in the Consumer cyclical sector and lowest in the Consumer non-cyclical and Utilities sectors.

4.2. Empirical Models and Testing Methodology

As described in Section 3., the Merton model posits that credit spreads are a function of the value and volatility of the assets, the face value and maturity of the debt and the risk-free interest rate. As discussed in that section, the Merton model also implies that the relationship between CDS spreads and default factors is highly non-linear.

In order to test for the capacity of the Merton model to explain observed CDS spreads, we run the following univariate regression:

$$s(i,t) = \beta_0 + \beta_1 \bar{s}(i,t) + \varepsilon(i,t), \qquad \text{(Model 1)}$$

where $i = 1,\ldots,n$ denotes a specific firm and $t = 1,\ldots,m$ a specific time period. The variable $\bar{s}$ is the theoretical CDS spread calculated using the Merton model with the following assumptions: the face value of the debt, whose maturity is assumed to be equal to 5 years, is equal to the total of balance sheet liabilities net of cash; the value of the equity is equal to the market capitalization of the firm; the volatility of the equity is equal to the mean of implied volatilities calculated from call and put options; the risk-free interest rate is given by the 5-year zero-coupon rate on US government bonds.

Since Model 1 may not be able to fully describe the relationship between observed CDS spreads and default factors because of its simplifying assumptions, we also estimate the following three-factor linear model which has been used in other empirical works on the determinants of CDS spreads (e.g. Ericsson et al., 2009):

$$s(i,t) = \beta_0 + \beta_1 \sigma_E(i,t) + \beta_2 L(i,t) + \beta_3 r(t) + \varepsilon(i,t). \qquad \text{(Model 2)}$$

As for the explanatory variables, σ_E is the implied volatility calculated as the mean of implied volatilities derived from call and put options, L is the leverage calculated as the ratio of total assets (current and non-current liabilities, net of cash and equivalents, plus market capitalization) to market capitalization, and r is the 5-year zero-coupon rate on US government bonds. We opted to use implied volatility as a proxy of equity volatility to partially correct for the backward-looking nature of the historical volatility of share prices and because of its superiority in explaining CDS spreads (see Campbell and Taksler, 2003).

If the non-linearities implied by the Merton model had some additional explanatory power we would expect that, once we add the theoretical spread to the linear model, the portion of total variation explained by the model increases and the linear terms lose significance. Thus, we also estimate a third model which is a combination of the previous two models:

$$s(i,t) = \beta_0 + \beta_1 \bar{s}(i,t) + \beta_2 \sigma_E(i,t) + \beta_3 L(i,t) + \beta_4 r(i,t) + \varepsilon(i,t). \qquad \text{(Model 3)}$$

Finally, we estimate an extended model in which we include other variables, generally used in the literature on the determinants of credit spreads, such as the (log) returns of the firms' stocks, the slope of the yield curve (the difference between the 10-year and the 1-year zero-coupon rates on US government bonds), an index of the premium required by investors to hold riskier assets (the difference between the average OASs of the Merrill Lynch indices for US industrial companies with BBB and AA ratings), an equity market index (the log of the S&P Composite index), and an index of market uncertainty (the VIX index).

$$\begin{aligned} s(i,t) = {} & \beta_0 + \beta_1 \bar{s}(i,t) + \beta_2 \sigma_E(i,t) + \beta_3 L(i,t) + \beta_4 r(i,t) \\ & + \beta_5 STOCK(t) + \beta_6 SLOPE(t) + \beta_7 OAS(t) \\ & + \beta_8 SPCI(t) + \beta_9 VIX(t) + \varepsilon(i,t). \end{aligned} \qquad \text{(Model 4)}$$

The expected signs for the additional variables are:

- *STOCK*: a negative sign is expected, as higher stock values should signal higher future profitability and higher capacity of the firms to meet their obligations;

- *SLOPE*: the sign is uncertain. On the one hand, higher values for the slope should predict higher future risk-free rates, which should have a negative impact on CDS spreads. On the other hand, the increase in expected future interest rates may reduce the number of profitable projects available to the company and, in turn, increase credit spreads. Moreover, it has to be pointed out that we are already including a 5-year interest rate in our regressions. In our setting, a higher level for the slope would imply, *ceteris paribus*, a lower level for the short-term interest rate which is usually associated with worsening economic conditions and higher credit spreads;

- *OAS*: a positive sign is expected, as the higher the premium required by investors to hold riskier securities the higher should be the compensation required to hold credit risk;

- *SPCI*: the sign is uncertain. On the one hand a broad market increase of equity values should signal better economic conditions and a lower probability of default for the companies, and have a negative impact on CDS spreads. On the other hand, in our regressions we have already included individual stock returns that should take into account firm-specific expectations about profitability much better than broad market measures. In our setting, a broad market increase of equity values signals, *ceteris paribus*, a relatively bad performance of individual firms, so that a positive effect on CDS spreads could otherwise be expected;

- *VIX*: a positive sign is expected, as the higher the uncertainty in the market the higher the value of the put option that the bondholders implicitly sell to the shareholders when buying credit risk.

The four models are estimated in first-differences by running pooled OLS regressions with standard errors that allow for time correlation at firm level. As we said, models in first-differences are preferred to those in levels in order to isolate unobserved individual factors which do not vary over time and account for the possible problem of non-stationarity of the processes for CDS spreads.[7] As a robustness check, we also estimate Model 4 with a panel regression with fixed effects.[8]

We then compare the results across groups of firms defined according to the level of leverage or the economic sector. We abstract from factors not linked to credit risk which the literature has documented are significant in the corporate bond market (such as taxes, liquidity and supply and demand shocks) on the assumption that for the CDS market they are less relevant. However, we recognize that the lack of liquidity in the CDS market following the onset of the crisis could have an impact on our estimates and so we try to control for that by using the CDS bid-ask spread change as an instrument to distinguish between contracts that were hit by different liquidity shocks during the crisis. In particular, we run a set of regressions for subgroups of contracts defined according to the size of the change in the average bid-ask spread on CDS contracts from before to after the onset of the crisis.[9]

Finally, we perform a principal component analysis on CDS spread changes and regression residuals from Model 4 in order to assess to what extent the model reduces the weight of the first components of spreads variation. This analysis is conducted on a balanced sub-sample of 34 firms with complete monthly data from January 2003 to December 2008.

5. Results

In this section we report the results of our estimates. In order to have a comparison with previous literature we first discuss results for the four models presented in Section 4 in the pre-crisis period (January 2002 to June 2007) and then we asses how results change after the onset of the crisis (July 2007 to March 2009).

[7]We found that the augmented Dickey-Fuller test, run separately for each CDS time series, does not reject the null hypothesis of the presence of a unit-root in almost all cases.

[8]The test by Hausman (1978) implies that the model with random effects cannot be rejected; a panel data analysis with random effects did not result in appreciable differences.

[9]We were not able to estimate directly the effect of liquidity on spreads as our dependent variable is defined as the average between the bid and the ask prices and adding the bid-ask spread as an extra right-hand variable would have resulted in a misspecified model. For a study on the determinants of CDS bid-ask spreads, see Meng and ap Gwilym (2008).

Table 4. The Determinants of CDS Spread Changes

	Model 1			Model 2			Model 3			Model 4		
	Pre Crisis	Crisis	Diff.	Pre Crisis	Crisis	Diff.	Pre Crisis	Crisis	Diff.	Pre Crisis	Crisis	Diff.
Theoretical spread	0.32***	0.20***	−0.12***				0.18***	0.00	−0.18	0.16***	−0.03	−0.20
Volatility				2.72***	1.29***	−1.43***	1.22*	1.25	0.03	0.99	1.67	0.68
Leverage				0.35***	0.92***	0.57***	0.37***	0.92***	0.55***	0.35***	0.91***	0.56***
Interest rate				−3.56***	−41.21***	−37.65***	−2.49***	−41.26***	−38.78***	−3.19**	−15.61	−12.42
Stock return										−0.42***	−0.17	0.26
Slope yield curve										3.29*	9.44**	6.15
Corporate spread										0.56***	0.65***	0.09
S&P Composite										1.01***	1.01	0.00
VIX										0.27	−0.53	−0.79
Intercept	−0.64**	14.26***	14.9***	−0.13	−1.17	−1.04	−0.35	−1.16	−0.81	0.44*	−3.10**	−3.54**
Adjusted R^2	0.25	0.07		0.48	0.50		0.52	0.50		0.54	0.51	
No. obs.	8,140	2,944		8,140	2,944		8,140	2,944		8,140	2,944	

The values in the table are obtained by running a pooled OLS regression for all observations in the selected period, with standard errors that allow for time correlation at firm level. Monthly data from January 2002 to March 2009; the pre-crisis period goes from January 2002 to June 2007; the post-crisis period from July 2007 to March 2009. The explanatory variables are changes in the monthly averages of: the estimated theoretical spread for firm i at time t; the implied volatility of options written on the stocks of firm i at time t; the leverage ratio of firm i at time t; the 5-year zero-coupon interest rate on the US government bond at time t; the log of the stock value of firm i at time t; the slope of the zero-coupon curve on US government bonds (10-1 yrs) at time t; the Merrill Lynch industrial bond average spread (BBB-AA) at time t; the log of the S&P Composite stock index at time t; the VIX volatility index at time t; a constant term. Observed and theoretical spreads and the corporate spread are in basis points, all other variables are in percentages. Significance levels: *** = 1%; ** = 5%; * = 10%.

5.1. The Pre-Crisis Period

As shown in Table 4, by regressing observed CDS spreads on the theoretical spreads obtained using the Merton model for the period before the onset of the crisis we find that, as expected, the coefficient of the theoretical spread (0.32) is positive and highly significant, and the explanatory power of the model (adjusted R^2 statistics equal to 0.25) is comparable to previous studies on the determinants of CDS spread changes (e.g. Ericsson et al., 2009). However, the coefficient is significantly different from the value of one that is predicted by theory.

Turning to Model 2, all the estimated coefficients have the expected signs and are strongly significant. In particular, a one percentage point increase in the levels of volatility and leverage raises the CDS spread by 2.72 and 0.35 basis points, respectively. A similar increase in the interest rate level determines a drop of 3.56 basis points for the CDS spread. The adjusted R^2 statistics (0.48) is much higher than in Model 1; this aspect suggests that the Merton model constrains the effects of the single factors on CDS spreads in ways that are not fully consistent with market data.

In Model 3, where the theoretical spread is added to the more traditional three-factors model, the coefficients of the theoretical spread, volatility and interest rate are all lower in absolute terms when compared with the previous models. Moreover, the coefficient of volatility shows a large loss of significance, which is probably due to the high level of correlation with the theoretical spread (70 per cent). The linear contribution of leverage, on the contrary, remains basically unchanged and highly significant; this could be due to the fact that the Merton model is not very sensitive to changes in leverage (see Figure 1). The adjusted R^2 statistics increases further from 0.48 to 0.52, highlighting the positive contribution to the model of the theoretical spread, which should partly take into account the non-linearities embedded in the pricing of CDSs.

In Model 4, the other explanatory variables that the literature has indicated as important determinants of credit spreads (such as, individual stock returns, the slope of the yield curve, an indicator of risk aversion in the bond market, and a broad market stock index return) have the expected signs and all but the indicator of broad market uncertainty (the VIX index) have significant effects on CDS spreads.[10] However, their overall contribution to the explanatory power of the model is marginal, as the adjusted R^2 statistic only rises from 0.52 to 0.54.

Tables 5 shows that results obtained running a panel regression with fixed effects confirm those obtained with the pooled OLS regression, both in terms of absolute values and the significance of the coefficients. We also checked that our results are robust to the filtering procedures applied to the original data such as the dropping of stale quotations and of observations referring to months with few CDS quotes. We also verified that results remain basically unchanged when we limit the analysis to a balanced dataset including only a subset of companies with complete data in the period from 2003 to 2008.

[10] The coefficients of *SLOPE* and *SPCI*, whose signs are theoretically uncertain, are positive.

All in all, results suggest that factors predicted by the theory as being relevant for credit spreads have indeed a good explanatory power. Moreover, the theoretical spread calculated using the Merton model does convey specific information on credit risk that cannot be captured by the linear models, supporting the hypothesis that non-linearities are important in explaining credit spreads.

5.2. The Crisis Period

The financial crisis has disrupted credit markets, causing spreads and volatility to surge and market liquidity to evaporate (e.g. International Monetary Fund, 2008). The impact of these events on the pricing of credit risk is a matter of debate. On the one hand, one might expect that the crisis, by amplifying the importance of systemic risk factors, has caused a generalized increase of spreads (almost) independently from the fundamental characteristics of firms. On the other hand, the crisis could have exacerbated the differences between firms belonging to different classes of risk, as investors have become more aware of idiosyncratic risk factors. In order to assess the impact of the financial crisis on the pricing of risk, we compare the results in the pre-crisis period with those obtained during the crisis period. Table 4 reports the results of the regressions for our four models in both periods, as well as the tests on the differences between the two periods.

As for Model 1, the striking fact is the drop in both the coefficient of the theoretical spread and the explanatory power of the model, from 0.32 and 25% before the start of the crisis, to 0.20 and just 7%, respectively. This indicates that during the crisis the empirical relationship between CDS spreads and default factors is no longer described by the specific functional form of the Merton model.

This interpretation is confirmed by looking at the results from Model 2, where the default factors are included in the regression separately and the functional form between the default factors and the CDS spreads is not determined by the theoretical model. In this case we actually find a moderate increase in the explanatory power of the model from before to during the crisis. Moreover, all the coefficients maintain the expected signs and are highly significant. However, the impact of equity volatility on CDS spreads more than halves, suggesting that the wide swings in implied volatility, which have characterized the crisis period, have probably made this indicator a poor proxy for long-term asset volatility. This fact could also explain the loss of importance in Model 1 of the theoretical spread, which is mostly driven by volatility changes (see Figure 1). At the same time, during the crisis spreads have become much more sensitive to changes in leverage (from 0.35 to 0.92) and interest rates (from -3.56 to -41.21). On the one hand, the increased importance of leverage may reflect a greater awareness by investors of firm-specific characteristics. On the other hand, the increased relevance of interest rates probably reflects the fact that during the crisis risk-free interest rates have been interpreted as better proxies of economic activity: lower interest rates should signal worse economic conditions and higher credit risks.

Table 5. The Determinants of CDS Spread Changes: Pooled and Panel Regressions

	Pre-Crisis		Crisis		Difference	
	Coeff.	t-Stud.	Coeff.	t-Stud.	Coeff.	t-Stud.
Pooled OLS Regression						
Theoretical spread	0.16***	2.63	−0.03	−0.25	−0.20	−1.29
Volatility	0.99	1.25	1.67	0.60	0.68	0.24
Leverage	0.35***	9.65	0.91***	5.19	0.56***	3.16
Interest rate	−3.19**	−2.52	−15.61	−1.61	−12.42	−1.26
Stock return	−0.42***	−3.57	−0.17	−0.32	0.26	0.51
Slope yield curve	3.29*	1.84	9.44**	2.27	6.15	1.34
Corporate spreads	0.56***	8.22	0.65***	4.37	0.09	0.61
S&P Composite	1.01***	4.27	1.01	1.64	0.00	−0.01
VIX	0.27	0.65	−0.53	−0.44	−0.79	−0.61
Intercept	0.44*	1.76	−3.10**	−2.02	−3.54**	−2.33
Adjusted R^2	0.54		0.51			
Panel Fixed Effect Regression						
Theoretical spread	0.16***	2.63	−0.04	−0.28	−0.20	−1.31
Volatility	0.96	1.22	1.62	0.61	0.69	0.24
Leverage	0.34***	9.59	0.93***	5.21	0.57***	3.18
Interest rate	−2.95**	−2.28	−15.76*	−1.73	−12.90	−1.35
Stock return	−0.44***	−3.59	0.05	0.09	0.34	0.68
Slope yield curve	3.04*	1.66	9.13**	2.18	6.60	1.46
Corporate spreads	0.56***	8.26	0.67***	4.56	0.10	0.64
S&P Composite	1.05***	4.29	0.70	1.10	−0.12	−0.20
VIX	0.30	0.75	−0.50	−0.43	−0.80	−0.62
Intercept	0.41*	1.82	−3.56	−1.30	−3.38**	−2.22
Adjusted R^2	0.54		0.50			
No. obs.	8,140		2,944			

The values in the table compares the result from pooled OLS and panel fixed-effect regressions run on the same sample. Standard errors allow for time correlation at firm level. Monthly data from January 2002 to March 2009; the pre-crisis period goes from January 2002 to June 2007; the post-crisis period from July 2007 to March 2009. The explanatory variables are changes in the monthly averages of: the estimated theoretical spread for firm i at time t; the implied volatility of options written on the stocks of firm i at time t; the leverage ratio of firm i at time t; the 5-year zero-coupon interest rate on the US government bond at time t; the log of the stock value of firm i at time t; the slope of the zero-coupon curve on US government bonds (10-1 yrs) at time t; the Merrill Lynch industrial bond average spread (BBB-AA) at time t; the log of the S&P Composite stock index at time t; the VIX volatility index at time t; a constant term. Observed and theoretical spreads and the corporate spread are in basis points, all other variables are in percentages. Significance levels: *** = 1%; ** = 5%; * = 10%.

Changes in the results of Model 3 from the pre-crisis period to the crisis period are rather similar to those of Model 2, given the negligible impact of the theoretical spread during the crisis.

In Model 4, the interest rate coefficient also loses its significance during the crisis, possibly in favor of the slope of the yield curve. Given the negative relationship between the slope of the yield curve and short-term interest rates, for a given level of longer term yields – for which our regressions already control for – the positive coefficient on the slope of the yield curve seems to indicate that the CDS market has been looking at short-term interest rates as a better indicator of economic activity than longer-term interest rates. Lower short-term rates (and a higher slope) are associated with worsening economic conditions and greater CDS spreads.

Overall, during the crisis the proportion of explained variations decreases only slightly, from 54% to 51% in Model 4, confirming that the model works rather well also in this case. This result highlights that the underlying risk factors identified by the literature as relevant for the pricing of credit risk have maintained their explanatory power also in a period of remarkable stress for the CDS market. In this regard, the CDS market appears to have continued to price credit risk in much the same fashion as it did before the crisis.

Table 5 shows that our estimates for the crisis period are also confirmed by a panel regression with fixed effects.

Finally, we performed a principal component analysis on CDS spread changes and regression residuals from Model 4. The analysis shows that during the crisis CDS spreads appear to have been moving increasingly together, as reported in Figure 3. The fraction of CDS variations explained by the first component increases from 45% to 62% during the crisis period. When the analysis is repeated using the residuals of Model 4, the two values drop to 25% and 40%, respectively, thus confirming the ability of the model to capture a substantial part of the common factors underlying the spread changes. Our result suggests that spread changes during the crisis are increasingly driven by common or systematic factors and less by firm-specific factors. In order to take into account time varying factors, we repeated the analysis including monthly dummy variables but the findings were mostly unchanged. Given that general indicators of economic activity, uncertainty, and risk aversion are already included in our model, our results seem to point to the presence of a market-specific factor that hit CDSs during the crisis in forms that are not fully reflected in other markets. A large part of CDS spread variations during the crisis is thus still to be explained.

5.3. Further Analyses

In order to dig deeper into previous results we repeated the analysis based on Model 4 on sub-groups of firms defined according to the level of leverage, the economic sector, and the size of the change in the average bid-ask spreads for CDSs from before to during the crisis.

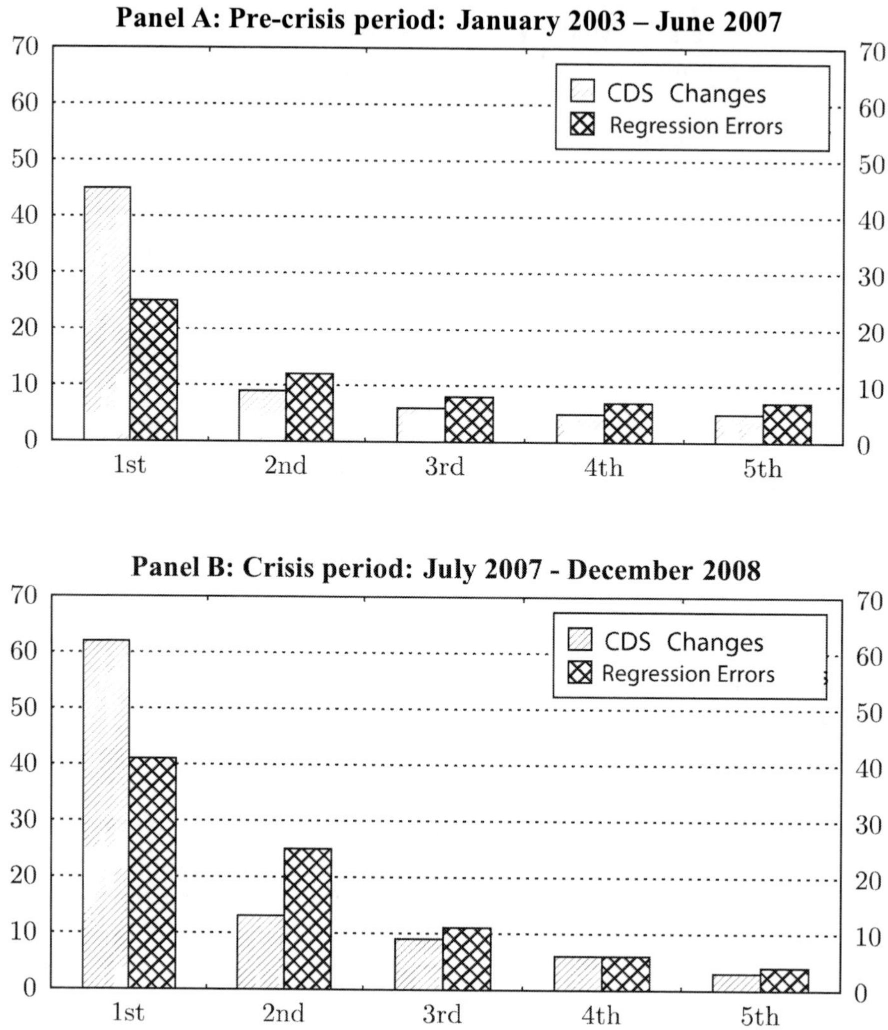

Figure 3. **Principal Component Analysis.** The principal component analysis has been conducted on a balanced sub-sample of 34 firms with complete data from January 2003 to December 2008 for the CDS changes and the regression residuals of Model 4. The explained variations by the first 5 components are expressed in percentages.

Table 6. The Determinants of CDS Spread Changes by Leverage

	1st quartile (< 148)			2nd quartile (148 – 186)			3rd quartile (186 – 242)			4th quartile (> 242)		
	Pre Crisis	Crisis	Diff.	Pre Crisis	Crisis	Diff.	Pre Crisis	Crisis	Diff.	Pre Crisis	Crisis	Diff.
Theoretical spread	0.17***	0.04	−0.13**	0.21***	0.09**	−0.12*	0.18**	0.03	−0.15	0.09	−0.18	−0.27
Volatility	0.09	−0.06	−0.15	−0.20	−0.67	−0.48	0.08	0.46	0.37	2.19**	4.04	1.84
Leverage	0.91**	0.95**	0.04	0.21	0.66***	0.45*	0.46**	0.75***	0.29	0.28***	0.86***	0.58***
Interest rate	1.19	−20.61***	−21.80***	−4.43**	−28.24***	−23.81***	−3.64**	−28.66***	−25.01***	−5.83	8.56	14.38
Stock return	−0.05	−0.26	−0.22	−0.59***	−0.47	0.12	−0.05	−0.16	−0.11	−0.96***	−0.49	0.47
Slope yield curve	0.36	8.67**	8.31*	3.95*	9.95**	6.00	2.43	2.17	−0.26	5.04	8.71	3.68
Corporate spreads	0.24***	0.44***	0.20**	0.39***	0.40***	0.01	0.52***	0.57***	0.05	1.15***	1.15**	0.00
S&P Composite	0.35	0.76***	0.41	0.82***	0.57	−0.25	0.46	0.78	0.33	2.70***	1.62	−1.08
VIX	0.74	0.13	−0.61	0.83**	0.11	−0.72	0.63	−0.44	−1.08	0.35	−0.49	−0.84
Intercept	−0.47	−3.45***	−2.98***	0.05	−2.95*	−2.99*	0.24	−3.76***	−3.99***	1.24*	−0.64	−1.87
Adjusted R^2	0.25	0.35		0.43	0.33		0.30	0.39		0.63	0.52	
No. obs.	2,009	780		2,023	786		2,174	720		1,934	658	

The values in the table are obtained by running a pooled OLS regression for all observations in the selected period and quartile of the firms' average leverage, with standard errors that allow for time correlation at firm level. Monthly data from January 2002 to March 2009; the pre-crisis period goes from January 2002 to June 2007; the post-crisis period from July 2007 to March 2009. The explanatory variables are changes in the monthly averages of: the estimated theoretical spread for firm i at time t; the implied volatility of options written on the stocks of firm i at time t; the leverage ratio of firm i at time t; the 5-year zero-coupon interest rate on the US government bond at time t; the log of the stock value of firm i at time t; the slope of the zero-coupon curve on US government bonds (10-1 yrs) at time t; the Merrill Lynch industrial bond average spread (BBB-AA) at time t; the log of the S&P Composite stock index at time t; the VIX volatility index at time t; a constant term. Observed and theoretical spreads and the corporate spread are in basis points, all other variables are in percentages. Significance levels: *** = 1%; ** = 5%; * = 10%.

Table 7. The Determinants of CDS Spread Changes by Sector

	Industrial			Communications & Technology			Basic materials & Energy		
	Pre Crisis	Crisis	Diff.	Pre Crisis	Crisis	Diff.	Pre Crisis	Crisis	Diff.
Theoretical spread	0.27**	0.04	−0.22*	0.16***	0.05	−0.11	0.04	0.05	0.02
Volatility	−0.71**	1.33	2.04*	0.01	0.20	0.18	0.12	0.34	0.22
Leverage	0.14	0.51	0.37*	0.89***	0.81***	−0.08	0.41*	0.36***	−0.05
Interest rate	0.12	−21.34***	−21.46***	−9.95**	−44.12*	−34.17	−1.53	−30.19***	−28.66***
Stock return	−0.49*	−0.11	0.37	−0.55*	0.40	0.96	0.07	−0.46*	−0.53*
Slope yield curve	1.08	−0.14	−1.22	10.39**	−8.36	−18.75	2.03	2.21	0.18
Corporate spreads	0.41***	0.36*	−0.05	0.71***	1.13***	0.42	0.51***	0.29***	−0.23
S&P Composite	0.40	−0.35	−0.75	2.02***	0.66	−1.36	0.45*	0.06	−0.39
VIX	0.41	−1.81**	−2.21**	2.02**	−0.87	−2.89	0.56*	−1.08*	−1.64**
Intercept	0.11	−2.87	−2.98	−0.16	−5.28	−5.12	0.29	−1.48	−1.77
Adjusted R^2	0.33	0.40		0.46	0.18		0.25	0.50	
No. obs.	1,416	568		1,328	410		1,432	541	

(Cont.)

The values in the table are obtained by running a pooled OLS regression for all observations in the selected sector and period, with standard errors that allow for time correlation at firm level. Monthly data from January 2002 to March 2009; the pre-crisis period goes from January 2002 to June 2007; the post-crisis period from July 2007 to March 2009. The explanatory variables are changes in the monthly averages of: the estimated theoretical spread for firm i at time t; the implied volatility of options written on the stocks of firm i at time t; the leverage ratio of firm i at time t; the 5-year zero-coupon interest rate on the US government bond at time t; the log of the stock value of firm i at time t; the slope of the zero-coupon curve on US government bonds (10-1 yrs) at time t; the Merrill Lynch industrial bond average spread (BBB-AA) at time t; the log of the S&P Composite stock index at time t; the VIX volatility index at time t; a constant term. Observed and theoretical spreads and the corporate spread are in basis points, all other variables are in percentages. Significance levels: *** = 1%; ** = 5%; * = 10%.

Table 7.Continued

	Consumer Cyclical			Consumer Non cyclical			Utilities		
	Pre Crisis	Crisis	Diff.	Pre Crisis	Crisis	Diff.	Pre Crisis	Crisis	Diff.
Theoretical spread	0.06	−0.14	−0.19	0.11	0.07**	−0.04	0.40***	0.08***	−0.33***
Volatility	2.11*	2.57	0.46	1.01***	0.03	−0.97**	−0.50	−0.54	−0.03
Leverage	0.30***	0.94***	0.63***	−0.16***	0.23***	0.39***	0.74**	−0.21	−0.95**
Interest rate	0.00	19.49	19.48	−2.42	−25.43***	−23.01***	−14.18**	−31.25***	−17.06*
Stock return	−0.75***	−1.86	−1.11	−0.60*	−0.64***	−0.04	0.79	−1.26***	−2.04**
Slope yield curve	−2.27	16.89	19.16	3.98	19.41***	15.44**	23.40***	−2.32	−25.72***
Corporate spreads	0.90***	1.45***	0.55	0.16***	0.19**	0.03	0.75***	0.41***	−0.34
S&P Composite	1.67**	2.11	0.44	−0.10	0.89***	0.99**	1.51	1.83***	0.32
VIX	0.05	−0.25	−0.30	−0.66	0.42	1.08	1.75	1.90***	0.15
Intercept	0.70	−4.04	−4.74	0.57	−4.19***	−4.75***	0.79	−0.82	−1.61
Adjusted R^2	0.64	0.62		0.20	0.57		0.74	0.40	
No. obs.	2,026	726		1,285	467		653	232	

The values in the table are obtained by running a pooled OLS regression for all observations in the selected sector and period, with standard errors that allow for time correlation at firm level. Monthly data from January 2002 to March 2009; the pre-crisis period goes from January 2002 to June 2007; the post-crisis period from July 2007 to March 2009. The explanatory variables are changes in the monthly averages of: the estimated theoretical spread for firm i at time t; the implied volatility of options written on the stocks of firm i at time t; the leverage ratio of firm i at time t; the 5-year zero-coupon interest rate on the US government bond at time t; the log of the stock value of firm i at time t; the slope of the zero-coupon curve on US government bonds (10-1 yrs) at time t; the Merrill Lynch industrial bond average spread (BBB-AA) at time t; the log of the S&P Composite stock index at time t; the VIX volatility index at time t; a constant term. Observed and theoretical spreads and the corporate spread are in basis points, all other variables are in percentages. Significance levels: *** = 1%; ** = 5%; * = 10%.

Table 8. The Determinants of CDS Spread Changes by Liquidity Change

	1st quartile (< −0.9)			2nd quartile (−0.9 – 1.1)			3rd quartile (1.1 – 5.5)			4th quartile (> 5.5)		
	Pre Crisis	Crisis	Diff.	Pre Crisis	Crisis	Diff.	Pre Crisis	Crisis	Diff.	Pre Crisis	Crisis	Diff.
Theoretical spread	0.25***	0.02	−0.23**	0.20***	0.04*	−0.16**	0.21***	0.01	−0.20***	0.20***	−0.22	−0.42
Volatility	0.07	0.36	0.29	0.44**	0.07	−0.37	−0.06	0.72*	0.77	−0.04	3.76	3.81
Leverage	0.26**	1.46***	1.21***	0.11	0.65**	0.55**	0.09	0.32***	0.23*	0.43***	0.86***	0.43**
Interest rate	−6.65**	−18.20***	−11.55***	−0.87	−17.03***	−16.16***	−2.01**	−24.84***	−22.83***	−1.08	9.14	10.21
Stock return	−0.66*	0.86**	1.52**	−0.13	0.16	0.28	−0.03	−0.33	−0.30	−0.71***	−0.63	0.08
Slope yield curve	10.84***	7.93**	−2.91	−0.52	6.73***	7.25***	2.01	4.92	2.92	−1.13	3.76	4.90
Corporate spreads	0.65***	0.2***	−0.45***	0.15***	0.24***	0.09*	0.38***	0.74***	0.36***	0.84***	1.58***	0.75
S&P Compos-ite	0.91**	0.57*	−0.33	0.11	0.03	−0.08	0.41***	0.41	0.00	2.18***	0.31	−1.87
VIX	0.50	0.46	−0.04	0.09	−0.07	−0.16	0.92**	−0.81*	−1.73***	1.42*	0.07	−1.36
Intercept	0.28	−3.37***	−3.65***	−0.26	−3.17***	−2.91***	−0.03	−4.01***	−3.98***	0.13	−3.11	−3.24
Adjusted R^2	0.51	0.48		0.21	0.43		0.33	0.41		0.47	0.52	
No. obs.	2,155	709		1,953	750		1,757	733		1,811	752	

The values in the table are obtained by running a pooled OLS regression for all observations in the selected period and quartile of the firms' liquidity change, with standard errors that allow for time correlation at firm level. The liquidity change is defined as the change in the average bid-ask spread of the CDSs, at the firm level, from before to after the onset of the crisis. Monthly data from January 2002 to March 2009; the pre-crisis period goes from January 2002 to June 2007; the post-crisis period from July 2007 to March 2009. The explanatory variables are changes in the monthly averages of: the estimated theoretical spread for firm i at time t; the implied volatility of options written on the stocks of firm i at time t; the leverage ratio of firm i at time t; the 5-year zero-coupon interest rate on the US government bond at time t; the log of the stock value of firm i at time t; the slope of the zero-coupon curve on US government bonds (10-1 yrs) at time t; the Merrill Lynch industrial bond average spread (BBB-AA) at time t; the log of the S&P Composite stock index at time t; the VIX volatility index at time t; a constant term. Observed and theoretical spreads and the corporate spread are in basis points, all other variables are in percentages. Significance levels: *** = 1%; ** = 5%; * = 10%.

Analysis by Leverage Quartiles

In Table 6 we report the results for an analysis based on the average level of leverage of the firms. First of all, we note that the explanatory power of the model is highest for the companies with leverage in the highest quartile (0.63 in the pre-crisis period) and lowest for the companies in the lowest quartile (0.25). As the two groups are also associated with the highest and lowest levels of CDS spreads, these results confirm previous findings that structural models can better explain the credit spreads for firms with relatively lower credit quality (e.g. Collin-Dufresne et al. 2001, for an analysis on corporate spreads, and Greatrex, 2008, for comparable results on CDSs). We also note that for firms with low leverage the explanatory power of the model increases substantially during the crisis, to 0.35. The increased explanatory power of the model for firms with low levels of leverage does not derive from factors related to firm-specific characteristics (such as leverage and volatility), but from market-wide factors such as the interest rate and the market price of risk (as captured by the significant increase of the coefficient of the corporate bond spread). For firms with the highest levels of leverage, the leverage itself is the variable whose coefficient increased more significantly during the crisis, pointing to the fact the investors became more concerned about the particular weaknesses of the balance sheets of those firms.

Analysis by Economic Sector

Table 7 reports the results for the sectoral analysis. We notice that, across sectors, the model explains the highest proportion of variation for companies in the Utilities and Consumer Cyclical sectors, which are also the ones with the highest levels of leverage. During the crisis model performance sharply increases for firms in the Basic materials/Energy and Consumer non cyclical sectors, which are characterized by relatively low levels of leverage, volatility, and CDS spreads, probably reflecting the fact that these firms have been perceived as relatively riskier than before the crisis. Actually, for these sectors the theoretical spreads calculated using the Merton model show the highest levels of relative increase from before to after the onset of the crisis (see Table 3). Overall, this is further evidence of the capacity of the model to price CDSs of riskier companies better.

Analysis by Liquidity Change

In order to check whether the change of liquidity in the CDS market had any impact on the capacity of the model to explain CDS spread variations, we repeated our analysis on the basis of the bid-ask spread on CDS contracts. In particular, we grouped firms into four quartiles according to the change in the average bid-ask spread they experienced from before to after the onset of the crisis. The results are reported in Table 8. The interesting result is that the overall explanatory power of the model remains broadly the same during the crisis period for both the contracts in the lowest and highest quartiles of bid-ask spread changes. For firms in the highest quartile, moreover, all coefficients of the regression, except for that related to leverage, do not show any significant change during the crisis. These results suggest that the lack of liquidity experienced in the CDS market during the crisis, as proxied by larger bid-ask spreads, did not modify the basic relationships between CDS spread changes and their explanatory factors.

6. Conclusion

In this paper we analyze the determinants of CDS spread changes (based on a sample of 167 US non-financial firms over the period between January 2002 and March 2009), using the variables that the literature has found to have a theoretical and empirical impact on CDS spreads. We include in our regressions the theoretical spread implied by the Merton model in order to deal with the non-linear relationships between the individual characteristics of the firms and CDS spreads. We find that the inclusion of this additional term improves the capacity of changes in the fundamental variables to explain changes in CDS spreads. When the theoretical spread calculated using the Merton model is introduced in the regressions, the coefficient of the equity volatility decreases significantly, because of the high sensitivity of the Merton model to this parameter. On the contrary, leverage, which has only second-order effects on the theoretical spreads, maintains its usefulness in explaining CDS spread changes. The extended model is able to explain 54% of the variations in CDS spreads in the pre-crisis period and 51% in the crisis period, which is higher than previous findings of studies on corporate bond and CDS spread changes.

We also analyze how the financial crisis has changed the way in which credit risk is priced in the CDS market. We find that the contribution of the leverage of the firms to the explanation of CDS spread changes is much higher during the crisis than before, as investors appear to have become more aware of individual risk factors. At the same time, the impact of equity volatility substantially decreases, possibly because the large swings in implied volatility during the crisis period have made this indicator a poor proxy for long-term asset volatility. We also find that the overall capacity of the model to explain CDS changes is almost the same before and during the turmoil, thus highlighting that the underlying risk factors identified by the literature as relevant for the pricing of the credit risk have maintained their explanatory power even in a period of remarkable stress for the CDS market.

Finally, we show that during the crisis CDS spreads appear to have been moving increasingly together, driven by a common factor that our model was only partly able to explain. Given that the model includes general indicators of economic activity, uncertainty, and risk aversion, our results point to the presence of a market-specific factor that hit the CDS market during the crisis in forms not fully reflected in other markets. The exact identification of this factor is an interesting topic for further research.

References

Abid, F., & Naifar, N. (2006). The determinants of credit default swap rates: An explanatory study. *International Journal of Theoretical and Applied Finance,* **9** (1), 23-42.

Alexander, C., & Kaeck, A. (2008). Regime dependent determinants of credit default swap spreads. *Journal of Banking & Finance,* **32** (6), 1008-1021.

Amato, J., & Remolona, E. M. (2005). The Pricing of Unexpected Credit Losses. *BIS Working Papers*, No. **190**.

Anderson, R., & Sundaresan, S. (2000). A Comparative Study of Structural Models of Corporate Bond Yields: An Explanatory Investigation. *Journal of Banking & Finance,* **24** (1-2), 255-269.

Annaert, J., De Ceuster, M., Van Roy, P., & Vespro, C. (2009). What determines euro area bank CDS spreads? In National Bank of Belgium, *Financial Stability Review.*

Aunon-Nerin, D., Cossin, D., Hricko, T., & Huang, Z. (2002). Exploring for the determinants of credit risk in credit default swap transaction data: Is fixed-income markets' information sufficient to evaluate credit risk? *FAME Research Paper Series,* No. **65.**

Avramov, D., Jostova, G., & Philipov, A. (2007). Understanding changes in corporate credit spreads. *Financial Analysts Journal,* **63** (2), 90-105.

Black, F., & Scholes, M. (1973). The pricing of options and corporate liabilities. *Journal of Political Economy,* **81** (3), 637-654.

Blanco, R., Brennan, S., & Marsh, I. W. (2005). An empirical analysis of the dynamic relationship between investment-grade bonds and credit default swap. *Journal of Finance,* 60 (5), 2255-2281.

Byström, H. (2006). CreditGrades and the iTraxx CDS index market. *Financial Analysts Journal,* **62** (6), 65-76.

Campbell, J. Y., & Taksler, G. B. (2003). Equity volatility and corporate bond yields *Journal of Finance,* **58** (6), 2321-2349.

Collin-Dufresne, P., Goldstein, R. S., & Martin, J. S. (2001). The determinants of credit spread changes. *The Journal of Finance,* **56** (6), 2177-2207.

Committee on the Global Financial System (2003). *Credit risk transfer,* Bank for International Settlements.

Cossin, D., & Pirotte, H. (2001). *Advanced credit risk analysis.* Chichester, UK: John Wiley & Sons, Ltd.

Cremers, M., Driessen, J., Maenhout, P., & Weinbaum, D. (2008). Individual stock-option prices and credit spreads. *Journal of Banking & Finance,* **32** (12), 2706-2715.

Di Cesare, A. (2005). Do market-based indicators anticipate rating agencies? Evidence for international banks. *Economic Notes,* **35** (1), 121-150.

Driessen, J. (2005). Is default event risk priced in corporate bonds? *Review of Financial Studies, 18* (1), 165-195.

Elton, E. J., Gruber, M. J., Agrawal, D., & Mann, C. (2001). Explaining the rate spread on corporate bonds. *The Journal of Finance,* **56** (1), 247-277.

Eom, Y. H., Helwege, J., & Huang, J. Z. (2004). Structural Models of Corporate Bond Pricing: An Empirical Analysis. *The Review of Financial Studies,* **17** (2), 499-544.

Ericsson, J., Reneby, J., & Wang, H. (2007). Can structural models price default risk? Evidence from bond and credit derivative markets. Mimeo, electronic copy available at: http://ssrn.com/abstract=637042.

Ericsson, J., Jacobs, K., & Oviedo, R. (2009). The Determinants of credit default swap premia. *Journal of Financial and Quantitative Analysis,* **44** (1), 109-132.

European Central Bank (2009a). *Financial Stability Review*, June.

European Central Bank (2009b). *Credit default swaps and counterparty risk*. Frankfurt am Main, Germany.

Fitch Ratings (2006). *Global Credit Derivatives Survey.*

Giesecke, K. (2004). Credit risk modeling and valuation: An introduction. In D. Shimko (Ed.), *Credit Risk: Models and Management*. London: Riskbooks.

Granger, C. W. J., & Newbold, P. (1974). Spurious regressions in econometrics. *Journal of Econometrics, 2* (2), 111-120.

Greatrex, C. A. (2008). The credit default swap market's determinants. *Discussion Paper Series,* No. 2008-05, Department of Economics, Fordham University.

Guazzarotti, G. (2004). The determinants of changes in credit spreads of European corporate bonds. *Mimeo*, Bank of Italy, Economic Research Department.

Hausman, J. A. (1978). Specification tests in econometrics. *Econometrica,* **46** (6), 1251-1371.

Hull, J., Predescu, M., & White, A. (2004). The relationship between credit default swap spreads, bond yields, and credit rating announcements. *Journal of Banking and Finance,* **28** (11), 2789-2811.

International Monetary Fund (2008). *Global financial stability report.* October.

Leland, H. E., & Toft, K. B. (1996). Optimal capital structure, endogenous bankruptcy, and the term structure of credit spreads. *The Journal of Finance,* **51** (3), 987-1019.

Meng, L., & ap Gwilym, O. (2008).The determinants of CDS bid-ask spreads. *The Journal of Derivatives,* **16** (1), 70-80.

Merton, R. C. (1974). On the pricing of corporate debt: The risk structure of interest rates. *Journal of Finance,* **29** (2), 449-470.

Norden, L., & Weber, M. (2004). Informational efficiency of credit default swap and stock markets: The impact of credit rating announcements. *Journal of Banking and Finance,* **28** (11), 2813-2843.

Pires, P., Pereira, J. P., & Martins, L. (2009). The complete picture of credit default swap spreads – A quantile regression approach. Mimeo, electronic copy available at: http://ssrn.com/abstract=1125265.

Raunig, B., & Scheicher, M. (2009). Are banks different? Evidence from the CDS market. Oesterreichische Nationalbank, *Working Paper* No. **152**.

Tarashev, N. A. (2005). An empirical evaluation of structural credit risk models. *BIS Working Papers*, No. **179**.

Zhang, B. Y., Zhou, H., & Zhu, H. (2005). Explaining credit default swap spreads with equity volatility and jump risks of individual firms. *BIS Working Papers,* No. **181**.

Zhu, H. (2004). An empirical comparison of credit spreads between the bond market and the credit default swap market. *BIS Working Papers,* No. **160**.

In: The Financial Crisis
Editors: Barbara L. Campos and Janet P. Wilkins

ISBN: 978-1-61209-281-2

Chapter 6

INSOLVENCY OF SYSTEMICALLY SIGNIFICANT FINANCIAL COMPANIES: BANKRUPTCY VS. CONSERVATORSHIP/RECEIVERSHIP

David H. Carpenter*

SUMMARY

One clear lesson of the 2008 recession, which brought Goliaths such as Bear Sterns, CitiGroup, AIG, and Washington Mutual to their knees, is that no financial institution, regardless of its size, complexity, or diversification, is invincible. Congress, as a result, is left with the question of how best to handle the failure of systemically significant financial companies (SSFCs). In the United States, the insolvencies of depository institutions (i.e., banks and thrifts with deposits insured by the Federal Deposit Insurance Corporation (FDIC)) are not handled according to the procedures of the U.S. Bankruptcy Code. Instead, they and their subsidiaries are subject to a separate regime prescribed in federal law, called a conservatorship or receivership. Under this regime, the conservator or receiver, which generally is the FDIC, is provided substantial authority to deal with virtually every aspect of the insolvency. However, the failure of most other financial institutions within bank, thrift, and financial holding company umbrellas (including the holding companies themselves) generally are dealt with under the Bankruptcy Code.

In March of 2009, Treasury Secretary Timothy Geithner proposed legislation that would impose a conservatorship/receivership regime, much like that for depository institutions, on insolvent financial institutions that are deemed systemically significant. In order to make a policy assessment concerning the appropriateness of this proposal, it is important to understand both the similarities and differences between insured depositories and other financial institutions large enough or interconnected enough to pose systemic risk to the U.S. economy upon failure, as well as the differences between the U.S. Bankruptcy Code and the FDIC's conservatorship/receivership authority.

This report first discusses the purposes behind the creation of a separate insolvency regime for depository institutions. The report then compares and contrasts the characteristics of depository institutions with SSFCs. Next, the report provides a brief analysis of some important differences between the FDIC's conservatorship/receivership authority and that of the Bankruptcy Code. The specific differences discussed are: (1)

* E-mail address: dcarpenter@crs.loc.gov, 7-9118. Legislative Attorney

overall objectives of each regime; (2) insolvency initiation authority and timing; (3) oversight structure and appeal; (4) management, shareholder, and creditor rights; (5) FDIC "superpowers," including contract repudiation versus Bankruptcy's automatic stay; and (6) speed of resolution. This report makes no value judgment as to whether an insolvency regime for SSFCs that is modeled after the FDIC's conservatorship/receivership authority is more appropriate than using (or adapting) the Bankruptcy Code. Rather, it simply points out the similarities and differences between SSFCs and depository institutions, and compares the conservatorship/receivership insolvency regime with the Bankruptcy Code to help the reader develop his/her own opinion.

INTRODUCTION

One clear lesson of the 2008 recession, which brought Goliaths such as Bear Sterns, CitiGroup, AIG, and Washington Mutual to their knees, is that no financial institution, regardless of its size, complexity, or diversification, is invincible. Congress, as a result, is left with the question of how best to handle the failure of systemically significant financial companies (SSFCs). In the United States, the insolvencies of depository institutions (i.e., banks and thrifts with deposits insured by the Federal Deposit Insurance Corporation (FDIC)) are not handled according to the procedures of the U.S. Bankruptcy Code.[1] Instead, they and their subsidiaries are subject to a separate regime prescribed in federal law, called a conservatorship or receivership.[2] Under this regime, the conservator or receiver, which generally is the FDIC, is provided substantial authority to deal with virtually every aspect of the insolvency. However, the failure of most other financial institutions within bank, thrift, and financial holding company umbrellas (including the holding companies themselves) generally are dealt with under the Bankruptcy Code.[3]

In March of 2009, Treasury Secretary Timothy Geithner proposed legislation that would impose a conservatorship/receivership regime, much like that for depository institutions, on insolvent financial institutions that are deemed systemically significant.[4] In order to make a policy assessment concerning the appropriateness of this proposal, it is important to understand both the similarities and differences between insured depositories and other financial institutions large enough or interconnected enough to pose systemic risk to the U.S.

---

[1] 11 U.S.C. §§ 109(b)(2) and (d).

[2] The basic difference between a conservatorship and a receivership is that a conservatorship involves operating the institution as a going concern to protect its assets until it stabilizes or is closed and a receiver appointed. A receiver is charged with liquidating the institution and winding up its affairs. A conservatorship may indicate that the FDIC aims to restore the institution to solvency or that the FDIC had to act quickly without the usual lead time for investigation. In either case, a conservatorship may be followed by a receivership if a determination is made that the institution is not viable. For an in-depth analysis of the FDIC's conservatorship/receivership powers, *see* CRS Report RL34657, *Financial Institution Insolvency: Federal Authority over Fannie Mae, Freddie Mac, and Depository Institutions*, by David H. Carpenter and M. Maureen Murphy. Fannie Mae, Freddic Mac, and the Federal Home Loan Banks are subject to a conservatorship/receivership regime modeled after that for insured depositories.

[3] 11 U.S.C. § 109.

[4] The proposal is to be known as the "Resolution Authority for Systemically Significant Financial Companies Act of 2009). Text can be found at http://www.ustreas.gov/press/releases/reports/032509%20legislation .pdf. It is unclear exactly which financial firms would be considered "systemically significant." For a detailed analysis of the proposal, *see* CRS Report R40526, *Insolvencies of "Systemically Significant Financial Companies" (SSFCs): Proposal for Federal Deposit Insurance Corporation (FDIC) Resolution*, by M. Maureen Murphy

economy upon failure, as well as the differences between the U.S. Bankruptcy Code and the FDIC's conservatorship/receivership authority.

This report first discusses the purposes behind the creation of a separate insolvency regime for depository institutions. The report then compares and contrasts the characteristics of depository institutions with SSFCs. Next, the report provides a brief analysis of some important differences between the FDIC's conservatorship/receivership authority and that of the Bankruptcy Code. The specific differences discussed are: (1) overall objectives of each regime; (2) insolvency initiation authority and timing; (3) oversight structure and appeal; (4) management, shareholder, and creditor rights; (5) FDIC "superpowers," including contract repudiation versus Bankruptcy's automatic stay; and (6) speed of resolution. This report makes no value judgment as to whether an insolvency regime for SSFCs that is modeled after the FDIC's conservatorship/receivership authority is more appropriate than using (or adapting) the Bankruptcy Code. Rather, it points out the similarities and differences between SSFCs and depository institutions and compares the conservatorship/receivership insolvency regime with the Bankruptcy Code to help readers develop their own opinions.

Comparison of Depository Institutions and Systemically Significant Financial Institutions

The idea of having a separate insolvency regime for banks goes back at least as far as 1837 when President Van Buren proposed such legislation. A special insolvency system for depositories has existed in some form in the United States since the enactment of the National Bank Act in 1864.[5]

The reasons for having special regimes may have evolved since the creation of federal deposit insurance in 1933. However, many of the justifications for a special regime relate specifically to the functions of and services provided by depositories, which hold true regardless of deposit insurance. Some of these justifications are:

- Large portions of American citizens' wealth are held by depositories;
- Banks and thrifts serve as financial intermediaries for individuals, businesses, and governments;
- Banks and thrifts are crucial to credit and payment systems;
- A large portion of depository assets are highly liquid, thus making depository institutions especially susceptible to runs and insider abuse;[6]
- "Some [banks and thrifts] are individually large relative to GDP ... [and] are closely interconnected through interbank deposits and loans."[7]

---

[5] Peter P. Swire, *Bank Insolvency Law Now That It Matters Again*, 42 Duke L. J. 469 (1992).

[6] *See*, Peter P. Swire, *Bank Insolvency Law Now That It Matters Again*, 42 Duke L. J. 469 (1992) and Robert R. Bliss and George G. Kaufman, *U.S. Corporate and Bank Insolvency Regimes: A Comparison and Evaluation*, 2 Va. L. & Bus. Rev. 143 (2007).

[7] Robert R. Bliss and George G. Kaufman, *U.S. Corporate and Bank Insolvency Regimes: A Comparison and Evaluation*, 2 Va. L. & Bus. Rev. 143, 147-48 (2007).

For these reasons, it is argued that the pivotal role banks and thrifts play in mainstream economic life exceeds that of most other commercial firms, thus justifying a special regime designed specifically for bank and thrift insolvencies.[8] The corporate bankruptcy code, rather than being tailored to a specific type of firm, applies to all non-exempt companies conducting business or having property in the country.[9] It serves as a one-stop shop for all firms, except for the minority of businesses expressly exempted.

This raises the question: Do SSFCs, as a result of their inherent traits, warrant a special insolvency regime modeled after that of depositories? While SSFCs do not hold insured deposits, it is entirely possible that large portions of individuals' wealth could be held by these institutions in other forms. While non-deposit financial products may not be explicitly insured like deposits, financial firms that are truly systemically significant arguably have an implicit backing by the federal government, which considers them too big or interconnected to fail, and thus would warrant federal financial investment to avoid their failure (at least under the current insolvency process).

Aside from the above differences, non-depository financial institutions seem to share other attributes often used to justify a special insolvency regime for banks and thrifts. Non-depositories, just like banks and thrifts, serve as financial intermediaries for individuals, governments, and businesses. They also serve an important role in the payment system, for instance by establishing a more liquid derivatives market from otherwise illiquid, long-term debts. A large portion of their assets can be highly liquid. Finally, SSFCs could hold assets that account for a proportionally large percentage of GDP and that are highly interconnected to other financial firms, including banks and thrifts.

DIFFERENCES BETWEEN THE FDIC'S CONSERVATORSHIP/RECEIVERSHIP POWERS AND THE BANKRUPTCY CODE

Overall Objectives of Each Regime

The FDIC is a federal agency that administers the deposit insurance fund, which is comprised of premiums assessed on the basis of the amount of insured deposits held by an institution[10] under the authority of the Federal Deposit Insurance Act (FDI Act).[11] The primary object of the FDIC when any bank or thrift with FDIC-insured deposits fails is to see to it that insured deposits are protected (i.e., that any insured deposits in the failed bank or thrift are either paid

---

[8] *See, e.g.*, Eva Hüpkes, *Insolvency: Why a Special Regime for Banks?*, CURRENT DEVELOPMENTS IN MONETARY AND FINANCIAL LAW, Vol. 3, pp. 472-74 (2003) and David A. Skeel, Jr., *The Law and Finance of Bank and Insurance Insolvency Regulation*, 76 Tex. L. Rev. 723 (1998). However, some commentators believe a special insolvency regime for banks and thrifts is not justified. *See, e.g.*, Charles W. Calomiris, *Runs on Banks and the Lessons of the Great Depression*, CATO Regulation Magazine Vol. 22, No. 1 (Spring 1999) [http://www.cato.org/pubs/regulation/regv22n1/deplesson.pdf].

[9] 11 U.S.C. § 109.

[10] For a description of deposit insurance, *see* CRS Report RS20724, *Federal Deposit and Share Insurance: Proposals for Change*, by Walter W. Eubanks. The FDIC currently sets the Designated Reserve Ratio at 1.25 percent or $1.25 on every dollar of insured deposits. 72 *Fed. Reg.* 65576 (November 21, 2007).

[11] 12 U.S.C. §§ 1811 - 1835a.

off or transferred to another institution). This process generally requires significant disbursements from the deposit insurance fund and results in the FDIC being the largest creditor of the failed institution.

Federal deposit insurance is backed by the full faith and credit of the United States;[12] therefore, if the deposit insurance fund is exhausted, the funds of the federal government are at risk. This means that if there were multiple bank or thrift failures that exhausted the deposit insurance fund, federal appropriations would be necessary to supplement the deposit insurance fund and protect insured depositors.[13] Because of the possible threat to the federal fisc,[14] one of the guiding principles imposed upon the FDIC in resolving institutional failures is the "least-cost resolution" requirement. Under the FDI Act, the FDIC is prohibited from resolving failing institutions in any manner unless it determines that (1) the action is necessary to protect insured deposits and (2) the total to be expended will cost the deposit fund less than any other possible method. It may not take any action to protect depositors for more than the insured portions of their deposits or protect creditors other than depositors. There is, however, a provision that permits the FDIC to arrange purchase and assumption transactions in which the acquirer may take on uninsured deposit liabilities if the insurance fund does not incur any loss with respect to them that is greater than it would have been had the institution been liquidated.[15]

However, depositor protection is only one slice of the overall objective of the current depository insolvency regime. Another goal of resolving depository institutions is to limit the impact of failures on the overall economy and on local markets. This is achieved by authorizing the FDIC to waive the least-cost resolution requirement to prevent systemic risk, i.e., when complying with that requirement "would have serious adverse effects on economic conditions or financial stability" and when action or assistance under this provision "would avoid or mitigate such adverse effects."[16] In fact, one of the intents of establishing the least-cost resolution was to promote the early intervention of financially troubled depository institutions so as to limit the long-term costs of intervention and, thus, to avoid systemic risk.[17]

---

[12] 12 U.S.C. § 1828(a)(1)(B).

[13] According to Timothy Curry and Lynn Shibut, *The Cost of the Savings and Loan Crisis: Truth and Consequences*, 13 FDIC Banking Rev. 26, 33 (2000), in the savings and loan crisis of 1985-1995, 1,043 thrifts failed with assets of over $500 billion, costing taxpayers $124 billion and the thrift industry, $29 billion.

[14] The FDIC has authority to borrow "for insurance purposes" up to $30 billion from the U.S. Treasury. 12 U.S.C. § 1824. FDIC's borrowing is limited to the sum of cash in the deposit insurance fund, the fair market value of assets held by the insurance fund, and the $30 billion Treasury borrowing limit. 12 U.S.C. § 1825.

[15] 12 U.S.C. § 1823(c)(4)(A).

[16] 12 U.S.C. § 1823(c)(4)(G)(i). Such a waiver requires a determination by the Secretary of the Treasury, in consultation with the President, and upon the recommendation of the FDIC and Board of Governors of the Federal Reserve System (with 2/3's vote from each). This section of the FDI Act also includes provisions requiring the FDIC to impose emergency special assessments on members of the insurance fund; the Secretary of the Treasury to document any determination; and the Comptroller General of the United States to review any determination to provide assistance with respect to, among other things, "the likely effect of the determination and such action on the incentives and conduct of insured depository institutions and uninsured depositors." 12 U.S.C. §§ 1823(d)(4)(G)(ii), (iii), and (iv).

[17] Under § 143 of the Federal Deposit Insurance Corporation Improvement Act of 1991, P.L. 102-242, there is a sense of Congress urging the FDIC to favor early resolution of troubled institutions when doing so involves the least possible long-term cost to the insurance fund. To achieve this end, the FDIC is exhorted to follow various practices: entering into competitive negotiation; requiring substantial private investment; requiring owners and holding companies of troubled institutions to make concessions; making sure that there is qualified

Corporate bankruptcy, on the other hand, does not have a systemic risk analog. Its primary objectives are to either liquidate a company's assets so as to maximize returns to creditor classes based on a statutorily-defined priority scheme[18] (liquidation, usually under Ch. 7[19]) or to reorganize a company's debts so that creditor classes receive more than they would have through liquidation while also maximizing the company's "going concern value" (reorganization, usually under Ch. 1 1[20]).[21] One commentator explained it this way:

> Bankruptcy law, in contrast, is not concerned with maintaining confidence in a certain system, but in promoting two fundamental goals. First, bankruptcy law gives debtors an opportunity to make a "fresh start" by granting them a second chance at becoming economically viable. Second, bankruptcy law stops the "race to the courthouse" by placing all similarly situated creditors on an equal footing such that all such creditors receive ratable recoveries.[22]

Insolvency Initiation Authority and Timing

The decision to appoint a receiver or conservator over a bank or thrift is at the discretion of the depository institution's regulators and is to be based on one or more grounds specified in section 11 of the FDI Act.[23] Neither the creditors of an institution nor its managers have the authority to declare the institution insolvent.

Under section 11, the FDIC may be appointed conservator or receiver for any insured depository institution, i.e., any state- or federally-chartered bank or thrift, the deposits of which are insured by the FDIC. If a receivership of a *federally*-chartered bank or thrift is involved, the FDIC *must* be the appointed receiver.[24] Appointment of a conservator or receiver for a federally-chartered depository institution is generally at the discretion of the institution's chartering authority.[25] In the case of a *state*-chartered depository institution, appointment of a conservator or receiver may be at the discretion of the state chartering authority, the primary federal regulator, or, in certain cases, the FDIC.[26]

---

management for resulting institutions; assuring FDIC participation in the resulting institution; and structuring transactions so that the FDIC does not acquire too much of a troubled institution's problem assets.

18 11 U.S.C. § 507.

19 11 U.S.C. § 701, *et seq.*

20 11 U.S.C. § 1101, *et seq.*

21 Eva H.G. Hüpkes, THE LEGAL ASPECTS OF BANK INSOLVENCY: A COMPARATIVE ANALYSIS OF WESTERN EUROPE, THE UNITED STATES AND CANADA, pp. 17-20 (2000).

22 John R. Ashmead, *In re Colonial Realty Co.*, 60 Brook. L. Rev. 517, 519 (1994).

23 12 U.S.C. § 1821.

24 The decision to appoint a receiver for a national bank is to be determined by the OCC "in the Comptroller's discretion." 12 U.S.C. § 191. OCC's decision is generally not subject to judicial review. United Sav. Bank v. Morgenthau, 85 F. 2d 811 (D.C. Cir. 1936), *cert. denied*, 299 U.S. 605 (1935). In addition to the grounds specified in the FDI Act, 12 U.S.C. § 1821(c)(5), the OCC may appoint a receiver upon determining that the bank's board of directors consists of less than five members. 12 U.S.C. § 191(2).

25 12 U.S.C. §§ 1821(c)(2) and (6) (appointment of the FDIC as conservator or receiver of federally-chartered depository institution at the discretion of the chartering agency)

26 12 U.S.C. §§ 1821(c)(3), (4), (9), and (10) (appointment of the FDIC as conservator or receiver of state-chartered depository institution). The FDIC may appoint itself as conservator or receiver for a state-chartered, FDIC-insured depository institution upon determining that (1) a state-appointed conservator or receiver has been appointed and 15 consecutive days have passed and one or more depositors has been unable to withdraw any

Under the FDI Act, the appointment of a conservator or receiver need not wait until insolvency, i.e., when the institution has insufficient assets to meet its obligations. The regulators are given sufficient authority to intervene before a deteriorating situation worsens. For example, a conservator or receiver may be appointed if the depository has incurred, or is likely to incur, losses that will deplete capital with no reasonable likelihood of becoming adequately capitalized without federal assistance.[27]

The bankruptcy of firms subject to the Bankruptcy Code may be initiated either by management of the companies or by their creditors.[28] Involuntary bankruptcy initiated by creditors generally requires acts of default.[29] Management may strategically initiate bankruptcy proceedings in advance of default, but management may not have economic incentives to do so. Where corporate management does petition for bankruptcy protections in advance of default, it is likely to do so in order to remain in control of the reorganization process or maximize the firm's going concern, rather than for the benefit of the overall economy.[30]

Acceleration clauses and closeout agreements, which are common in derivative contracts and other short-term financing arrangements, that require a company to post collateral or capital upon a triggering event (e.g., credit rating downgrade) may precipitate default. Financial institutions are especially prone to being parties to these contractual arrangements. As will be discussed in greater detail in the *FDIC "Superpowers," Including Contract Repudiation Versus the Automatic Stay* section of this report, many of the short-term financing contracts that tend to include acceleration and closeout arrangements are given unique treatment under both the Bankruptcy Code and the banking laws.[31]

Oversight Structure and Appeal

The conservatorship/receivership regime for insured-depositories is almost entirely administrative in nature with only limited judicial appeal. When an insured bank or thrift becomes insolvent, the institution's charterer,[32] its primary federal regulator, or the FDIC is

amount of insured deposit or (2) the institution has been closed under state law and the FDIC determines that one of the grounds specified in 12 U.S.C. § 1821(c)(4) exists or existed. If the FDIC acts to appoint itself conservator or receiver under any of those circumstances, the institution is provided with an opportunity for judicial review. 12 U.S.C. § 1821(c)(7). There is also authority for the FDIC to appoint itself as conservator or receiver for any insured depository institution "to reduce loss to the deposit insurance fund." 12 U.S.C. § 1821(c)(10).

27 12 U.S.C. § 1821(c).

28 11 U.S.C. §§ 301, 303.

29 11 U.S.C. § 303.

30 Robert R. Bliss and George G. Kaufman, *U.S. Corporate and Bank Insolvency Regimes: A Comparison and Evaluation*, 2 Va. L. & Bus. Rev. 143, 156-57 (2007).

31 Robert R. Bliss and George G. Kaufman, *Derivatives and Systemic Risk: Netting, Collateral, and Closeout*, Federal Reserve Bank of Chicago (2005) [http://www.chicagofed.org/publications/workingpapers/wp 2005_03.pdf].

32 State-chartered banks are chartered by state banking authorities. The primary federal regulator of a federally chartered bank or thrift is its chartering authority. National banks are chartered by the Office of the Comptroller of the Currency (OCC); federal thrifts or savings associations are chartered by the Office of Thrift Supervision (OTS). The primary federal regulator of state-chartered banks is either the Board of Governors of the Federal Reserve System (Fed) or the FDIC, depending upon whether the institution is a member bank, i.e., a member of the Federal Reserve System (FRS).

authorized to act *ex parte* (i.e., without notice or a hearing) to seize the institution and its assets and install the FDIC as conservator or receiver.[33] Unless time is of the essence, prior to taking such action, however, there is consultation between the institution's regulator and the FDIC concerning the imminent failure. This gives the FDIC time to investigate the situation and determine a resolution strategy before releasing information to the public of the looming insolvency.

The powers conferred on the FDIC as conservator or receiver are broad. The FDIC may "take any action authorized by ... [the FDI Act], which the Corporation determines is in the best interests of the depository institution, its depositors, or the Corporation."[34] A bank or thrift in conservatorship remains subject to "banking agency supervision."[35] Otherwise, the FDIC as conservator or receiver is not subject to any other authority in exercising its powers.[36]

Judicial review of the FDIC's actions as conservator or receiver is limited to a handful of situations. For instance, the FDI Act specifies judicial review for only one type of conservatorship or receivership appointment—FDIC's appointment of itself as receiver or conservator if depositors have been unable to access their funds 15 days after the appointment by the state of a receiver or conservator.[37] Additionally, disputes about claims for insured deposits are to be resolved first by the FDIC in accordance with its regulations, subject to judicial review under the Administrative Procedure Act.[38] Also, the FDIC has the power to

---

[33] The FDI Act specifies judicial review for only one type of conservatorship or receivership appointment—FDIC's appointment of itself as receiver or conservator if depositors have been unable to access their funds 15 days after the appointment by the state of a receiver or conservator. 12 U.S.C. § 1821(c)(4). There are also other statutes that provide for post- seizure judicial review in certain instances. E.g. 12 U.S.C. § 203(b) (appointment of a conservator for a national bank). It has also been held that judicial review is available under the Administrative Procedure Act. James Madison Ltd. By Hecht v. Ludwig, 82 F. 3d 1085 (D.C. Cir. 1996).

[34] 12 U.S.C. § 1821(d)(J)(ii).

[35] 12 U.S.C. §§ 1821(c)(2)(D) and (3)(D). For example, the FDIC was named conservator of IndyMac Bank, F.S.B., Pasadena, California, closed by OTS on July 8, 2008. As conservator, the FDIC transferred all non-brokered insured deposit accounts and substantially all of the assets to a newly chartered federal thrift, seemingly serving the same function as a bridge bank. *See*, Failed Bank Information, Information for IndyMacBank, F.S.B., Pasadena, CA, http://www.fdic.gov/bank/individual/failed/IndyMac.html. Under 12 U.S.C. § 1821(d)(2)(F), the FDIC may organize and operate a new institution chartered by OCC or OTS, and transfer to it some or all of the failed institution's assets and liabilities. There is also authority for the FDIC to charter a bridge depository institution with a limited life of two years with the possibility of a one-year extension. 12 U.S.C. § 1821(n). Prior to enactment of the Housing and Economic Recovery Act of 2008, P.L. 110-289, § 1604(a), this authority was limited to creation of bridge banks. According to the FDIC's Resolution Handbook, the use of bridge banks is "generally ... limited to situations in which more time is needed to permit the least-costly resolution of a large or complex institution." FDIC, Resolution Handbook 90, http://www.fdic.gov/bank/historical/reshandbook/index.html.

[36] 12 U.S.C. § 1821(c)(2)(C). This provision states: "When acting as conservator or receiver ..., the Corporation shall not be subject to the direction or supervision of any other agency or department of the United States or any State in the exercise of the Corporation's rights, powers, and privileges." *See also* 12 U.S.C. § 1821(j), which provides: "Except as provided in this section no court may take any action except at the request of the Board of Directors by regulation or order, to restrain or affect the exercise of powers or functions of the Corporation as a conservator or receiver."

[37] 12 U.S.C. § 1821(c)(4). There are also other statutes that provide for post-seizure judicial review in certain instances. *See, e.g.*, 12 U.S.C. § 203(b) (appointment of a conservator for a national bank). It has also been held that judicial review is available under the Administrative Procedure Act. James Madison Ltd. By Hecht v. Ludwig, 82 F. 3d 1085 (D.C. Cir. 1996).

[38] 12 U.S.C. §§ 1821(f)(3) and (4).

repudiate certain contracts entered into by the institution, under certain conditions.[39] The statute limits damages to "actual direct compensatory damages."[40] Conflicts as to the amount of "actual direct compensatory damages" may be settled in court.

Even when judicial review is allowed, the only remedy generally available is damages. In other words, aggrieved parties usually cannot stop or reverse FDIC decisions.[41]

Bankruptcy proceedings are judicial. They are performed under the supervision of a federal court with individual parties having their own legal representation. Bankruptcy proceedings are coordinated by a court-appointed representative (e.g., a trustee in Ch. 7 or the firm's management in Ch. 11), with the approval and oversight of a bankruptcy judge. Most decisions affecting the bankruptcy estate may be appealed to a higher court, and some decisions may not go into effect until such litigation is settled.[42]

Management, Shareholder, and Creditor Rights

As successor to the institution, the FDIC is authorized to operate the institution and endowed with "all the powers of the members or shareholders, the directors, and the officers of the institution."[43] As a result, the FDIC usually removes and replaces senior management of a failed depository and eliminates shareholders' rights and powers.[44] These decisions are not subject to judicial review. Creditors also have no say in the decisions made by the FDIC as conservator or receiver. Instead, decisions are primarily guided by the least-cost resolution.

In contrast, creditors and management wield control over major decisions during corporate reorganizations. During reorganization proceedings, management generally remains in control of a firm, for instance, disposing of property in the ordinary course of business.[45] Creditors and management, as well as shareholders, can play a role in adopting a reorganization plan. As one scholar explains:

> All creditors have "standing" to be represented in the proceedings, although the dynamics of voting [based on creditor classes] may lead to certain minority blocks being effectively

[39] 12 U.S.C. § 1821(e)(1). The statute contains specific provisions relating to various types of contracts and leases. These include contracts for the sale of real property, 12 U.S.C.§ 1821(e)(6); service contracts, 12 U.S.C. § 1821(e)(7); and any certain securities contract, commodity contract, forward contract, repurchase agreement, swap agreement, or similar agreement that the FDIC determines to be a "qualified financial contract." 12 U.S.C. §§ 1821(e)(8) - (10). Contracts with a Federal Home Loan Bank and the Federal Reserve Bank may not be repudiated. 12 U.S.C. § 1921)(e)(13).

[40] 12 U.S.C. § 1821(e)(3).

[41] Robert R. Bliss and George G. Kaufman, *U.S. Corporate and Bank Insolvency: An Economic Comparison and Evaluation*, Federal Reserve Bank of Chicago (2006) [http://www.chicagofed.org/publications/ working papers/wp2006_01 .pdf].

[42] *Id.*

[43] 12 U.S.C. § 1821(d)(2).

[44] Eva H.G. Hüpkes, THE LEGAL ASPECTS OF BANK INSOLVENCY: A COMPARATIVE ANALYSIS OF WESTERN EUROPE, THE UNITED STATES AND CANADA, pp. 64-66 (2000).

[45] 11 U.S.C. § 363.

frozen out. Each creditor group, and in reorganizations also management and shareholders, must vote to approve the plans proposed by management, receiver, or trustee.[46]

When creditors cannot agree to a reorganization plan, the bankruptcy court has "cram down" authority, i.e. the authority to approve a plan over creditor objections as long as it meets certain statutory standards.[47] As previously mentioned, decisions made or approved by a bankruptcy court are appealable to a higher court.

FDIC "Superpowers," Including Contract Repudiation, versus Bankruptcy's Automatic Stay

A "stay" is a power by which creditors are, at least temporarily, prevented from pursuing their claims against a default entity. As one commentator explains:

> Stays permit the resolution authority [the time to] collect and validate claims, to determine the best way to dispose of assets in an orderly, non-fire-sale manner, and to treat all like- priority creditors equally. Stays prevent creditor runs and keep contracts in force – the counter party is bound by the contract; claims on the insolvent firm remain pending; and collateral may usually not be liquidated. This facilitates the coordination of creditor claims.[48]

The stay is an important tool under the U.S. Bankruptcy Code, especially for reorganizations. The Code establishes a general stay automatically upon petitioning for bankruptcy.[49] However, the Code provides a number of exceptions to the automatic stay, including for many securities contracts, commodity contracts, forward contracts, repurchase agreements, swap agreements, and netting arrangements.[50] These contracts that are exempted from the automatic stay are very similar to "qualified financial contracts," which, as discussed below, are provided special protections under the bank and thrift insolvency regime, as well. As previously mentioned, it is especially common for financial institutions to be parties to these contractual arrangements, making special protections provided for them all the more important in case of a financial institution's insolvency.

Additionally, the Bankruptcy Code provides trustees the authority to avoid, i.e. claw-back or reverse, certain transfers (subject to certain limitations[51]) made by debtors if five conditions are met: (1) the transfer was made "to or for the benefit of a creditor"; (2) the transfer was for a debt owed before the transfer; (3) the transfer "was made while the debtor was insolvent"; (4) the transfer occurred "on or within 90 days" of the petition or within one

---

46 Robert R. Bliss and George G. Kaufman, *U.S. Corporate and Bank Insolvency: An Economic Comparison and Evaluation*, Federal Reserve Bank of Chicago (2006)[http://www.chicagofed.org/publications/ workingpapers/ wp2006_01.pdf].

47 11 U.S.C. § 1129(b).

48 Robert R. Bliss and George G. Kaufman, *U.S. Corporate and Bank Insolvency: An Economic Comparison and Evaluation*, Federal Reserve Bank of Chicago (2006).

49 11 U.S.C. § 362(a).

50 11 U.S.C. § 362(b).

51 *See, e.g.*, 11 U.S.C. §§ 546, 547, 555, 556, 559, 560, 561.

year if the transfer was made to an "insider"[52]; and (5) the creditor received more from the transfer than it would have through bankruptcy proceedings.[53] The purpose of this avoidance power is to facilitate the equitable distribution of the bankruptcy estate's assets among credit classes and to limit the "race to the courthouse" problem.[54] Most securities contracts,[55] commodity contracts,[56] forward contracts,[57] repurchase agreements,[58] swap agreements,[59] and netting arrangements[60] are exempted from the trustees' general avoidance power. The Code also provides trustees the authority to avoid certain fraudulent transfers made within two years of petition under limited circumstances.[61]

Whereas the general rule under the Bankruptcy Code is the implementation of the automatic stay to provide time for similarly situated creditors to negotiate their claims, the FDIC as conservator or receiver is primarily focused on a seamless continuation of access to deposits and the administration of other bank affairs.[62] The FDIC has a number of tools, called "superpowers," to deal with insolvent depository institutions that stem from long-standing judicial decisions, many of which were later codified into law. These powers, in some respects, exceed the authority of a bankruptcy court. They include the power to reorganize the institution, to sell its assets, as well as to disaffirm and repudiate certain claims, with little judicial oversight.[63]

The FDIC, as conservator or receiver, may disaffirm or repudiate certain contracts if allowing performance would be "burdensome" and "disaffirmance or repudiation ... will promote the orderly administration of the institution's affairs."[64]

There are, however, statutory exceptions to the FDIC's broad repudiation/disaffirmance powers, including for "qualified financial contracts." A "qualified financial contract" is defined as "any securities contract, commodity contract, forward contract, repurchase agreement, swap agreement, and any similar agreement that the ... [FDIC] determines by regulation, resolution, or order to be a qualified financial contract.... "[65] Counterparties to these contracts are given greater protection than other creditors.

---

52 The term "insider" is defined at 11 U.S.C. § 101(31).

53 11 U.S.C. § 547(b).

54 Collier on Bankruptcy § 5-547.0 1 (15th ed. rev.).

55 11 U.S.C. § 555.

56 11 U.S.C. § 556.

57 11 U.S.C. § 556.

58 11 U.S.C. § 559

59 11 U.S.C. § 560.

60 11 U.S.C. § 561.

61 11 U.S.C. § 548.

62 Robert R. Bliss and George G. Kaufman, *U.S. Corporate and Bank Insolvency Regimes: A Comparison and Evaluation*, 2 Va. L. & Bus. Rev. 143, 158-59 (2007).

63 *See, e.g.*, Thomas C. Baxter, Jr., Joyce M. Hansen, and Joseph H. Sommer, *Two Cheers for Territoriality: An Essay on International Bank Insolvency Law*, 78 Am. Bankr. L. J. 57, 72 (2004); Robert W. Norcross, Jr., *The Bank Insolvency Game: FDIC Superpowers, the D 'Oench Doctrine, and Federal Common Law*, 103 Banking L. J. 316, 328 (1986); Fred Galves, *Might Does Not Make Right: The Call for Reform of the Federal Government's D 'Oench, Duhme and 12 U.S.C. 1823(e) Superpowers in Failed Bank Litigation*, 80 Minn. L. Rev. 1323 (1996); Robert W. Norcross, Jr., *The Bank Insolvency Game: FDIC Superpowers, the D 'Oench Doctrine, and Federal Common Law*, 103 Banking L. J. 316, n.137 (1986).

64 12 U.S.C. § 1821(e)(1).

65 12 U.S.C. § 1821(e)(8)(D)(i).

The FDIC, as conservator or receiver, is free to repudiate and disaffirm qualified financial contracts, as long as the decision to do so is made within a reasonable time,[66] and only if the FDIC repudiates or disaffirms all qualified financial contracts with a particular counterparty and its affiliates.[67] In other words, the FDIC must either repudiate or disaffirm all qualified financial contracts with a particular party and its affiliates or may not repudiate or disaffirm any of them. Also, the damages available to counterparties of qualified financial contracts that are repudiated are more expansive than the "actual direct compensatory damages" available for the repudiation of other contracts. The damages available in such a situation would include "normal and reasonable costs of cover or other reasonable measures of damages utilized in the industries for such contract and agreement claims."[68]

Counterparties to qualified financial contracts are granted additional protections under the FDIC's conservatorship/receivership powers. Counterparties to qualified financial contracts generally are free to exercise rights (to net, terminate, or liquidate) under such contracts that are triggered by the appointment of a *receiver*,[69] except that counterparties whose rights are triggered either as a result of the appointment of a receiver or as a result of the financial condition of a depository for which a receiver was appointed shall be stayed (prevented) from exercising such rights until the counterparties are notified of a transfer of the qualified financial contract or until 5:00 p.m. of the business day after the appointment of the receiver.[70]

Counterparties to qualified financial contracts whose rights would be triggered by the appointment of a *conservator* or by the financial condition that results in the appointment of a conservator, *may not* exercise such rights.[71] However, counterparties are free to exercise rights under qualified financial contracts triggered by the default *of the contracts* (as opposed to the insolvency of the depository institution) when a depository is in *conservatorship*.[72]

The FDIC, as conservator or receiver, is free to transfer qualified financial contracts as long as certain notice requirements are met. But the FDIC must either transfer all qualified financial contracts with a particular party and its affiliates to a single financial institution, or it may not transfer any of them.[73]

Finally, the FDIC as conservator or receiver may not avoid (i.e., reverse or claw-back) any property transfer pursuant to a qualified financial contract unless the transfer was performed with the "actual intent to hinder, delay, or defraud."[74]

Another superpower given to the FDIC, both as receiver and in its corporate capacity, is the power to defeat claims against its interests in assets it has acquired in a receivership or through open institution assistance. To prevail on a claim that tends to defeat or diminish the FDIC's interest in such an asset, the claimant must show that there was a written agreement, executed contemporaneously with the institution's acquisition of the assets, approved by the

---

66 12 U.S.C. §§ 1821(e)(1) and (8)(F).

67 12 U.S.C. § 1821(e)(11).

68 12 U.S.C. § 1821(e)(3)(C).

69 12 U.S.C. § 1821(e)(8)(A).

70 12 U.S.C. § 1821(e)(10)(B)(i).

71 12 U.S.C. § 1821(e)(10)(B)(ii).

72 12 U.S.C. § 1821(e)(8)(E).

73 12 U.S.C. §§ 1821(e)(8)(F), (9), and (10).

74 12 U.S.C. § 1821(e)(8)(C).

institution's board of directors or its loan committee, and continuously reflected on the institution's books.[75] This power provides the FDIC protection "from unwritten or unrecorded agreements."[76] There also are statutory exemptions from the contemporaneous execution requirement—agreements lawfully collateralizing deposits or other loans by governmental entities, bankruptcy estate funds, extensions of credit from Federal Home Loan Banks and Federal Reserve Banks and "qualified financial contracts."[77]

In addition, the FDIC may acquire a court-issued temporary stay from "judicial actions or proceedings to which [a depository] institution is or becomes a party." The stay can last up to 45 days after the appointment of a conservator or 90 days after the appointment of a receiver.[78]

Speed of Resolution

The U.S. insolvency regime for banks and thrifts is designed to provide the FDIC the ability to intervene early and resolve financially troubled banks and thrifts quickly. The FDIC is granted vast powers to make unilateral decisions, grounded in statutorily defined guidance, in an administrative setting with only limited judicial review, and where generally only ex post damages are available. The focus is primarily on protecting depositors, and little emphasis is placed on attempting to rehabilitate insolvent institutions.[79]

The Bankruptcy Code, on the other hand, is designed to give creditors and management in reorganizations a say in major decisions of bankruptcy proceedings. All bankruptcy proceedings are judicial in nature. Most decisions are reviewable by a higher court, and in some situations, decisions receive ex ante review. While the majority of corporate bankruptcies are liquidations, the Code puts much greater emphasis on rehabilitating default firms than the depository counterpart. As a result, complex bankruptcies can take years to complete.[80]

---

[75] 12 U.S.C. § 1823(e)(1).

[76] Rebecca J. Simmons, *Bankruptcy and Insolvency Provisions Relating to Swaps and Derivatives*, NUTS AND BOLTS OF FINANCIAL PRODUCTS 2001: UNDERSTANDING THE EVOLVING WORLD OF CAPITAL MARKETS & INVESTMENT MANAGEMENT PRODUCTS, Corporate Law and Practice Handbook Series 937, 968 (2004).

[77] 12 U.S.C. § 1823(e)(2).

[78] 12 U.S.C. § 1821(d)(12).

[79] Eva H.G. Hüpkes, THE LEGAL ASPECTS OF BANK INSOLVENCY: A COMPARATIVE ANALYSIS OF WESTERN EUROPE, THE UNITED STATES AND CANADA (2000).

[80] Robert R. Bliss and George G. Kaufman, *U.S. Corporate and Bank Insolvency Regimes: A Comparison and Evaluation*, 2 Va. L. & Bus. Rev. 143 (2007).

In: The Financial Crisis
Editors: Barbara L. Campos and Janet P. Wilkins
ISBN: 978-1-61209-281-2

Chapter 7

FINANCIAL MARKET INTERVENTION

Edward V. Murphy* and Baird Webel
Financial Economics

SUMMARY

Financial markets continue to experience significant disturbance and the banking sector remains fragile. Efforts to restore confidence have been met with mixed success thus far. This report provides answers to some frequently asked questions concerning ongoing financial disruptions and the Troubled Asset Relief Program (TARP), enacted by Congress in the Emergency Economic Stabilization Act of 2008 (EESA, Division A of H.R. 1424/P.L. 110-343). It also summarizes legislation in the 111th Congress such as H.R. 384, the TARP Reform and Accountability Act of 2009 and H.R. 703, "Promoting Bank Liquidity and Lending Through Deposit Insurance, Hope for Homeowners, and other Enhancements." The report also describes the option of a good-bank, bad-bank split.

CURRENT CONCERNS

What, if Anything, is Wrong with the Financial System?

Banks and other financial institutions have been reluctant to lend or otherwise engage with other institutions for fear of exposure to the bad assets of troubled counterparties. That is, a relatively healthy bank is afraid to sign a contract with other institutions because of the fear that the other institution will not be able to fulfill its obligations. For similar reasons, banks that need to raise capital have had trouble doing so because potential investors are afraid that the full extent of damage to banks' assets has not yet been revealed. Furthermore, the possibility that a future intervention by the government will dilute shareholder value might also deter private investors from recapitalizing banks. Under these conditions it is difficult for people who depend on regularly accessing credit markets to get loans, which in turn can affect the broader economy. Often, this lack of confidence in other financial institutions

* Email: tmurphy@crs. loc. gov

expresses itself in wide spreads between market interest rates and the yield on Treasury securities. These spreads have been relatively wide for the past year. They spiked following recent interventions intended to prevent disorderly bankruptcies, an indication of significant loss of confidence.[1]

In addition to the financial turmoil that initially arose from higher than expected default rates among residential real estate loans and lower than expected returns on mortgage-backed securities and related financial derivatives, the banking sector is experiencing increasing stress as the broader economy weakens. If the recession deepens and unemployment increases, as many economists project, then default rates will increase for non-real estate loans. Worsening performance rates, and expectations of further declines, for broad classes of loans has caused banking regulators to remind each bank to maintain "... the adequacy of its loan loss allowance."[2] Because loan losses are rising, banks are attempting to increase the funds they keep available for loan loss provisions.

When did Trouble in the Financial Markets Start?

Loss of market confidence can be proxied by spreads in interest rates between Treasury securities and riskier assets of similar maturities. These spreads first spiked in August 2007.[3] Although spreads declined following policy responses by the Federal Reserve, the Treasury, and the passage of the 2008 stimulus package, the spreads did not return to their pre-August 2007 level. The persistence of historically wide spreads during 2007-2008 suggests that full confidence has not been restored.

What Caused Financial Market Turmoil?

Most observers agree that rising defaults among residential mortgage borrowers sparked the initial loss in financial market confidence.[4] Reasonable people will continue to disagree as to the initial cause of rising defaults and how these defaults were multiplied through the financial system. Some believe that low interest rates and loose monetary policy caused a housing bubble that was bound to burst when interest rates rose.[5] Others place more emphasis on loose lending standards that may have been fostered by a lack of regulation of non-bank lenders and a lack of market discipline by mortgage-backed securities issuers who sold the loans to other investors.[6] Another group places the blame on the failure of officials to regulate

---

[1] CRS Report RS22956, *The Cost of Government Financial Interventions, Past and Present*, by Baird Webel, N. Eric Weiss, and Marc Labonte.

[2] Office of Thrift Supervision, OTS 08-053 - Interagency Statement on Meeting the Needs of Creditworthy Borrowers, press release, November 12, 2008, available at http://www.ots.treas.gov/?p=PressReleases&ContentRecord_id=912275af-1e0b-8562-eb24-7c8442d1e8d3.

[3] CRS Report RL34182, *Financial Crisis? The Liquidity Crunch of August 2007*, by Darryl E. Getter et al.

[4] RS Report RL33775, *Alternative Mortgages: Causes and Policy Implications of Troubled Mortgage Resets in the Subprime and Alt-A Markets*, by Edward V. Murphy.

[5] CRS Report RL33666, *Asset Bubbles: Economic Effects and Policy Options for the Federal Reserve*, by Marc Labonte.

[6] CRS Report RS22722, *Securitization and Federal Regulation of Mortgages for Safety and Soundness*, by Edward V. Murphy.

relatively recent innovations in finance. Still others emphasize potentially irresponsible marketing practices or fraud by subprime lenders. Some observers blame investors and borrowers who did not adequately investigate the risks of their decisions.

If 97% of Mortgage Borrowers are not in Foreclosure, Why is the Financial Turmoil So Large?

Several factors magnify the effects of loan defaults on the financial system. First, banks are leveraged, which means that for a given dollar reduction in the value of their assets they must either raise additional capital or reduce their lending by a multiple of the loss.[7] Second, banks have become less transparent because of changes in accounting and risk management. This lack of transparency has made it more difficult for banks to raise additional capital as an alternative to reducing lending or selling assets. Third, the use of financial derivatives that should have reduced risk in the banking system may have had the effect of increasing leverage and making it even harder to identify sound counterparties.

Where are the Problem Loans Located?

Two of the problem loan categories, subprime and Alt-A, are disproportionately located in areas that had previously experienced rapid price appreciation. This includes Florida, California, Arizona, and Nevada. In addition, subprime loans are disproportionately located in relatively low income and minority neighborhoods across the country.[8]

Who is Affected by the Financial Turmoil?

The financial turmoil also affects anyone seeking credit, including troubled home owners who wish to refinance out of a troubled mortgage. Restrictions in credit have contributed to a downward spiral in home prices. The people most directly affected by financial market turmoil are investment bankers and investors. These people may lose their jobs and livelihood. Business firms are also affected because their cost of financing possible projects has risen, which in turn can hurt the broader economy.

How have Policymakers Responded to Financial Turmoil?

Policymakers have responded in several ways. The tools of standard macroeconomics have been used to try to stimulate the broader economy. The tools of banking and financial regulators have been used to try to restore order in financial markets. Congress has given

---

[7] CRS Report RL34412, *Containing Financial Crisis*, by Mark Jickling.
[8] CRS Report RL34232, *The Process, Data, and Costs of Mortgage Foreclosure*, by Darryl E. Getter et al.

Treasury and housing finance regulators additional tools to stabilize mortgage markets and address troubled financial assets.

Many modern macroeconomists believe that there are two basic policy responses to avoid an economic slowdown.[9] First, the Federal Reserve can provide expansionary monetary policy by lowering interest rates, as it did starting in the fall of 2007.[10] Second, the government can provide expansionary fiscal policy by spending more than it collects in taxes, as it did with the stimulus package.[11] These expansionary macroeconomic policies have not prevented further financial turmoil.

In addition to pursuing both of these responses, financial regulators have tried to restore order in the financial sector using existing authority. Liquidity was increased by expanding the range of collateral accepted at the Federal Reserve's discount window and by holding regular liquidity auctions.[12] The Federal Reserve and Treasury have also tried to help arrange buyers of distressed firms, as it did for Bear Stearns and Lehman Brothers even though the government was unwilling to also provide funding to facilitate a purchase of Lehman Brothers). Similarly, the Federal Deposit Insurance Corporation (FDIC) has sought buyers for distressed banks. In addition, the FDIC and the Department of Housing and Urban Development (HUD) have tried to help organize loan servicers through the HOPE Now program. The Securities and Exchange Commission (SEC) and Internal Revenue Service (IRS) have issued rules clarifying the ability of loan servicers to modify loans held in securitized trusts.[13]

Congress gave HUD and the newly created Federal Housing Finance Agency (FHFA) additional authority to address mortgage markets. The Housing and Economic Recovery Act (HERA) (P.L. 110-289) contains a voluntary plan to allow banks to write down the balance of existing loans so that borrowers can refinance into FHA to avoid foreclosure.[14] The act also provided some Community Development Block Grant (CDBG) funds to allow local communities to acquire and redevelop vacant and foreclosed properties.[15] The act also created a new regulator for the government-sponsored enterprises (GSEs), Fannie Mae, Freddie Mac, and the Federal Home Loan Banks.[16] The act gave Treasury the temporary authority to purchase debt and equity securities of the GSEs.

Fall 2008 saw a series of financial market interventions. First, the FHFA placed the GSEs in a conservatorship with agreements by the Federal Reserve Bank of New York to assure liquidity and by the Treasury to purchase enough preferred stock and securities to ensure adequate capitalization.[17] On a single weekend, policymakers helped broker a deal to sell investment bank Merrill Lynch to Bank of America and failed to broker a similar deal for Lehman Brothers, reportedly because the government declined to provide financial support.

---

[9] CRS Report RL34349, *Economic Slowdown: Issues and Policies*, by Jane G. Gravelle et al.

[10] CRS Report RS22371, *The Pattern of Interest Rates: Does It Signal an Impending Recession?*, by Marc Labonte and Gail E. Makinen.

[11] CRS Report RS22850, *Tax Provisions of the Economic Stimulus Package*, by Jane G. Gravelle.

[12] CRS Report RL34427, *Financial Turmoil: Federal Reserve Policy Responses*, by Marc Labonte

[13] CRS Report RL34372, *The HOPE NOW Alliance/American Securitization Forum (ASF) Plan to Freeze Certain Mortgage Interest Rates*, by David H. Carpenter and Edward V. Murphy.

[14] CRS Report RL34623, *Housing and Economic Recovery Act of 2008*, by N. Eric Weiss et al.

[15] CRS Report RS22919, *Community Development Block Grants: Legislative Proposals to Assist Communities Affected by Home Foreclosures*, by Eugene Boyd and Oscar R. Gonzales.

[16] CRS Report RL33940, *Reforming the Regulation of Government-Sponsored Enterprises in the 110th Congress*, by Mark Jickling, Edward V. Murphy, and N. Eric Weiss.

[17] CRS Report RS22950, *Fannie Mae and Freddie Mac in Conservatorship*, by Mark Jickling.

Lehman Brothers subsequently declared bankruptcy. A policy of no financial support did not survive the week, as insurer AIG was granted a Federal Reserve loan three days later. The next day financial markets froze up and Treasury announced a proposal to buy mortgage-related assets from financial institutions.

Congress also gave Treasury additional tools to address financial market instability. The Emergency Economic Stabilization Act of 2008 (EESA, Division A of P.L. 110-343) created a Troubled Asset Relief Program (TARP) that allows Treasury to purchase up to $700 billion of assets from financial institutions. Although the plan was originally discussed in terms of purchasing assets from financial institutions similar to the Resolution Trust Corporation (RTC), some policymakers argued that it would be preferable to purchase stock in banks similar to the Reconstruction Finance Corporation (RFC). The definition of troubled asset is broad enough to encompass both approaches. The troubled assets purchase proposal has been used primarily to inject capital into banks. In addition to support of the banks, TARP funds have also been used for the automobile industry and as a backstop for Federal Reserve programs to support consumer finance markets through the purchases of commercial paper.

Why Have The Federal Reserve's Traditional Tools Not Restored Order In Financial Markets?[18]

The Federal Reserve's primary tools help provide liquidity but do not restore capital levels. Liquidity generally refers to the ability to access markets, either as a firm issuing bonds or as a person selling a good, without suffering "fire-sale" prices. An adequate capital level is generally determined as a relation between assets and liabilities. All of a firm's assets can be completely liquid (cash) but the firm can remain undercapitalized if small losses can reduce its capital to near insolvency. These concepts are related. Even if a firm has liquid assets, it may have difficulty accessing credit markets to borrow more funds because it is too close to insolvency to be perceived as a good credit risk. Complexities of mortgage-related securities have made it difficult to ascertain their value, thus those assets have become less liquid. Furthermore, investors know that some banks have suffered loan losses that reduced their capital, but the complexities of the mortgage-related assets have made it difficult to identify which banks are undercapitalized. As a result, the liquidity of mortgage-related assets has been reduced, and the liquidity of financial firms has been reduced. The Federal Reserve has taken steps to increase the liquidity of particular assets, for example, by expanding the categories of assets that it will accept as collateral for loans.

The TARP program has been used to provide additional capital to banks. Thus far, these programs have not been sufficient to restore confidence in the financial sector. .

[18] CRS Report RL34427, *Financial Turmoil: Federal Reserve Policy Responses*, by Marc Labonte.

What is Contained in EESA, P.L. 110-343?[19]

The expressed purpose of EESA (Division A of P.L. 110-343) is to " ... provide authority and facilities that the Secretary of the Treasury can use to restore liquidity and stability to the financial system." This measure addressed some of the concerns that some policymakers may have had regarding the original three-page Treasury plan. A short description of some of the provisions of the Troubled Asset Relief Program (TARP) follows.

- It has two definitions of troubled assets. The first definition specifies mortgages and mortgage-related assets. The second definition is more general, and includes any asset that the Treasury, in consultation with the Federal Reserve, believes the purchase of which from financial institutions would help restore financial stability.
- It includes an asset insurance program as an alternative to, or in addition to, purchasing troubled assets.
- It excludes foreign central banks from the definition of eligible financial institutions but includes institutions in U.S. territories, such as Guam and the Virgin Islands.
- It includes a variety of oversight mechanisms including a Financial Stability Oversight Board of executive branch officers to review the exercise of authority under the program; ongoing oversight by the Comptroller General; a Congressional Oversight board; and a special inspector to be appointed by the President and confirmed by the Senate.[20]
- The Treasury will manage the acquisition and sale of assets with any proceeds accruing to the general fund for reduction of the public debt.
- The measure instructs the Secretary of Treasury to implement a plan to maximize assistance for homeowners and to encourage loan servicers to participate in the Hope for Homeowners program. Assistance to homeowners includes consent to reasonable loan modification requests.
- The measure puts limits on executive compensation of institutions that participate. Under certain circumstances, these include limits on incentive compensation for risk-taking during the period that the program has an equity or debt position in the firm, recovery of incentive bonuses paid to senior executives based on financial statements that are later shown to be false, and a prohibition of golden parachutes.
- The debt limit is raised to $11.3 trillion.
- The SEC is given the authority to suspend mark-to-market accounting rules.

---

[19] CRS Report RL34730, *The Emergency Economic Stabilization Act and Current Financial Turmoil: Issues and Analysis*, by Baird Webel and Edward V. Murphy.

[20] CRS Report RL34713, *Emergency Economic Stabilization Act: Preliminary Analysis of Oversight Provisions*, by Curtis W. Copeland and CRS Report R40099, *The Special Inspector General (SIG) for the Troubled Asset Relief Program (TARP)*, by Vanessa K. Burrows.

- The limit on FDIC insurance for accounts at depository institutions is raised from \$100,000 to \$250,000 per individual until the end of TARP (December 31, 2009).

What has Treasury done under the EESA?

While the initial Treasury focus was on purchasing troubled mortgage-related assets, this portion of TARP has not been implemented. Instead, Treasury has focused on direct capital injections though preferred stock purchases. On October 14, 2008, Treasury announced the Capital Purchase Plan (CPP). Under the initial CPP announcement, nine large banks received \$125 billion in capital with another \$125 billion intended for the rest of the banking system. Approximately

\$62.5 billion of the second \$125 billion had been disbursed as of December 31, 2008. In addition to the general capital purchase plan, there have been several other case-by-case interventions since the passage of the EESA. AIG received \$40 billion in preferred share purchases as part of a revamp of an earlier rescue package. Citigroup received an additional \$20 billion in preferred share purchases after an initial \$25 billion from the CPP, along with a package of federal guarantees to cover losses on a \$306 billion pool of assets, with \$5 billion in losses covered under TARP. The U.S. automakers also received financial assistance through TARP, with a \$5 billion preferred share purchase from GMAC, up to \$14.4 billion in loans to GM and \$4 billion in loans to Chrysler. Treasury also committed up to \$20 billion in TARP funds to absorb losses on a \$200 billion Federal Reserve credit facility intended to assist the credit markets in accommodating the credit needs of consumers and small businesses. In total, over \$350 billion in funds have been committed through TARP, although less than this has actually been disbursed.

What Legislation is being Considered in the 111 Congress?

On January 9, 2009, House Financial Services Chairman Barney Frank introduced H.R. 384, the TARP Reform and Accountability Act of 2009, which is scheduled for floor action during the week of January 12, 2009. H.R. 384 substantially amends the EESA to address several criticisms of the TARP since enactment. The bill includes provisions to: (1) increase reporting on the use of TARP funds; (2) apply stricter executive compensation rules to institutions receiving TARP funds; (3) condition the release of the second \$350 billion on usage of at least \$40 billion in foreclosure mitigation; (4) confirm the authority to provide assistance to automobile manufactures and conditions the assistance on long-term restructuring; (5) clarify authority to provide support to consumer loans, commercial real estate loans, and municipal securities; (6) amend the Hope for Homeowners program to expand availability; (7) make permanent the increase in deposit insurance included in the EESA.

On Wednesday, February 4, 2009, the Financial Services Committee is due to markup H.R. 703, “Promoting Bank Liquidity and Lending Through Deposit Insurance, Hope for Homeowners, and other Enhancements”. If enacted, H.R. 703 would make permanent the increase in FDIC deposit insurance for individual accounts, which Section 136 of EESA temporarily increases from $100,000 to $250,000. The FDIC's automatic line of credit from Treasury would be raised from $30 billion to $100 billion. The FDIC line of credit refers to the funds that the FDIC can draw from Treasury if the Deposit Insurance Fund (DIF) proves insufficient to cover the FDIC's guarantees. H.R. 703 also makes several changes to the Hope for Homeowner's Program that may increase the incentive of people to participate in the program. It changes the initial loan write-down from 90% to 93% of the current appraised value of the house. It allows for reduced insurance premiums if Secretary determines that conditions warrant a decrease. It possibly reduces some barriers to modifying securitized mortgages by providing a safe harbor for loan servicers who modify loans as long as the servicers comply with several criteria, including a that default was reasonably foreseeable and that the expected net recovery of funds is not diminished.

What is a Bad Bank?

A bad bank is an institution set up to hold problem assets. In a good-bank, bad-bank split, a bank or a group of banks will have their bad assets removed with the intent of making the remaining bank or banks healthy.[21] Once healthy, these good banks can offer new loans and may be in a position to attract private capital. The bad bank or banks will have the job of trying to recover the value of impaired assets or liquidating them. For nonperforming loans, the bad bank may sometimes choose to restructure the loans with the current borrower. Because the troubled assets in the bad bank are not necessarily expected to return zero, it is sometimes possible to find private investors to provide partial financing or managerial expertise.

A good-bank, bad bank split requires consideration of funding sources. That is, the original institution is presumably undercapitalized in part because the bad assets are not performing as expected and, therefore, their current market price is less than the original price. Somehow, these losses must be recognized and absorbed. One method is for the bad bank to purchase the nonperforming assets from the good bank. If the purchases occur at current market prices then the losses are absorbed by the good bank (the original) and the good bank will remain undercapitalized if no other action is taken. If the bad bank is underwritten by a third party, such as the government, and the bad bank pays the original price of the asset then the bad bank and the third party absorb the losses. Programs can be created that share losses. It is likely that a bad-bank would be at least partially funded with TARP money. Many of the features of a bad bank were part of the original TARP discussion.

There have been a number of variations on the good-bank, bad-bank split. In the United States, the use of the good-bank, bad bank structure was often used during the Savings and Loan Crisis. In some ways, the Resolution Trust Corporation itself was a form of a bad bank because it acquired and disposed of nonperforming assets while allowing some thrifts to re-emerge with more healthy balance sheets. Similar procedures are sometimes used by the FDIC when it serves as a receiver or conservator of troubled banks. Because of this expertise,

---

[21] See IMF proposal for dealing with troubled assets through a bad bank, "Governments Must Take Stronger Measures to Strengthen Banks," January 28, 2009, available at http://www.imf.org/external/pubs/ft/ survey/ so/2009/RES012809B.htm.

some have proposed that the FDIC administer a larger bad bank program for the current financial turmoil.

In: The Financial Crisis
Editors: Barbara L. Campos and Janet P. Wilkins
ISBN: 978-1-61209-281-2

Chapter 8

THE DEBT LIMIT: HISTORY AND RECENT INCREASES

D. Andrew Austin[1]* and Mindy R. Levit[2]
[1]Economic Policy
[2]Public Finance

SUMMARY

Total debt of the federal government can increase in two ways. First, debt increases when the government sells debt to the public to finance budget deficits and acquire the financial resources needed to meet its obligations. This increases *debt held by the public*. Second, debt increases when the federal government issues debt to certain government accounts, such as the Social Security, Medicare, and Transportation trust funds, in exchange for their reported surpluses. This increases *debt held by government accounts*. The sum of *debt held by the public* and *debt held by government accounts* is the total federal debt. Surpluses generally reduce debt held by the public, while deficits raise it.

A statutory limit has restricted total federal debt since 1917 when Congress passed the Second Liberty Bond Act. Congress has raised the debt limit seven times since 2001. Deficits each year since 2001 and the persistent increases in debt held by government accounts repeatedly raised the debt to or near the limit in place at the time. Congress raised the limit in June 2002, and by December 2002 the U.S. Department of the Treasury asked Congress for another increase, which was passed in May 2003. In June 2004, the Treasury asked for another debt limit increase. After Congress recessed in mid-October 2004 without acting, the Secretary of the Treasury told Congress that the actions he was taking to avoid exceeding the debt limit would suffice only through mid-November. Congress approved a debt limit increase in a post-election session, which the President signed on November 19, 2004.

In 2005, Congress included debt limit raising reconciliation instructions in the FY2006 budget resolution (H.Con.Res. 95). Approval of the budget resolution in April 2005 triggered the automatic passage of a debt limit increase in the House. With no action having been taken by December 2005, the Secretary of the Treasury sent several letters warning Congress that the Treasury would exhaust its options to avoid default by mid-March 2006. Congress passed an increase in mid-March, which the President signed on March 20.

* Email: aaustin@crs.loc.gov

The House's adoption of the conference report on the FY2008 budget resolution in the spring of 2007 automatically created and deemed passed legislation (H.J.Res. 43) raising the debt limit by $850 billion to $9,815 billion. The Senate approved the resolution on September 27, 2007, and it was signed by the President two days later.

The current economic slowdown has led to sharply higher estimates of the FY2008 deficit, raising the prospect of another debt limit increase. A debt limit increase was included in the Housing and Economic Recovery Act of 2008 (H.R. 3221) and signed into law (P.L. 110-289) on July 30. The Emergency Economic Stabilization Act of 2008 (H.R. 1424), signed into law on October 3 (P.L. 110-343), raised the debt limit for the second time in. The debt limit was increased for the third time in less than a year with the passage of American Recovery and Reinvestment Act of 2009 on February 13, 2009 (ARRA; H.R. 1). ARRA was signed into law on February 17, 2009 (P.L. 111-5), which raised the debt limit to $12,104 billion, where it now stands. This report will be updated as events warrant.

INTRODUCTION

The statutory debt limit applies to almost all federal debt.[1] The limit applies to federal debt held by the public (that is, debt held outside the federal government itself) and to federal debt held by the government's own accounts. Federal trust funds, such as Social Security, Medicare, Transportation, and Civil Service Retirement accounts, hold most of this internally held debt.[2] The government's surpluses or deficits determine essentially all of the change in debt held by the public.[3] The government's on-budget fiscal balance, which excludes a small U.S. Postal Service net surplus or deficit and a large Social Security surplus of payroll taxes net of paid benefits, does not directly affect debt held in government accounts.[4] Increases or decreases in debt held by government accounts result from net financial flows into accounts holding the debt, such as the Social Security Trust Fund. Legal requirements and government accounting practices also affect levels of debt held by government accounts.[5]

---

[1] About 0.6% of total debt is excluded from debt limit coverage. As of December 2008, total public debt outstanding was $10,700 billion; debt subject to limit was $10,640 billion or 99.4% of total public debt outstanding. The Treasury defines "Total Public Debt Subject to Limit" as "the *Total Public Debt Outstanding* less the *Unamortized Discount on Treasury Bills and Zero-Coupon Treasury Bonds*, old debt issued before 1917, and old currency called United States Notes, as well as Debt held by the Federal Financing Bank and Guaranteed Debt."

[2] Although there are hundreds of trust funds, the overwhelming majority are very small. The 12 largest trust funds hold 98.8% of the federal debt held in government accounts.

[3] Other means of financing—including cash balance changes, seigniorage, and capitalization of financing accounts used to fund federal credit programs—have relatively little effect on the changes in debt held by the public.

[4] In future years, when some trust funds are projected to pay out more than they take in, funds that the Treasury would use to redeem those intergovernmental debts must be obtained via higher taxes or lower government spending.

[5] Trust fund surpluses by law must be invested in special federal government securities.

The Debt Limit and the Treasury

Standard methods of financing federal activities or meeting government obligations used by the U.S. Department of Treasury (Treasury) can be hobbled when federal debt nears its legal limit. If the limit prevents the Treasury from issuing new debt to manage short-term cash flows or to finance an annual deficit, the government may be unable to obtain the cash needed to pay its bills or it may be unable to invest the surpluses of designated government accounts (federal trust funds) in federal debt as generally required by law. In either case, the Treasury is left in a bind; the law requires that the government's legal obligations be paid, but the debt limit may prevent it from issuing the debt that would allow it to do so.

The government's income and outlays vary over the course of the year, producing monthly surpluses and deficits that affect the level of debt, whether or not the government has a surplus or deficit for the entire year. The government accounts holding federal debt also can experience monthly deficits and surpluses, even if most of them currently show annual surpluses.

Why Have a Debt Limit?

The debt limit can hinder the Treasury's ability to manage the federal government's finances, as noted above. In extreme cases, when the federal debt is very near its statutory limit, the Treasury must take unusual and extraordinary measures to meet federal obligations.[6] While the debt limit has never caused the federal government to default on its obligations, it has at times caused great inconvenience and has added uncertainty to Treasury operations.

The debt limit also provides Congress with the strings to control the federal purse, allowing Congress to assert its constitutional prerogatives to control spending.[7] The debt limit also imposes a form of fiscal accountability, which compels Congress and the President to take visible action to allow further federal borrowing when the federal government spends more than it collects in revenues. In the words of one author, the debt limit "expresses a national devotion to the idea of thrift and to economical management of the fiscal affairs of the government."[8]

A Brief History of the Federal Debt Limit

Origins of the Federal Debt Limit

The statutory limit on federal debt began with the Second Liberty Bond Act of 1917,[9] which helped finance the United States' entry into World War I.[10] By allowing the Treasury to issue

[6] U.S. General Accounting Office (GAO), *Analysis of Actions Taken during the 2003 Debt Issuance Suspension Period,* GAO-04-526, May 2004, available at http://www.gao.gov/new.items/d04526.pdf.

[7] For a vigorous assertion of the utility of the debt ceiling, see Anita S. Drishnakumar, "In Defense of the Debt Limit Statute," *Harvard Journal on Legislation*, vol. 42, 2005, pp. 135-185.

[8] Marshall A. Robinson, *The National Debt Ceiling: An Experiment in Fiscal Policy*, Washington, DC: The Brookings Institution, 1959, pp.5.

[9] P.L. 65-43, 40 Stat. 288, enacted September 24, 1917. Currently codified as amended as 31 U.S.C. § 3101.

long-term Liberty Bonds, which were marketed to the public at large, the federal government held down its interest costs.[11]

Before World War I, Congress authorized specific loans, such as the Panama Canal loan, or allowed the Treasury to issue specific types of debt instruments, such as certificates of indebtedness, bills, notes and bonds.[12] In other cases, Congress provided the Treasury with limited discretion to choose debt instruments.[13]

With the passage of the Second Liberty Bond Act, Congress enacted aggregate constraints on certificates of indebtedness and on bonds that allowed the Treasury greater ability to respond to changing conditions and more flexibility in financial management. Debt limit legislation in the following two decades also set separate limits for different categories of debt, such as bills, certificates, and bonds.

In 1939, Congress eliminated separate limits on bonds and on other types of debt, which created the first aggregate limit that covered nearly all public debt. [14] This measure gave the Treasury freer rein to manage the federal debt as it saw fit. In particular, the Treasury could choose to issue debt instruments with maturities that would reduce interest costs and minimize financial risks stemming from future interest rate changes given the conditions in financial markets. [15] On the other hand, although the Treasury was delegated greater independence of action, the debt limit on the eve of World War II was much closer to total federal debt than it had been at the end of World War I. For example, the 1919 Victory Liberty Bond Act (P.L. 65-3 28) raised the maximum allowable federal debt to $43 billion, far above the $25.5 billion in total federal debt at the end of FY19 19.[16] By contrast, the debt limit in 1939 was $45 billion, only about 10% above the $40.4 billion total federal debt of that time.

World War II and After

The debt ceiling was raised to accommodate accumulating costs for World War II in each year from 1941 through 1945, when it was set at $300 billion.[17] After World War II ended, the debt limit was reduced to $275 billion. Because the Korean War was mostly financed by

---

[10] H. J. Cooke and M. Katzen, "The Public Debt Limit," *Journal of Finance*, vol. 9, no. 3 (September 1954), pp. 298- 303.

[11] Robert D. Hormats, *The Price of Liberty,* (New York: Henry Holt, 2007), ch. 4.

[12] Treasury certificates of indebtedness were short-term, interest-bearing securities. Treasury bills are securities with a maturity of a year or less. Treasury notes are interest-bearing securities that generally have maturities of two to five years. Treasury bonds are interest-bearing securities that generally have maturities of 10 or more years.

[13] Marshall A. Robinson, *The National Debt Ceiling: An Experiment in Fiscal Policy*, (Washington, DC: The Brookings Institution, 1959), pp.1-6.

[14] P.L. 76-201. Some authors claimed the aggregate limit was first created in Public Debt Act of 1941 (P.L. 77-7). The 1939 Senate floor debate, however, makes clear that Congress intended to lift categorical debt restrictions. See Senate debate, *Congressional Record*, vol. 84, part 6 (June 1, 1939), pp. 6480, 6497-650 1.

[15] This limit did not apply to certain previous public debt issues that constituted a minor portion of the federal debt.

[16] U.S . Bureau of the Census, *Historical Statistics of the United States: Colonial Times to 1970*, H. Doc. 93-78 (Washington: GPO, 1975), Series Y 493-504.

[17] Public Debt Acts of 1941 (P.L. 77-7), 1942 (P.L. 77-510), 1943 (78-34), 1944 (P.L. 78-333), and 1945 (P.L. 79-48).

higher taxes rather than by increased debt, the limit remained at $275 billion until 1954. After 1954, the debt limit was reduced twice and increased seven times, until March 1962 when it again reached $300 billion, its level at the end of World War II. Since March 1962, Congress has enacted 73 separate measures that have altered the limit on federal debt.[18] Most of these changes in the debt limit were, measured in percentage terms, small in comparison to changes adopted in wartime or during the Great Depression. Some recent increases in the debt limit, however, were large in dollar terms. For instance, in May 2003, the debt limit increased by $984 billion.

THE DEBT CEILING IN THE LAST DECADE

During the four years (FY1998-FY2001) the government ran surpluses, federal debt held by intergovernmental accounts grew by $855 billion and debt held by the public fell by almost $450 billion. Since FY200 1, however, debt held by the public grew continuously due to persistent and substantial budget deficits, as shown in Table 1, which shows components of debt in current dollars and as percentages of gross domestic product (GDP). [19] Debt held in government accounts also continued to grow.

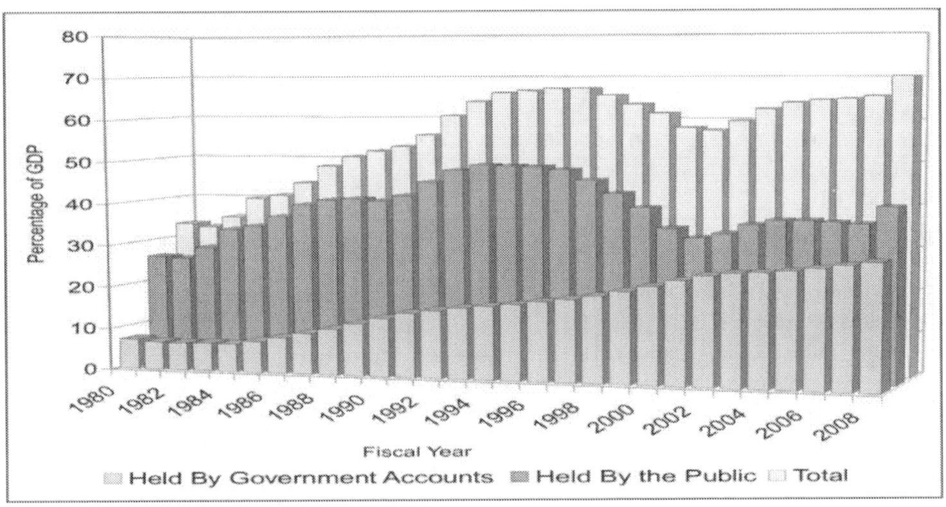

Source: OMB, Budget of the United States for FY2009, Historical Tables, February 2008; CBO.

Figure 1. Components of Federal Debt As Percentage of GDP, FY1980-FY2008,

Figure 1 shows the components of federal debt as shares of gross domestic product (GDP) from FY1980 through FY2008.[20] Federal debt held by government accounts has

[18] U.S. Office of Management and Budget, *FY2008 Budget of the U.S. Government: Historical Tables*, Table 7-3.

[19] Until 2001, government publications did not divide debt subject to limit into the portions held by the public and held by government accounts. This discussion and Table 1 use CRS calculations that approximate the amounts of debt subject to limit held in these two categories for fiscal years prior to 2001.

[20] The data show components of debt compared to the size of the economy. This avoids possible distortions resulting from changing price levels over time and includes changes in per capita incomes. This percentage increases when debt grows faster than GDP and falls when it grows more slowly than GDP.

grown steadily since 1980. Debt held by the public, which changes in response to total surpluses or deficits, grew as a share of GDP through the mid-1990s. After FY1992, deficits

Table 1. Components of Debt Subject to Limit, FY1 996-FY2008 (in billions of current dollars and as percentage of GDP)

End of fiscal year	Debt limit	Debt subject to limit					
		Total		Held by government accounts		Held by the public	
		$ billion	% of GDP	$ billion	% of GDP	$ billion	% of GDP
1996	$5,500	$5,137.2	65.7%	1,432.4	18.3%	3,704.8	47.4%
1997	5,950	5,327.6	64.2%	1,581.9	19.0%	3,745.8	45.1%
1998	5,950	5,439.4	62.2%	1,742.1	19.9%	3,697.4	42.3%
1999	5,950	5,567.7	60.1%	1,958.2	21.1%	3,609.5	38.9%
2000	5,950	5,591.6	57.0%	2,203.9	22.4%	3,387.7	34.5%
2001	5,950	5,732.8	56.6%	2,436.5	24.1%	3,296.3	32.5%
2002	6,400	6,161.4	58.9%	2,644.2	25.3%	3,517.2	33.6%
2003	7,384	6,737.6	61.4%	2,846.7	25.9%	3,890.8	35.5%
2004	7,384	7,333.4	62.5%	3,056.6	26.0%	4,276.8	36.4%
2005	8,184	7,871.0	64.0%	3,301.0	26.9%	4,570.1	37.2%
2006	8,965	8,420.3	64.2%	3,610.4	27.5%	4,809.8	36.7%
2007	9,815[a]	8,921.3	65.4%	3,903.7	28.6%	5,017.6	36.8%
2008	10,615[b]	9,960.0	70.0	4,180.0	29.4	5,780.3	40.6
Change During FY1998 - FY2001		$405.2		$854.6		$-449.5	
Change During FY2002 - FY2008		$3,798.6		$1,535.8		$2,263.1	

Source: U.S. Department of the Treasury, Financial Management Service, *Treasury Bulletin*, June 2001 and December 2006. Bureau of the Public Debt, *Monthly Statement of Public Debt*, September 2007 and September 2008. CRS calculations. Totals may not sum due to rounding.

Note: For the fiscal years 1996 through 2000, the amounts held by government accounts and held by the public are approximations. In 2001, the Treasury publications began distinguishing holders of debt subject to limit. The numbers in the table showing this breakdown for FY 1996 through FY2000 were calculated by subtracting debts of the Federal Financing Bank, an arm of the Treasury whose debt is not subject to limit, from total debt held by government accounts. This calculation approximates the amount of that debt subject to limit. This approximation overestimates debt by billions of dollars because estimates of unamortized discount are unavailable. This adjusted amount was then subtracted from total debt subject to limit to produce an approximate measure of debt held by the public subject to limit. Because the amount held by government accounts is overestimated, the resulting measure of debt held by the public subject to limit is underestimated. Nevertheless, these approximations reported in the table above suffice to show how the two categories have changed over the time.

a. Debt limit increased September 29, 2007 to $9,815 billion.

b. The debt limit was increased twice in 2008—to $10,615 billion on July 30 and then to $11,315 billion on October 3, at the start of FY2009.

shrank, and from FY1998 through FY2001 the federal government ran surpluses.[21] Those surpluses, along with rapid GDP growth, reduced debt held by the public as a percentage of GDP. When large deficits returned and GDP growth slowed in the early 2000s, debt held by the public as a share of GDP again increased. Smaller deficits in FY2006 and FY2007 led to smaller increases in publicly held debt. The total FY2007 deficit fell to 1.2% of GDP according to the Congressional Budget Office (CBO).[22] As a result of the recession, which began in December 2007, and federal action taken to stabilize the housing and financial markets, deficits rose in FY2008 to 3.2% of GDP. Federal debt is on track to exceed the debt limit before the end of FY2009.

The Debt Limit Issue in 2002

Accumulating debt in government accounts produced most of the pressure on the debt limit that occurred early in 2002. As deficits reemerged in FY2002, increases in debt held by the public added to the pressure on the debt limit in the spring of 2002. During the four fiscal years with surpluses (FY1998-FY2001), the increases in federally held debt and decreases in debt held by the public produced a net increase of $405 billion in total debt subject to limit. At the beginning of FY2002 (October 1, 2001), debt subject to limit was within $217 billion of the existing $5,950 billion debt limit.[23] Between then and the end of May 2002, debt subject to limit increased by another $217 billion, divided between a $117 billion increase in debt held by government accounts and a $100 billion increase in debt held by the public, putting the debt close to the $5,950 billion limit. Table A-1, presented in the Appendix, shows month-by-month debt totals and accumulations from September 2001 through December 2008.

In the fall of 2001, the Administration recognized that a deteriorating budget outlook and continued growth in debt held by government accounts were likely to lead to the debt limit soon being reached. In early December 2001, it asked Congress to raise the debt limit by $750 billion to $6.7 trillion. As the debt moved closer to and reached the debt limit over the first six months of FY2002, the Administration asked Congress repeatedly to increase the debt limit, warning of adverse financial consequences were the limit not raised.

On April 4, 2002, the Treasury held debt below the limit by invoking its legislatively mandated authority to suspend reinvestment of government securities in the G-Fund of the federal employees' Thrift Savings Plan (TSP). This allowed the Treasury to issue new debt and meet the government's obligations. On April 15, debt subject to limit stood at $5,949,975 million, just $25 million below the limit. Once April 15 tax revenues flowed in, the Treasury "made whole" the G- Fund by restoring all of the debt that had not been issued to the TSP

---

[21] Federal on-budget receipts and outlays nearly matched in FY1999, and the on-budget surplus in FY2000 was 0.9% of GDP. Prior to FY1999, the federal government last had an on-budget surplus in FY1960. Social Security receipts in excess of benefits make up most of the off-budget surplus, which has been positive since FY1985.

[22] U.S. Congress, Congressional Budget Office, An Analysis of the President's Budgetary Proposals for Fiscal Year 2009, March 2008, available at http://www.cbo.gov/ftpdocs/89xx/doc8990/03-19-AnalPresBudget.pdf.

[23] The debt limit was raised from $5,500 billion to $5,950 billion on August 5, 1997, as part of the Balanced Budget Act of 1997 (P.L. 105-33, 111 Stat. 251).

over this period and crediting the fund with interest it would have earned on that debt.[24] By the end of April, debt subject to limit had fallen back $35 billion below the limit.

Resolving the Debt Limit Issue in 2002

By the middle of May 2002, debt subject to limit had again risen to within $15 million of the statutory limit. At the FY2002 average spending rate, $15 million equaled about five minutes of federal outlays. The Treasury, for the second time in 2002, used its statutory authority to avoid a default. The Treasury's financing problems, however, would persist without an increase in the debt limit. On May 14, the Treasury asked Congress to raise the debt limit or enact other statutory changes allowing the Treasury to issue new debt. A Treasury news release stated "absent extraordinary actions, the government will exceed the statutory debt ceiling no later than May 16," and that a "debt issuance suspension period" will begin no later than May 16 [2002].... [This] allows the Treasury to suspend or redeem investments in two trust funds, which will provide flexibility to fund the operations of the government during this period.[25]

The Treasury reduced federal debt held by these government accounts by replacing it with noninterest-bearing, non-debt instruments, which enabled it to issue new debt to meet the government's obligations. The Treasury claimed these extraordinary actions would suffice, at the latest, through June 28, 2002. Without a debt limit increase by that date, the Treasury indicated it would need to take other actions to avoid breaching the ceiling. By June 21, the Treasury had postponed a regular securities auction, but took no other actions. With large payments and other obligations due at the end of June and at the beginning of July, the Treasury stated it would soon exhaust all options to issue debt and fulfill government obligations, putting the government on the verge of a default.

During May and June 2002, Congress took steps to increase the debt limit. The FY2002 supplemental appropriations bill (H.R. 4775) passed by the House on May 24 included, after extended debate, language allowing any eventual House-Senate conference on the legislation to increase the debt limit. However, the Senate's supplemental appropriations bill (S. 2551; incorporated as an amendment to H.R. 4775, June 3, 2002) omitted debt-limit-increasing language. The Senate leadership expressed strong reluctance to include a debt limit increase in the supplemental appropriation bill. Instead, on June 11, the Senate adopted a bill (S. 2578), without debate, to raise the debt limit by $450 billion to $6,400 billion. At that time, a $450 billion debt limit increase was thought to provide enough borrowing authority for government operations through the rest of calendar year 2002, if not through the summer of 2003. With the possibility of default looming over it, the House passed the $450 billion debt limit increase by a single vote on June 27. The President signed the bill into law on June 28 (P.L. 107-199, 116 Stat. 734), ending the 2002 debt limit crisis.[26]

---

[24] For a comprehensive discussion of the Treasury's previous uses of its short-term ability to avoid breaching the debt limit, see U.S. General Accounting Office, *Debt Ceiling: Analysis of Actions During the 1995-1996 Crisis*, GAO/AIMD-96-130, August 1996.

[25] U.S. Department of the Treasury, Treasury News, *Treasury Statement on the Debt Ceiling*, May 14, 2002.

[26] For additional details, see U.S. General Accounting Office, *Debt Ceiling: Analysis of Actions During the 2002 Debt Issuance Suspension Period*, GAO-03-134, December 2002.

The Debt Limit Issue in 2003

On Christmas Eve, 2002, Kenneth Dam, Deputy Secretary of the Treasury sent a letter to Congress requesting an unspecified increase in the debt limit by late February 2003, signaling that the $6,400 billion debt limit would then be reached.[27] The 108th Congress, still in the process of organizing itself, did not immediately respond. Through the winter and into the spring, the Treasury repeatedly requested that the debt limit be raised to avoid serious financial problems. By February 20, 2003, the Treasury, as in 2002, used legislatively mandated measures to manage debt holdings of certain government accounts to avoid reaching the debt limit. These actions included the replacement of internally held government debt with non-debt instruments in certain government accounts and not issuing new debt to these accounts. These actions allowed the Treasury to issue additional debt to the public to acquire the cash needed to pay for the government's commitments or to issue new debt to other federal accounts.

Through the rest of February and into May, the Treasury held debt subject to limit $15 million below the debt ceiling.[28] The adoption of the conference report on the FY2004 budget resolution (H.Con.Res. 95; H.Rept. 108-71) on April 11, 2003, in the House triggered the "Gephardt rule" (House Rule XXVII) that deems to have passed legislation (in this case, H.J.Res. 51) raising the debt limit to accommodate the spending and revenue levels approved in the adopted budget resolution.[29]

The Senate received the debt-limit legislation on April 11, but did not act until May 23, after receiving further Treasury warnings of imminent default. On that day, debt subject to limit was $25 million (or 0.0004%) below the existing $6,400 billion limit. The Senate adopted the legislation, after rejecting eight amendments and sent it to the President, who signed it on May 27. This legislation raised the debt limit to $7,384 billion (P.L. 108-24, 117 Stat. 710).

The Debt Limit Issue in 2004

In January 2004, CBO estimated that the debt limit, then set at $7,384 billion, would be reached the following summer.[30] In June 2004, the Treasury asked Congress to raise the debt limit in order to avoid the disruptions to government finances experienced in the previous two years.[31] In August, and again in September, the Treasury declared that the debt limit would be reached in the first half of October. On October 14, debt subject to limit reached $7,383,975

[27] Kenneth Dam, Deputy Secretary of the Treasury, letter to Speaker of the House, Dennis Hastert, December 24, 2002, available at http://www.treas.gov/press/releases/po3718.htm.

[28] The Treasury reduced the amount of debt held by selected federal accounts while it sold an equal (or smaller) amount of debt to the public. This raised cash needed to pay for ongoing obligations and kept the debt below the limit.

[29] The House Budget Committee has some discretion in setting the debt limit level in the House Joint resolution generated by the Gephardt rule. SeeCRS Report 98-453, *Debt-Limit Legislation in the Congressional Budget Process*, by Bill Heniff Jr. and CRS Report RL3 1913, *Developing Debt-Limit Legislation: The House's "Gephardt Rule"*, by Bill Heniff Jr..

[30] U.S. Congress, Congressional Budget Office, *The Budget and Economic Outlook: Fiscal Years 2005 to 2014*, January 2004.

[31] Alan Fram, "Congress May Duck Debt Limit Raise," *Oakland Tribune*, June 5, 2004.

million, just $25 million below the existing limit. The Treasury employed methods used in the previous two years to keep debt under the legal limit. On October 14, Secretary of the Treasury John Snow informed Congress, just before the election recess, that available measures to avoid breaching the debt limit would be exhausted by mid-November.[32] Without an increase in the debt limit, the Treasury would be unable to meet all of the government's existing obligations, and the government could default.[33]

Although the House passed a budget resolution for FY2005 in the spring of 2004, it did not reach final agreement with the Senate on the measure. Without a budget resolution passed by Congress, no resolution to raise the debt limit could be deemed passed by the House automatically under the Gephardt rule. Consequently, no measure was available to send to the Senate. As the debt approached the limit through the summer and into the fall, no legislation was moved to raise the debt limit.

Earlier, in September 2004, the House had added an amendment to the FY2005 Transportation- Treasury appropriations (H.R. 5025) in an effort to remove the Treasury's flexibility in financing the government as federal debt approached and reached the existing limit. Without that flexibility, the government would be unable to meet its financial obligations as the amount of debt neared the limit. The legislation cleared the House, but the Senate did not act on it.

After the elections, Senator Frist, on November 16, 2004, introduced legislation (S. 2986) to raise the debt limit by $800 billion, from $7,384 billion to $8,184 billion. The Senate approved the increase on November 17, 2004. The House considered and approved the increase on November 18. The President signed the legislation into law (P.L. 108-415, 118 Stat. 2337) on November 19, 2004. Estimates made at that time anticipated the new limit would be reached between August and December 2005.

Shortly before the increase in the debt limit, the Treasury delayed a debt auction and informed Congress that it would invoke a "debt limit suspension period" as it had in previous years. The increase in the debt limit in mid-November allowed the Treasury to reschedule the debt auction and cancel, before it began, the "debt limit suspension period."

The Debt Limit Issue in 2005, 2006, and 2007

Debt limit increases in 2005, 2006, and 2007 took a less dramatic path than those in President Bush's first term. In 2005, Congress included three reconciliation instructions in the FY2006 budget resolution (H.Con.Res. 95, 109th Congress; April 28, 2005), the third of which directed the House Committee on Ways and Means and the Senate Finance Committee to report bills raising the debt limit. The instructions specified a $781 billion debt limit increase, to $8,965 billion, with a reporting date of no later than September 30, 2005. Neither committee reported a bill to raise the debt limit.

---

[32] John W. Snow, Secretary of the U.S. Treasury, letter to Senate Majority Leader Bill Frist, October 14, 2004, available at http://www.treas.gov/press/releases/reports/frist.pdf.

[33] Although not all the possible consequences of a government default are known, it would mean that the government could no longer meet all of its legal obligations. Not only the default, but the efforts to resolve it would arguably have negative repercussions on both domestic and international financial markets and economies.

The adoption of the conference report on the FY2006 budget resolution in late April 2005 also triggered the Gephardt rule (House Rule XXVII), producing a House Joint Resolution (H.J.Res. 47) that also would raise the debt limit by $781 billion to $8,965 billion. Under the rule, the resolution was automatically deemed passed by the House and sent to the Senate. Through the end of the first session of the 109th Congress, the Senate had not considered H.J.Res. 47, nor had Congress considered a reconciliation bill raising the debt limit as called for in the budget resolution.

At the end of December 2005, Secretary of the Treasury Snow wrote Congress that the debt limit would probably be reached in mid-February 2006, although the Treasury could take actions that maintain the debt below its limit until mid-March. He therefore requested an increase in the debt limit.[34] In two more letters, sent on February 19 and March 6, Secretary Snow advised Congress that the Treasury was taking measures within its legal discretion to avoid reaching the limit and that these measures would suffice only until the middle of March 2006. Secretary Snow authorized actions used previously by the Treasury, including declaring a debt issuance suspension period. As March began, the government was again close to becoming unable to meet its obligations. During the week of March 13 the Senate took up H.J.Res. 47. On March 16, the Senate passed a debt limit increase after rejecting several amendments. The President's signature on March 20, 2006, then raised the debt limit (P.L. 109-182) to $8,965 billion.

In mid-May 2007, Congress passed the conference report (H.Rept. 110-153) on the FY2008 budget resolution. The House's Gephardt rule, triggered by the adoption of the conference report on the budget resolution, resulted in the automatic engrossment of a joint resolution (in this case, H.J.Res. 43, 110th Congress) raising the debt limit by $850 billion to $9,815 billion, and sending it to the Senate. At the end of July 2007, the Treasury asked Congress to raise the debt limit, stating the limit would be reached in early October 2007. In August, the CBO Director said that projections suggested that the limit would be reached in late October or early November. Without an increase, the Treasury indicated that it would take steps within its legal authority to avoid exceeding the debt limit. The Senate Finance Committee approved the House resolution (H.J.Res. 43) without changes on September 12, 2007. The Senate then passed the measure on September 27, which the President signed on September 29, 2007 (P.L. 110-91).

The Economic Slowdown and Federal Debt

Fiscal Policy Considerations

The United States is currently in the midst of a recession, which began in December 2007. The economic slowdown began with a rapid deceleration of housing prices and a rise in interest rate spreads between private lending rates and benchmark Federal Reserve rates, indicating an increasing reluctance of major financial institutions to lend to each other as well as to firms and individuals. This led to sharply higher federal deficit spending in FY2008 spurred by several major actions taken by Congress to unfreeze credit markets, boost consumption, and increase spending. CBO projects deficit spending to increase even further

---

[34] John W. Snow, Secretary of the Treasury, letter to Senator Max Baucus, December 29, 2005, available at http://www.ombwatch.org/budget/pdf/snow_debtlimit_2006.pdf.

in FY2009, with higher than average deficits as a percentage of GDP persisting into the next decade. Congress is currently considering additional economic stimulus measures. If these proposals are enacted, they will likely lead to higher deficits well into the next decade, leading to increases in the federal debt and debt limit.

An economic recession affects the federal deficit in several ways. First, falling prices of many assets and equities can sharply reduce federal revenues from capital gains taxes and from the corporate tax. Second, individual income taxes, the largest component of federal revenues, may also fall if jobs are cut and unemployment increases due to economic conditions. Third, "automatic stabilizers" such as unemployment insurance and income support programs pay out more money as unemployment rises and the number of households eligible for means-tested benefits rises, thus increasing federal spending.

Boosting the economy through deficit spending provides a fiscal stimulus if the output levels of goods and services produced in the nation are below their potential levels. Deficit spending, however, can help accelerate inflation if output levels are near or at potential levels, and in addition, exacerbates long-term fiscal challenges. Several economists have expressed concerns that inflation, which had been relatively low since the early 1980s, could accelerate due to rising prices of food, energy, and primary commodities. While inflation would reduce the market value of the federal deficit, it would require Treasury to pay higher nominal interest rates on federal debt.

Raising the Debt Ceiling in 2008 and 2009

In a March 2008 report, CBO estimated the President's budget would lead to a $396 billion deficit in FY2008 and a $342 billion deficit in FY2009.[35] The actual deficit for FY2008 reached $455 billion. In January 2009, CBO predicted a $1,186 billion deficit for FY2009 and $703 billion deficit for FY20 10.[36] As a result of the current economic conditions and the actions of the federal government to bring the economy out of recession, several increases to the federal debt limit were enacted in 2008. One debt limit increase has been enacted thus far in 2009.

The House Concurrent Resolution on the Budget (H.Con.Res. 312) recommended policies that would result in a $10,200 billion debt in FY2009. The Senate Concurrent Resolution on the Budget (S.Con.Res. 70) recommended policies that would result in a total debt of $10,278 billion in FY2009.[37] Implementing either set of policies would require an increase in the federal debt limit. The conference agreement (H.Rept. 110-659) also recommended spending levels that would lead to a debt subject to limit of $10,207 billion in FY2009, a level that would require an increase in the statutory debt limit. The budget conference report passed the Senate on a 48-45 vote on June 4, 2008. The House passed the measure on the next day by a 214-210 vote. Agreement on the FY2009 budget resolution automatically created and deemed passed in the House legislation (H.J.Res. 92) that would

---

[35] U.S. Congress, Congressional Budget Office, *An Analysis of the President's Budgetary Proposals for Fiscal Year 2009*, Table 1.1, March 2008, available at http://www.cbo.gov/ftpdocs/89xx/doc8990/03-19-AnalPresBudget.pdf.

[36] Goldman Sachs U.S. Research, "US Daily: The Fiscal 2008 Deficit—Likely to Top $500 Billion," March 25, 2008.

[37] U.S. Congress, House Committee on the Budget, *Report to Accompany H. Con. Res. 312,* 110th Cong., 2nd sess., H.Rept. 110-543, March 2008, p. 99; U.S. Congress, Senate Committee on the Budget, *Report to Accompany S. Res. 70*, S.Prt. 110-039, March 2008.

increase the debt limit from its current level of $9,815 billion to $10,615 billion. Because the Senate did not take up H.J.Res. 92, the debt limit remained at $9,815 billion.

Subsequently, the House passed an amended version of the Housing and Economic Recovery Act of 2008 (H.R. 3221) by a vote of 272-152 that included a debt limit increase to $10,615 billion on July 23, 2008. The Senate then passed the measure on July 26 on a 72-13 vote. The President signed the bill on July 30 (P.L. 110-289), increasing the debt limit. In addition to increasing the debt limit, the act also contained provisions that would temporarily authorize the Secretary of Treasury to extend a line of credit to mortgage guarantee agencies Freddie Mac and Fannie Mae. The act also created the a new independent agency called the Federal Housing Finance Agency (FHFA), which replaced the Department of Housing and Urban Development Office of Federal Housing Enterprise Oversight (OFHEO) and the Federal Housing Finance Board (FHFB).

While CBO indicated that it was more likely than not that such intervention would not be needed, it also estimated a 5% chance of a cost to taxpayers of more than $100 billion.[38] Because debt subject to limit was just $339 billion less than the debt ceiling of $9,815 billion when the Senate passed H.R. 3221, some financial market participants may have worried that the debt limit, without an increase, might have hindered the Treasury Secretary's ability to intervene to support Freddie Mac and Fannie Mae. On September 7, 2008, the FHFA placed Fannie Mae and Freddie Mac in conservatorship, providing FHFA with the full powers to control the assets and operations of the firms.

Since the deprivatization of Fannie Mae and Freddie Mac, the federal government has acted to provide stability to financial markets.[39] On September 20, 2008, the U.S. Treasury submitted a proposal to Congress to authorize the Treasury Secretary to buy mortgage-related assets in order to stabilize financial markets. The Treasury proposal would allow Treasury holdings of mortgage- related securities up to $700 billion and would raise the debt limit to $11,315 billion.[40] The House introduced the Emergency Economic Stabilization Act of 2008 (H.R. 3997), which incorporated the main tenets of the Treasury proposal including raising the debt limit to $11,315 billion.[41] On September 29, 2008, however, the House rejected this measure. On October 1, 2008, the Senate voted on, and passed, a different version of the Emergency Economic Stabilization Act of 2008 (H.R. 1424) that included the same debt limit increase.[42] The House passed H.R. 1424 on October 3, 2008 and it was signed into law by the President (P.L. 110-343) on the same day, raising the debt limit to $11,315 billion.

Current economic conditions led Congress to consider another economic stimulus measure. This measure contains both tax cuts and spending increases, which will increase the deficit by reducing revenues and increasing outlays. The American Recovery and

---

[38] U.S. Congress, Congressional Budget Office, *Cost Estimate for H.R. 3221 "Housing and Economic Recovery Act of 2008" As passed by the Senate on July 11, 2008, with an amendment transmitted to CBO on July 22, 2008*, July 24, 2008, available at http://www.cbo.gov/ftpdocs/95xx/doc9597 /hr3221.pdf.

[39] For additional information see CRS Report RS22956, *The Cost of Government Financial Interventions, Past and Present*, by Baird Webel, Marc Labonte, and N. Eric Weiss.

[40] U.S. Department of Treasury, "Fact Sheet: Proposed Treasury Authority to Purchase Troubled Assets," Press release hp-1150, Sept. 20, 2008, available at http://www.treas.gov/press/releases/hp1150.htm.

[41] U.S. Congress, House Financial Services Committee, Emergency Economic Stabilization Act of 2008 (Amendment to the Senate Amendment to H.R. 3997), available at http://www.house.gov/apps/list/press/ financial svcs_dem/ amend_001_xml.pdf.

[42] U.S. Congress, Senate Banking, Housing, and Urban Affairs Committee, Emergency Economic Stabilization Act of 2008 (In the Nature of a Substitute to H.R. 1424), available at http://banking.senate.gov/ public/_files/latestversionAYO08C32_xml.pdf.

Reinvestment Act of 2009 (ARRA) as passed by the Senate on February 10, 2009 (Division B of the Senate Substitute amendment to H.R. 1 and S. 350) contained a provision which would raise the debt limit to $12,140 billion. The version of this legislation originally passed by the House did not contain this provision. The final conference agreement on ARRA was passed by the House and Senate on February 13, 2009 and signed by the President on February 17, 2009 (P.L. 111-5). This measure contained a provision increasing the debt limit to $12,104 billion.

In its March 2009 report, CBO estimated that debt subject to limit would reach $11,990 billion by the end of FY2009. As federal debt approaches the current limit, another debt limit increase before the end of 2009 would become increasingly likely.

Revised Deficit Estimates

The size of the debt may remain a concern in the future due to the size of impending federal deficits necessitating further increases in the debt limit. CBO warns that the current trajectory of federal borrowing is unsustainable and could lead to slower economic growth in the long run as debt rises as a percentage of GDP.

Comparing the most recent reports from CBO and the budget documents from the Bush and Obama Administrations shows growth in the estimates of future budget deficits as a result of economic and financial market conditions. In March 2009, CBO published a deficit figure for FY2008 in the amount of $459 billion. This represents a $52 billion increase in the FY2008 figure from their report released in September 2008 and an increase of $102 billion from their estimate in March 2008. CBO estimated deficits of $1,667 billion in FY2009, $1,139 billion in FY20 10, and $693 billion in FY20 11 under the baseline scenario, which exclude annual tax extenders, including the alternative minimum tax patch (beyond FY2009), and any additional federal financial assistance programs. Under President Obama's budget proposal, CBO projects deficits of $1,845 billion in FY2009, $1,379 billion in FY2010, and $970 billion in FY2011.[43]

In its July 2008 *Mid-Session Review*, the Bush Administration estimated a FY2009 deficit of $482 billion, an increase of $75 billion from their February estimate.[44] The Administration's FY2009 estimate excluded some costs of the wars in Iraq and Afghanistan, the cost of the Housing and Economic Recovery Act of 2008 (P.L. 110-289), which became law on July 30, 2008, and the Medicare Improvements for Patients and Providers Act of 2008 (H.R. 6331, P.L. 110-275), which became law on July 15, 2008. Additionally, some military analysts believe that the Pentagon will request as much as $100 billion or more in early 2009 to replace damaged, destroyed, and depreciated equipment and to fund war costs for the last few months of FY2009.[45] At that time, the Administration projected a decline in the deficit beginning in FY20 10, in part because of the assumption of a prompt recovery from the economic slowdown of 2008, with economic growth rates sharply higher than those estimated by most private forecasters. Due to subsequently enacted legislation and to the extent that

---

[43] U.S. Congress, Congressional Budget Office, The Budget and Economic Outlook: An Update, September 2008 and A Preliminary Analysis of the President's Budget and an Update of CBO's Budget and Economic Outlook, March 2009.

[44] Office of Management and Budget, *Mid-Session Review*, July 2008, available at http://www.whitehouse.gov/omb/ budget/fy2009/pdf/09msr.pdf.

[45] CRS Report RS22926, *Costs of Major U.S. Wars*, by Stephen Daggett.

actual growth rates are less than the Administration's projections, future deficits will likely be higher than expected.

Concluding Comments

Since the late 1950s, the federal government increased its borrowing from the public in all years, except in FY1969 following imposition of a war surcharge and in the period FY1997-FY2001. The persistence of federal budget deficits has required the government to issue more and more debt to the public.[46] The accumulation of Social Security and other trust funds, particularly after 1983 when recommendations of the Greenspan Commission were implemented, led to sustained growth in government-held debt subject to limit.[47] The growth in federal debt held by the public and in intergovernmental accounts, such as trust funds, has periodically obliged Congress to raise the debt limit.

Between August 1997, when the debt limit was raised to $5,950 billion, and the beginning of FY2002 in October 2001, federal budget surpluses reduced debt held by the public. From the end of FY200 1, the last fiscal year with a surplus, until the end of FY2008, debt held by the public subject to limit grew by $2,484 billion. Federal debt held in intergovernmental accounts grew steadily throughout the period, rising by $1,743 billion since the beginning of FY2002.

In early 2001, the 10-year budget forecasts projected large and growing surpluses, indicating rapid reduction in debt held by the public. Some experts expressed concern about consequences of retiring all federal debt held by the public.[48] Most long-term forecasts computed at that time, however, showed large deficits emerging once the baby boomers began to retire. Short-term forecasts projected continuous growth in debt held by government accounts, largely due to the difference between Social Security tax revenues and benefit payments. The combination of falling levels of publicly held debt and rising levels of debt held by government accounts moderated the expected growth of total debt. The moderate growth in total debt those projections had forecast was expected to postpone the need to increase the debt limit until late into the decade, when accumulating debt in government accounts would overtake reductions in debt held by the public.

New budget projections released in early 2002 smashed expectations of large, persistent surpluses, and hopes for reductions in debt held by the public collapsed. The return to large federal deficits accelerated the growth of total debt. Increases in the debt limit would be necessary much sooner than previously expected.

Early in 2003, the FY2003 deficit and the persistent rise in debt held by government accounts drove the federal debt up to the $6,400 billion limit in effect at the time. The Treasury avoided breaching the limit into May. Congress adopted a debt limit increase of

---

[46] The ability to run fiscal deficits gives the federal government useful flexibility in managing its finances, although large deficits may harm economic performance. See CRS Report RL33657, *Running Deficits: Positives and Pitfalls*, by D. Andrew Austin.

[47] Report of the National Commission on Social Security Reform, January 1983, available at http://www.ssa.gov/ history/reports/gspan.html.

[48] Testimony of Federal Reserve Chairman Alan Greenspan, in U.S. Congress, Senate Committee on the Budget, *Outlook for the Federal Budget and Implications for Fiscal Policy*, hearings, 107th Cong., 1st sess., January 25, 2001, available at http://www.federalreserve.gov/boarddocs/testimony/2001 /20010125/default.htm.

$934 billion on May 23, 2003, that provided enough room for the growing federal debt through the fall of 2004. The debt limit increase passed by Congress late in 2004 was expected, at the time, to accommodate the government's debt growth well into 2005, if not into early 2006. In late December 2005, and early in 2006, the Treasury informed Congress that the limit would be reached between mid- February and mid-March 2006. On March 16, 2006, the Senate passed the House-initiated debt limit increase, raising the debt limit to $8,965 billion. The debt limit crisis was resolved when the President signed the debt limit increase on March 20.

Smaller than expected deficits in FY2006 and FY2007 postponed, but did not end the need for a new, higher debt limit. The House passed legislation in May 2007 (H.J.Res. 43) to raise the debt limit. The Senate passed the measure (P.L. 110-91) on September 27, which the President signed on September 29. Turmoil in some financial markets in August 2007, according to some observers, appeared to constrain contention over the debt limit increase.

The 2008 economic slowdown, which reduced federal tax revenues and increased federal outlays, caused federal deficit spending to rise, thus bringing forward the projected date when the federal debt will reach its current limit. The House passed an amended version of the Housing and Economic Recovery Act of 2008 (H.R. 3221) that included a debt limit increase to $10,615 billion on July 23, 2008. The Senate passed the measure on July 26, and the President signed it on July 30, raising the debt limit for the first time in 2008. Subsequently, the Emergency Economic Stabilization Act of 2008 (H.R. 1424), signed into law on October 3 (P.L. 110-343), raised the debt limit for the second time in 2008 to $11,315 billion. The debt limit was raised for the third time in less than a year as a result of passage of the American Recovery and Reinvestment Act of 2009. President Obama signed this measure on February 17, 2009 (P.L. 111-5), which raised the debt limit to $12,104 billion.

Over the next decade, without major changes in federal policies, persistent and possibly growing deficits, along with the ongoing growth in the debt holdings of government accounts, would increase substantially the amount of federal debt subject to limit. Unless federal policies change, Congress would repeatedly face demands to raise the debt limit to accommodate the growing federal debt in order to provide the government with the means to meet its financial obligations.

FURTHER READING

Drishnakumar, Anita S., "In Defense of the Debt Limit Statute," *Harvard Journal on Legislation*, vol. 42, 2005, pp. 135-185.

Gordon, John Steele, *Hamilton's Blessing: the Extraordinary Life and Times of Our National Debt*, New York: Penguin, 1998.

Hormats, Robert D., *The Price of Liberty: Paying for America's Wars from the Revolution to the War on Terror*, New York: Times Books, 2007.

Noll, Franklin, "The United States Public Debt, 1861 to 1975," EH.Net Encyclopedia, edited by Robert Whaples, May 26, 2004. Available at http://eh.net/encyclopedia/article/noll.publicdebt.

Wright, Robert E., *One Nation Under Debt: Hamilton, Jefferson, and the History of What We Owe*, New York: McGraw-Hill, 2008.

APPENDIX. DEBT SUBJECT TO LIMIT BY MONTH SINCE SEPTEMBER 2001

Table A-1, below, provides data on the dollar amount, in current dollars, of federal debt and the changes in these amounts by month between the end of September 2001 (the end of FY200 1) and the end of December 2008. The table shows outstanding monthly balances of total federal debt, debt held by government accounts, and debt held by the public. The final row shows the change for each category for the entire period, September 2001 to December 2008.

Table A-1. Components of Debt Subject to Limit by Month, September 2001-December 2008 (in millions of current dollars)

End of month	Total	Change from pevious period	Held by government accounts	Change from previous period	Held by the public	Change from previous period
Sept. 2001	$5,732,802	—	$2,436,521	—	$3,296,281	—
Oct. 2001	5,744,523	$11,721	2,451,815	$15,294	3,292,709	$-3,572
Nov. 2001	5,816,823	72,300	2,469,647	17,832	3,347,176	54,467
Dec. 2001	5,871,413	54,590	2,516,012	46,365	3,355,401	8,225
Jan. 2002	5,865,892	-5,521	2,525,755	9,743	3,340,138	-15,263
Feb. 2002	5,933,154	67,262	2,528,494	2,739	3,404,659	64,521
Mar. 2002	5,935,108	1,954	2,528,318	-176	3,406,789	2,130
Apr. 2002	5,914,816	-20,292	2,549,438	21,120	3,365,378	-41,411
May 2002	5,949,975	35,159	2,553,350	3,912	3,396,625	31,247
June 2002	6,058,313	108,338	2,630,646	77,296	3,427,667	31,042
July 2002	6,092,050	33,737	2,627,980	-2,666	3,464,070	36,403
Aug. 2002	6,142,835	50,785	2,620,946	-7,034	3,521,890	57,820
Sept. 2002	6,161,431	18,596	2,644,244	23,298	3,517,187	-4,703
Oct. 2002	6,231,284	69,853	2,680,812	36,568	3,550,472	33,285
Nov. 2002	6,294,480	63,196	2,680,788	-24	3,613,692	63,220
Dec. 2002	6,359,412	64,932	2,745,787	64,999	3,613,625	-67
Jan. 2003	6,355,812	-3,600	2,753,301	7,514	3,602,511	-11,114
Feb. 2003	6,399,975	44,163	2,750,471	-2,830	3,649,504	46,993
Mar. 2003	6,399,975	0	2,722,812	-27,659	3,677,163	27,659
Apr. 2003	6,399,975	0	2,731,042	8,230	3,668,933	-8,230
May 2003	6,498,658	98,683	2,755,895	24,853	3,742,763	73,830
June 2003	6,625,519	126,861	2,842,361	86,466	3,783,158	40,395
July 2003	6,704,814	79,295	2,835,566	-6,795	3,869,247	86,089
Aug. 2003	6,743,775	38,961	2,829,387	-6,179	3,914,388	45,141
Sept. 2003	6,737,553	-6,222	2,846,730	17,343	3,890,823	-23,565
Oct. 2003	6,826,668	89,115	2,869,493	22,763	3,957,175	66,352
Nov. 2003	6,879,626	52,958	2,879,117	9,624	4,000,509	43,334
Dec. 2003	6,952,893	73,267	2,940,736	61,619	4,012,157	11,648
Jan. 2004	6,966,851	13,958	2,951,219	10,483	4,015,633	3,476
Feb. 2004	7,049,163	82,312	2,953,123	1,904	4,096,040	80,407
Mar. 2004	7,088,648	39,485	2,941,195	-11,928	4,147,453	51,413
Apr. 2004	7,089,700	1,052	2,960,151	18,956	4,129,549	-17,904
Aug. 2004	7,305,531	34,203	3,037,149	3,753	4,268,382	30,449
Sept. 2004	7,333,350	27,819	3,056,590	19,441	4,276,760	8,378
Oct. 2004	7,383,975	50,625	3,096,207	39,617	4,287,768	11,008
Nov. 2004	7,464,740	80,765	3,087,834	-8,373	4,376,906	89,138
Dec. 2004	7,535,644	70,904	3,158,531	70,697	4,377,114	208

Table A-1. Continued

End of month	Total	Change from pevious period	Held by government accounts	Change from previous period	Held by the public	Change from previous period
Jan. 2005	7,567,702	32,058	3,171,089	12,558	4,396,615	19,501
Feb. 2005	7,652,726	85,024	3,176,406	5,317	4,476,320	79,705
Mar. 2005	7,715,503	62,777	3,175,460	-946	4,540,042	63,722
Apr. 2005	7,704,041	-11,462	3,185,364	9,904	4,518,677	-21,365
May 2005	7,717,574	13,533	3,207,232	21,868	4,510,342	-8,335
June 2005	7,778,128	60,554	3,280,914	73,682	4,497,214	-13,128
July 2005	7,829,029	50,901	3,278,725	-2,189	4,550,304	53,090
Aug. 2005	7,868,395	39,366	3,284,696	5,971	4,583,699	33,395
Sept. 2005	7,871,040	2,645	3,300,969	16,273	4,570,071	-13,628
Oct. 2005	7,964,782	93,742	3,345,589	44,620	4,619,193	49,122
Nov. 2005	8,028,918	64,136	3,351,093	5,504	4,677,826	58,633
Dec. 2005	8,107,019	78,101	3,424,304	73,211	4,682,715	4,889
Jan. 2006	8,132,290	25,271	3,442,543	18,239	4,689,747	7,032
Feb. 2006	8,183,975	51,685	3,457,409	14,866	4,726,567	36,820
Mar. 2006	8,281,451	97,476	3,443,602	-13,807	4,837,849	111,282
Apr. 2006	8,262,718	-18,733	3,479,623	36,021	4,783,095	-54,754
May 2006	8,263,812	1,094	3,492,648	13,025	4,771,165	-11,930
June 2006	8,330,646	66,834	3,566,186	73,538	4,764,460	-6,705
July 2006	8,352,614	21,968	3,569,550	3,364	4,783,064	18,604
Aug. 2006	8,423,321	70,707	3,576,166	6,616	4,847,155	64,091
Sept. 2006	8,420,278	-3,043	3,622,378	46,212	4,828,972	-18,183
Oct. 2006	8,498,016	77,738	3,650,241	27,863	4,847,775	18,803
Nov. 2006	8,545,715	47,699	3,649,736	-505	4,895,979	48,204
Dec. 2006	8,592,513	46,798	3,724,450	74,714	4,868,063	-27,916
Jan. 2007	8,619,499	26,986	3,737,894	13,444	4,881,605	13,542
Feb. 2007	8,690,921	71,422	3,744,299	6,405	4,946,622	65,017
Mar. 2007	8,760,735	69,814	3,740,127	-4,172	5,020,608	73,986
Apr. 2007	8,753,070	-7,665	3,778,255	38,128	4,974,815	-45,793
May 2007	8,740,892	-12,178	3,792,201	13,946	4,948,691	-26,124
June 2007	8,779,168	38,276	3,867,819	75,618	4,911,348	-37,343
July 2007	8,845,417	66,249	3,873,239	5,420	4,972,178	60,830
Aug. 2007	8,918,493	73,076	3,854,115	-19,124	5,064,377	92,199
Sept. 2007	8,921,343	2,850	3,903,710	49,595	5,017,633	-46,744
Oct. 2007	8,994,639	73,296	3,958,357	54,647	5,036,281	18,648
Nov. 2007	9,065,827	71,188	3,950,468	-7,889	5,115,358	79,077
Dec. 2007	9,144,715	78,888	4,038,566	88,098	5,106,149	-9,209
Jan. 2008	9,155,842	11,127	4,053,199	14,633	5,102,644	-3,505
Feb. 2008	9,275,683	119,841	4,045,007	-8,192	5,230,676	128,032
Mar. 2008	9,358,135	82,452	4,051,685	6,678	5,306,450	75,774
Apr. 2008	9,298,567	-59,568	4,080,887	29,202	5,217,680	-88,770
May 2008	9,324,137	25,570	4,071,992	-8,895	5,252,144	34,464
June 2008	9,427,901	167,869	4,169,509	134,950	5,258,392	32,920
July 2008	9,520,220	92,319	4,144,377	-25,132	5,375,843	117,451
Aug. 2008	9,580,508	60,288	4,129,413	-14,964	5,451,095	75,252
Sept. 2008	9,959,850	379,342	4,179,574	50,161	5,780,276	329,181
Oct. 2008	10,504,702	544,852	4,231,878	52,304	6,272,824	492,548
Nov. 2008	10,595,725	91,023	4,228,270	-3,608	6,367,454	94,630
Dec. 2008	10,640,274	44,549	4,298,482	70,212	6,341,792	-25,662
Change, Sept. 2001-Dec. 2008		4,907,472	—	1,861,961	—	3,045,511

Source: U.S. Treasury, Bureau of the Public Debt, *Monthly Statement of the Public Debt*, Sept. 2001-Dec. 2008, TreasuryDirect website; CRS calculations.

All three measures of debt subject to limit increased over this period. From the end of September 2001 (the end of FY200 1) to the end of September 2008 (the most recently completed fiscal year), total federal debt increased by $4,227 billion, debt held in government accounts increased by $1,743 billion, and debt held by the public increased by $2,484 billion. All three measures experienced periodic reductions in some months. Because federal receipts and outlays are spread unevenly over the fiscal year, debt may rise or fall in a given month, even if debt measures follow an overall increasing trend.

In: The Financial Crisis
Editors: Barbara L. Campos and Janet P. Wilkins
ISBN: 978-1-61209-281-2

Chapter 9

ECONOMIC STIMULUS: ISSUES AND POLICIES

Jane G. Gravelle[1]*, Thomas L. Hungerford[2] and Marc Labonte[3]
[1]Economic Policy
[2]Public Finance
[3]Macroeconomic Policy

SUMMARY

Recent policies have sought to contain damages spilling over from housing and financial markets to the broader economy, including monetary policy, which is the responsibility of the Federal Reserve, and fiscal policy, including a tax cut in February 2008 of $150 billion and two extensions of unemployment compensation in June and November of 2008.

Over the past few months, the government has also intervened in specific financial markets, including financial assistance to troubled firms and legislation granting authority to the Treasury Department to purchase $700 billion in assets. The broad intervention into the financial markets has been passed to avoid the spread of financial instability into the broader market but there are disadvantages, including leaving the government holding large amounts of mortgage debt.

With the worsening performance of the economy beginning in September 2008, Congress passed and President Obama signed a much larger stimulus packages comprised of spending and tax cuts. The American Recovery and Reinvestment Act of 2009 (ARRA, P.L. 111-5), a $787 billion package with $286 billion in tax cuts and the remainder in spending, was signed into law on February 17, 2009. It includes spending for infrastructure, unemployment benefits, and food stamps, revenue sharing with the States, middle class tax cuts, and business tax cuts.

The need for additional fiscal stimulus depends on the state of the economy. The National Bureau of Economic Research (NBER), in December 2008, declared the economy in recession since December 2007. Growth rates, after two strong quarters, were negative in the fourth quarter of 2007, positive in the first and second quarters of 2008, and a negative 0.5% in the third quarter. Preliminary estimates put growth at a negative 6.2% for the fourth quarter

* Email: aaustin@crs.loc.gov

of 2008, the worst since 1982. According to one data series, employment fell in every month of 2008. The unemployment rate, which rose slightly in the last half of 2007, declined in January and February of 2008, but began rising in March and in March 2009 stood at 8.5%. Some forecasters believe that the ongoing financial turmoil will result in a recession that is deeper and longer than average.

Fiscal policy temporarily stimulates the economy through an increase in the budget deficit which leads to an increase in total spending in the economy, either through direct spending by the government or spending by the recipients of tax cuts or government transfers. There is a consensus that certain proposals, ones that result in more spending, can be implemented quickly, and leave no long-term effect on the budget deficit, would increase the benefits and reduce the costs of fiscal stimulus relative to other proposals. Economists generally agree that spending proposals are somewhat more stimulative than tax cuts since part of a tax cut may be saved by the recipients. The most important determinant of the effect on the economy is the stimulus' size. The 2008 stimulus package increased the deficit by about 1% of GDP. The ARRA would increase the budget deficit by about 1.3% in 2009 and an additional 2.2% (or 3.5% overall) in 2010. CBO projects that the ARRA would raise GDP by a range of 1.4% to 3.8% in 2009 compared to what it otherwise would have been.

The National Bureau of Economic Research (NBER) has declared the U.S. economy to be in recession since December of 2007. With the worsening performance of the economy, congressional leaders and President Obama proposed much larger stimulus packages. The American Recovery and Reinvestment Act of 2009 (ARRA), an $820 billion package with $275 billion in tax cuts (offset by a $7 billion gain from the treatment of built in losses) and the remainder in spending, was passed by the House on January 28 (H.R. 1). It contained infrastructure spending, revenue sharing with the States, middle class tax cuts, business tax cuts, unemployment benefits, and food stamps. Similar legislation was passed in the Senate on February 10 (a substitute for H.R. 1) and would cost $838 billion, with $292 billion in tax cuts. The version of the bill signed into law on February 17, 2009, (P.L. 111-5) was a $787 billion package with $286 billion in tax cuts and the remainder in spending.

Numerous actions have already been taken to contain damages spilling over from housing and financial markets to the broader economy. These policies include traditional monetary and fiscal policy, as well as federal interventions into the financial sector. In February 2008, in response to weaker economic growth, an economic stimulus package of approximately $150 billion was adopted.[1] A provision that was considered (but not enacted) in the February stimulus bill was a 26-week extension of unemployment benefits; this extension was eventually enacted.[2]

A number of financial interventions have also been undertaken, before and after financial market conditions worsened significantly in September 2008. The Federal Reserve has reduced short- term interest rates to zero and introduced a number of facilities, providing direct assistance to the financial system that would eventually surpass $1 trillion. In October

1 A second stimulus plan (H.R. 7110) passed the House on September 26, but was not passed by the Senate. It included $36.9 billion on infrastructure ($12.8 billion highway and bridge, $7.5 billion water and sewer, $5 billion Corps of Engineers); $6.5 billion in extended unemployment compensation; $14.5 billion in Medicaid, and $2.7 billion in food stamp and nutrition programs.

2 For a discussion of the tax, housing, and unemployment legislation adopted in the 1 10th Congress see CRS Reports RS22850, *Tax provisions of the Economic Stimulus Package*, by Jane G. Gravelle; RS22172, *The Conforming Loan Limit*, by Eric Weiss and Mark Jickling, and RS22915, *Temporary Extension of Unemployment Benefits: Emergency Unemployment Compensation (EUC08)*, by Julie Whittaker.

2008, legislation granting the Treasury Department authority to purchase up to $700 billion in assets through the Troubled Assets Relief Program (TARP) was adopted.[3] On March 18, 2009, the Federal Reserve announced plans to purchase over $1 trillion in assets, including $750 billion in mortgage backed securities and $300 billion in long term Treasury debt. On March 23, 2009, the Treasury announced a plan for a public-private partnership to purchase troubled assets, including one part that uses the Federal Deposit Insurance Corporation (FDIC) to insure loans and another part that would allow access to the Federal Reserve's Term Asset-Backed Securities Loan Facility (TALF).[4]

This report first discusses the current state of the economy, including measures that have already been taken by the monetary authorities. The next section reviews the economic stimulus package. The following section assesses the need for, magnitude of, design of, and potential consequences of fiscal stimulus. The final section of the report discusses recent and proposed financial interventions.

The Current State of the Economy[5]

The need for fiscal stimulus depends, by definition, on the state of the economy. According to the National Bureau of Economic Research (NBER), the official arbiter of the business cycle, the economy has been in recession since December 2007. It defines a recession as a "significant decline in economic activity spread across the economy, lasting more than a few months" based on a number of economic indicators, with an emphasis on trends in employment and income.[6] But because a recession is defined as a lasting decline, the NBER typically does not declare a recession until it is well under way. The current recession was declared in late November of 2008.

After two strong quarters, economic growth fell by 0.2% in the fourth quarter of 2007. It then increased by 0.9% in the first quarter of 2008 and 2.8% in the second quarter of 2008. Real GDP decreased by 0.5% in the third quarter, however. Preliminary estimates of the fourth quarter indicate a decline of 6.2%, the worst since 1982. The latest consensus forecast predicts that GDP will continue to contract until the second half of 2009 and the rate of decline will accelerate, with output falling by 2.6% for 2009 and unemployment reaching a high of 8.6% in 2009 and 9.1% in 2010.[7] If correct, this recession would be the longest and deepest in the period since the Great Depression, although it is still expected to end in 2009.

According to one data series, employment fell in every month of 2008. The deepening of the downturn following September can also be seen in the movement of the unemployment rate. The unemployment rate, which was 4.8% in February 2008, rose to 6.1% in August and September, and has steadily risen since, reaching 8.5% in March 2009.

---

[3] See CRS Report RL34427, *Financial Turmoil: Federal Reserve Policy Responses*, by Marc Labonte, for a discussion of Federal Reserve Policy and CRS Report RL34730, *The Emergency Economic Stabilization Act and Current Financial Turmoil: Issues and Analysis*, by Baird Webel and Edward V. Murphy.

[4] For further discussion see CRS Report RL34730, *Troubled Asset Relief Program: Legislation and Treasury Implementation*, by Baird Webel and Edward V. Murphy.

[5] This section was prepared by Marc Labonte of the Government and Finance Division.

[6] National Bureau of Economic Research, *The NBER's Recession Dating Procedure*, January 7, 2008.

[7] Blue Chip, *Economic Indicators*, vol. 34, no. 3, March 10, 2009.

After a long and unprecedented housing boom, house prices have fallen 11% since their peak in April 2007,[8] and residential investment has fallen by almost half. This marked possibly the first year of falling house prices since the Great Depression, according to one organization which compiles the data.[9] The decline in residential investment has acted as a drag on overall GDP growth, while the other components of GDP grew at more healthy rates until the third quarter of 2008. Many economists argued that the housing boom was not fully caused by improvements in economic fundamentals (such as rising incomes and lower mortgage rates), and instead represented a housing *bubble*—a situation where prices were being pushed up by "irrational exuberance."[10]

Most economists believed that a housing downturn alone would not be enough to singlehandedly cause a recession.[11] But in August 2007, the housing downturn spilled over to widespread financial turmoil.[12] Triggered by a dramatic decline in the price of subprime mortgage-backed securities and collateralized debt obligations, large losses and a decline in liquidity spread throughout the financial system. Although the real production of goods and services showed unexpected resilience until the fourth quarter of 2008, the ability of private borrowers to access credit markets remained restricted throughout the year. Evidence of a credit crunch was seen in the persistence of wide spreads between the interest rates that private borrowers paid for credit and the yields on Treasury securities of comparable maturity.

The Federal Reserve (Fed) was forced to create unusually large amounts of liquidity to keep short-term interest rates from rising in August 2007, and has since reduced interest rates significantly. The Fed has gradually reduced the federal funds target rate from 5.25% to a range of 0 to 0.25%, as of December 16, 2008. In addition, the Fed has lent directly to financial institutions through an array of new facilities, and the amounts of loans outstanding has at times exceeded a trillion dollars.[13] A reduction in lending by financial institutions in response to uncertainty or financial losses is another channel through which the economy entered a recession.

To date, financial markets remain volatile, new losses have been announced at major financial institutions, and responses outside traditional monetary policy have been undertaken. Last March, the financial firm Bear Stearns encountered liquidity problems, was purchased, after a plummet in stock value, by JPMorgan Chase with financial assistance from the Fed. Then in July, the government sponsored enterprises (GSEs) Fannie Mae and Freddie Mac experienced rapidly falling equity prices in response to concerns about the value of their mortgage backed securities assets. In July, Congress authorized Treasury to extend the GSEs an unlimited credit line (which has not been utilized to date) in the Housing and Economic Recovery Act of 2008 (P.L. 110-289) because of concern that the failure of a GSE would

---

[8] Based on the Federal Housing Finance Administration's Purchase-Only House Price Index, a national measure of single-family houses with conforming mortgages based on resale data.

[9] Michael Grynbaum, "Home Prices Sank in 2007, and Buyers Hid," *New York Times*, January 25, 2008. Prices are compiled by the National Association of Realtors.

[10] For more information, see CRS Report RL34244, *Would a Housing Crash Cause a Recession?*, by Marc Labonte.

[11] See, for example, Frederic Mishkin, "Housing and the Monetary Transmission Mechanism," working paper presented at the Federal Reserve Bank of Kansas City symposium, August 2007.

[12] See CRS Report RL34182, *Financial Crisis? The Liquidity Crunch of August 2007*, by Darryl E. Getter et al.

[13] See CRS Report RL34427, *Financial Turmoil: Federal Reserve Policy Responses*, by Marc Labonte.

cause a systemic financial crisis. The federal government took control of Fannie Mae and Freddie Mac in early September.

According to news reports in the fall of 2008, government officials decided not to intervene on behalf of Lehman Brothers and Merrill Lynch;[14] on September 14, Bank of America took over Merrill Lynch without federal intervention, and on September 15, Lehman Brothers filed for bankruptcy. The Treasury and Federal Reserve were trying to engineer a private bailout of the nation's largest insurance company, AIG, but on September 16 seized control with an $85 billion emergency loan, which would later be increased.[15]

On September 18, Administration and Federal Reserve officials with the bipartisan support of the Congressional leadership, announced a massive intervention in the financial markets.[16] The proposal asked for authority to purchase up to $700 billion in assets over the next two years. The Treasury had also provided insurance for money market funds, where withdrawals have been significant. These proposals suggested that government economists see problems with the transmission of traditional monetary stimulus into the financial sector and ultimately into the broader economy, where a significant contraction of credit could significantly reduce aggregate demand. Although the legislation passed with some delay, the stock market fell significantly. The original proposal had discussed buying mortgage related assets, particularly mortgage-backed securities, but the Treasury indicated it will spend the initial $250 billion on preferred stock in financial institutions. The Federal Reserve has also announced purchases of commercial paper, $200 billion of asset backed securities, and $600 billion of mortgage-related securities; the government has also announced a plan to guarantee certain assets of Citigroup and Bank of America. On March 18, the Federal reserve announced plans to purchase over $1 trillion in assets, including $750 billion in mortgage backed securities and $300 billion in long term Treasury debt. On March 23, 2009, the Treasury announced a plan for a public-private partnership to purchase troubled assets, including one part that uses the Federal Deposit Insurance Corporation (FDIC) to insure loans and another part that would allow access to the Federal Reserve's Term Asset- Backed Securities Loan Facility (TALF).[17]

At the same time the economy and financial sector had been grappling with the housing downturn, energy prices had risen significantly, from $48 per barrel in January 2007 to $115 dollars on April 30, 2008, and $144 as of July 2, 2008. After that, oil prices began a downward trend, and had fallen below $70 by October and $60 by the end of November. The price reached $43 per barrel on December 10; and remains at around $50 per barrel. Most recessions since World War II, including the most recent, have been preceded by an increase in energy prices.[18] Energy prices had gone up almost continuously in the current expansion, however, without causing a recession, which may point to the relative decline in importance of energy consumption to production. Although a housing downturn, financial turmoil, or an

---

[14] David Cho and Neil Irwin, "No Bailout: Feds Made New Policy Clear in One Intense Weekend," *Washington Post*, September 16, 2008, pp. A1, A6-A7.

[15] Glenn Kessler and David S. Hilzenrath, "AIG at Risk; $700 Billion in Shareholder Value Vanishes," *Washington Post*, September 16, 2008; U.S. Seizes Control of AIG With $85 Billion Emergency Loan, *Washington Post*, September 17, 2008, pp. A1, A8.

[16] See CRS Report RS22957, *Proposal to Allow Treasury to Buy Mortgage-Related Assets to Address Financial Instability*, by Edward V. Murphy and Baird Webel.

[17] For further discussion see CRS Report RL34730, *Troubled Asset Relief Program: Legislation and Treasury Implementation*, by Baird Webel and Edward V. Murphy.

[18] For more information, see CRS Report RL31608, *The Effects of Oil Shocks on the Economy: A Review of the Empirical Evidence*, by Marc Labonte.

energy shock might not be enough to cause a recession in isolation, the combination was sufficient.

THE 2009 STIMULUS PACKAGE[19]

Preliminary Discussions

On December 15, House Speaker Pelosi suggested a $600 billion package with $400 billion of spending and $200 billion in tax cuts as a starting point for discussion. It was reported that the package would include infrastructure spending, aid to the states, unemployment compensation, and food stamps. Earlier, on December 11, Finance Committee Chairman Baucus suggested that half of an expected $700 billion plan might be in tax cuts; he mentioned child tax credits, state and local property tax deductions, the R&D tax credit, the marriage penalty, tax exempt bonds and energy incentives. House Republican Leader Boehner proposed a tax package that included increases in the child tax credit, suspending the capital gains tax on newly acquired assets, increasing expensing, extending bonus depreciation and raising the share of costs expensed from 50% to 75%, extending net operating loss carrybacks to three years, lowering the corporate tax rate from 35% to 25%, and expanding energy subsidies.

Reports on December 29 suggested that then President Elect Obama would propose a package of $670 billion to $770 billion, but that additions in Congress might raise the total to $850 billion. The package was reported to include $100 billion in aid to the States to fund Medicaid, possibly with additional grants, and at least $350 billion for public works, alternative energy, health care and school modernization, and expanding unemployment insurance and food stamp benefits. The package would also include middle class tax cuts, possibly including changes to the child credit, state and local property taxes, marriage penalties, the R&D tax credit and tax exempt bonds.

Following a meeting between President Elect Obama and Congressional leaders on January 5, news reports indicated that the share of the package directed at tax cuts would increase to about 40%, perhaps $300 billion. President Elect Obama suggested a credit for working families of up to $1,000 for couples and $500 for singles. Business provisions that were discussed included extensions of the bonus depreciation and small business expensing enacted in February 2008 that expired at the end of 2008 as well as an extended net operating loss carryback provision that was discussed but not enacted in 2008. Also discussed was an expansion of the first-time homebuyers credit adopted in the 2008 housing legislation and expanding renewable energy incentives. A payroll tax holiday was also discussed.

News reports on January 9 indicated some resistance of Congressional lawmakers to two provisions in President Elect Obama's plan: a $3,000 tax credit for employers who hire new workers and the working families credit which provides for a credit of 6.2% of earnings up to a ceiling of $500 for individuals and $1,000 for married couples. Some were concerned that the employer tax credit would not benefit distressed firms and will be difficult to administer. There were also concerns about the effects of a tax benefit of small magnitude having an

[19] This section was prepared by Jane Gravelle and Thomas Hungerford, Government and Finance Division.

effect if reflected in withholding, although many economists suggest that a larger fraction of income received in small increments is spent.

House Proposal

The House proposal of the American Recovery and Reinvestment Act (H.R. 1) was comprised of both spending and tax cuts. The spending proposals, which total $518.7 billion, include the following:

(1) $54 billion for energy efficiency ($32 billion to improve the energy grid and encourage renewable energy, $16 billion to repair and retrofit public housing; $6 billion to weatherize modest income homes).
(2) $16 billion for science and technology ($10 billion for research, $6 billion to expand broadband access in rural and underserved areas).
(3) $90 billion for infrastructure ($30 billion for highways, $31 billion for public infrastructure that leads to energy cost savings, $19 billion for clean water, flood control and environmental infrastructure, $10 billion for transit and rail).
(4) $141.6 billion for education ($41 billion to local school districts dedicated to specific purposes, $79 billion to prevent cutbacks in state and local services including $39 billion to local school districts and public colleges and universities distributed through existing formulas, $15 billion to states for meeting performance measures, $25 billion to states for other needs, $15.6 billion to increase the Pell grant by $500, $6 billion for higher education modernization).
(5) $24.1 billion for health ($20 billion in health information technology and $4.1 billion for preventive care).
(6) $102 billion for transfer payments ($43 billion for unemployment benefits and job transit benefits, $39 billion to cover health care for unemployed workers, $20 billion for food stamps)
(7) $91 billion to the States ($87 billion in general revenues by temporarily increasing the Medicaid matching rate and $4 billion for law enforcement)

The proposal also contained $275 billion in tax cuts, which was reduced by a small revenue gain from limits on built-in losses. The tax elements included:

(8) Temporary income tax cuts for individuals included the Making Work Pay tax credit—a 6.2% credit for earnings with a maximum of $500 for singles and $1,000 for couples, phased out for taxpayers with incomes over $75,000 ($150,000 for joint returns)—with a $145.3 billion 10-year cost, $4.7 billion for a temporary increase in the earned income credit, $18.3 billion to make the child credit fully refundable, $13.7 billion to expand higher education tax credits and make them 40% refundable (the refundability feature accounts for $3.5 billion).
(9) Tax provisions for business, which would have lost revenue in FY2009-FY20 10 and gain revenue thereafter, included $37.8 billion for extending bonus depreciation, $59.1 billion for a temporary five year loss carryback for 2008 and 2009 (except for

recipients of TARP funds; and electing firms would reduce losses by 10%), and $1.1 billion for extending small business expensing.

(10) A series of provisions related to tax exempt bonds aimed at aiding State and local governments, which would have cost $1.3 billion for FY2009-2010, but $37.3 billion from FY2009-FY2019. Almost half the revenue loss would have arisen from allowing taxable bond options which to make bonds attractive to tax exempt investors. Other major provisions measured by dollar cost were qualified school construction bonds, recovery zone bonds, and provisions to allow financial institutes more freedom to buy tax exempt bonds.

(11) A permanent provision would have repealed the 3% withholding for government contractors, which would not have lost revenue until 2011 and would have cost $10.9 billion for FY2009-20 19.

(12) Energy provisions, some permanent and some temporary, would have totaled $5.4 billion in FY2009-FY201 1 and $20.0 billion in FY2009-2019. There was also a provision substituting grants for credits for certain energy projects which would have shifted benefits to the present.

(13) The proposal also included a provision to eliminate the requirement for paying back credit for first time homebuyers unless they sell their homes within three years ($2.5 billion for 2009-20 19). There was also a substitution of grants for the low income housing credit, which would have shifted benefits to the current year ($3 billion).

(14) A minor provision ($208 million for FY2009-20 19) would have provided incentives for hiring unemployed veterans and disconnected youth.

(15) Repeal (prospectively) a Treasury ruling made in 2008 that allowed financial institutions to carry over losses in an acquisition (gains $7 billion for FY2009-FY2010).

The bill passed the House on January 28, with an additional of $3.7 billion, primarily for transit funds, bringing the total cost to $820 billion.

Senate Proposal

The Senate passed a bill (a substitute for H.R. 1) with $838 billion in spending and tax cuts. The higher cost was primarily due to the addition of the Alternative Minimum Tax (AMT) "patch" (see below).

The tax provisions were similar to the House tax bill in many respects. The bill, however, did not fully refund the child credit and made 30% of tuition credits refundable, but allowed an exclusion of up to $2,400 of unemployment benefits. The Senate bill also included a $15,000 homeownership tax credit at a 10-year cost of $35 billion and an above-the-deduction for certain costs of a new automobile purchase ($11 billion 10-year cost). It would not have required net operating losses to be reduced, as in the House bill. It added provisions for businesses including an election to accelerate alternative minimum tax and research and experimentation credits in lieu of bonus depreciation, a deferral of tax on income from cancellation of indebtedness, an increase in the exclusion for small business stock. It also altered the size and mix of tax exempt bond provisions, with the total cost of $22.6 billion, and changed some energy provisions. The bill also included a $300 per adult payment to individuals eligible for Social Security, Railroad Retirement, Veterans benefits, and Supplemental Security Income, at a cost of $17 billion, and provided a one year increase in the Alternative Minimum Tax exemption (the AMT "patch"), at a cost of $70 billion. Overall, the tax cuts were $368.4 billion. The measure also included $87 billion in Medicaid funding for the states, $20 billion to provide health insurance for unemployed workers, and $16 billion to provide for health information technology.

The details of the spending provisions amounted to $290 billion in discretionary spending and $260 billion in direct spending.[20] One category of provisions would have provided $116 billion for infrastructure and science including $5.9 billion for the Department of Homeland Security and border stations, $7 billion for broadband technology, provisions in infrastructure and science for a variety of federal programs (e.g. $4.6 billion for the corps of engineers, $9.3 billion for defense and veterans), $27 billion for highways, $8.4 billion for mass transit, $10.9 billion for grants and other transportation, $8.6 billion for public housing, $15 billion for environmental programs, and $4.3 billion for science. The bill would have provided $84 billion for education and training, with the majority, $79 billion, in grants to states and localities, and also included $13 billion in Title 1, and $3.9 billion in Pell grants. Energy programs accounted for $43 billion; $23 billion would have been provided for nutrition, early childhood and similar programs, and $14 billion for health. The Senate bill also contained a limit on executive compensation at firms receiving assistance from the Troubled Asset Relief Program (TARP).

The American Recovery and Reinvestment Act of 2009

The American Recovery and Reinvestment Act of 2009 (P.L. 111-5) was signed by President Obama on February 17, 2009. The version of the Act signed into law has several provisions similar to the House and Senate proposals. The total 10-year cost, at $787 billion, is lower than both versions initially passed by the House and Senate, however. The spending parts of the Act account for 63.7% of the total cost ($501.6 billion) and the tax provisions account for 36.3% ($285.6 billion). The Act includes the $70 billion AMT "patch" and an executive compensation limitation for TARP recipients.

Many of the tax and spending provisions of the Act were scaled down from the House and Senate proposals. The Making Work Pay tax credit was scaled back to $116.2 billion between FY2009 and FY2011 and provides a tax credit of up to $400 for a single taxpayer and $800 of joint taxpayers. The temporary increase in the earned income credit is projected to cost $4.7 billion over 10 years and the child tax credit is projected to cost $14.8 billion. The Act also includes a $8,000 first-time homebuyer credit with a 10-year cost of $6.6 billion, an above-the-line deduction for sales tax on a new automotive purchase ($1.7 billion), a $2,400 exclusion of unemployment compensation benefits ($4.7 billion), and a $250 payment to recipients of Social Security, SSI, Railroad Retirement benefits, and certain veterans benefits ($14.2 billion).[21]

The business tax provisions are projected to lose $75.9 billion in revenues for FY2009 and FY2010, but gain revenue in the future; the total 10-year revenue loss is projected to be

[20] The direct spending also includes $83.7 billion in the refundable portion of tax credits.

[21] There is also a $250 tax credit for federal and state pensioners not eligible for Social Security with a $218 million 10- year cost.

$6.2 billion. Other business tax provisions include an extension of bonus depreciation ($5.1 billion revenue loss), a five-year carryback of net operating losses for small businesses ($0.9 billion), delayed recognition of certain cancellation of debt income ($1.6 billion), an increase in the small business capital gains exclusion from 50% to 75% ($0.8 billion), and incentives to hire unemployed veterans and disconnected youth ($0.2 billion).

The energy tax provisions amount to $20 billion over 10 years and $3.4 billion for FY2009- FY2011. The major energy provision is a long-term extension and modification of renewable energy production tax credits ($13.1 billion over 10 years). The Act alters the size and mix of tax exempt bond provisions with a total 10-year cost of $25 billion.

The discretionary appropriations provisions of the Act provide $311 billion in appropriations between FY2009 and FY2019. Investments in infrastructure and science account for $120 billion and education and training programs are to receive $106 billion. Health programs are set to receive $14.2 billion, the Supplemental Nutrition Assistance Program (formerly food stamps) will receive $20 billion, Head Start $2.1 billion, and $2 billion for the child care development block grant. Almost $40 billion will be used for investments in energy infrastructure and programs. Increases for direct spending programs include $57.3 billion for assistance to unemployed workers and struggling families, $25.1 billion for health insurance assistance, $20.8 billion for health information technology, and $90.0 billion for state fiscal relief.

Discussion

Fiscal stimulus is only effective when the policy options increase aggregate demand. Many economists view fiscal policy as less effective than monetary policy in an open economy. As mentioned earlier in this report, however, several monetary policy options have already been employed for several months.

Fiscal stimulus can involve tax cuts, spending, or a combination of both. Tax cuts may be less effective than spending because some of the tax cut may be saved, which diminishes the effectiveness of the stimulus. Some argue that tax cuts that are temporary, that appear in a lump sum rather than in withholding, or that are aimed at higher income individuals are more likely to be saved. Some evidence suggests that two-thirds of the 2001 tax rebate was spent within two quarters.

The challenge to spending programs is that there may be a lag time for planning and administration before the money is spent. For that reason, infrastructure spending is often discussed in the context of "ready-to-go" projects where all of the planning is in place and the only missing factor is funding. The U.S. Conference of Mayors has identified $73 billion of these projects and urged some funds to be given directly to localities; the American Association of State highway and Transportation Officials has identified $64 billion of these projects; the National Association of Counties has identified $9.9 billion. Some analysts suggest that aid to state and local governments may be more quickly spent because these governments are likely to cut back on spending in downturns due to balanced budget requirements, and the aid may forestall these cuts.[22] The Congressional Budget Office (CBO)

---

[22] See CRS Report R40 107, *The Role of Public Works Infrastructure in Economic Stimulus*, coordinated by Claudia Copeland, and CRS Report 92-939, *Countercyclical Job Creation Programs*, by Linda Levine.

score for the spending (discretionary and direct) portion of the Act estimates that about 21% will be spent in FY2009, and 38% in FY20 10.[23] Overall, about 74% of the spending and tax provisions are estimated to reach the public by the end of FY20 10. However, if the AMT "patch" is omitted then about 70% is estimated to reach the public by the end of FY2010.

The receipt of tax cuts can also be delayed. For example, according to Joint Committee on Taxation estimates of the Making Work Pay credit revenue losses, 17% of the total would be received in FY2009.[24] The benefit is provided in the form of withholding; since the measure was not in place on January 1, some benefit would be delayed until tax returns are filed. Close to 50% would be received in FY2009 if a rebate mechanism were used (based on estimates of a similar provision considered in 2008 at about the same time of the year, 93% of the rebate was projected to be received in the current fiscal year). There is some limited evidence that periodic payments are more likely to be spent than lump sum payments, but that evidence is subject to uncertainty and is not of a magnitude that the withholding approach would result in a larger short run stimulus than a rebate.[25] In the second year, 57% would be received.

Several studies have estimated the effects of the proposed package on the economy. Romer and Bernstein estimate an increase of 3.7 million jobs by the fourth quarter of 2010; Zandi estimates 3.3 million in 2010.[26] Citing uncertainty surrounding the effects of fiscal stimulus, CBO projects that the ARRA would boost GDP in 2009 by a range of 1.4% to 3.8%

---

[23] CBO, Letter to the Honorable Nancy Pelosi, Estimated Budget Impact of the Conference Agreement for H.R. 1, February 13, 2009.

[24] [http://www.house.gov/jct/x-19-09.pdf].

[25] This issue does not address the difference between temporary and permanent tax cuts; economists expect the latter to have more effect on consumption, but a permanent tax cut would result in budget pressures after recovery. Alan S. Blinder, "Temporary Income Taxes and Consumer Spending" *The Journal of Political Economy*, Vol. 89, February 1981, pp. 26-53, found the rebate 38% as effective as a permanent change and a withholding approach 50%, suggesting that the rebate would be 75% as effective as withholding. James M. Poterba, "Are Consumers Forward Looking?" *American Economic Review*, Vol. 78, (May 1988), pp. 413-418 found only 20% spent. Many economists have reservations about estimates using aggregate data, however, because of the difficulties of determining the counterfactual. For that reason, many researchers turned to comparisons of households with different amounts of tax cuts. Two studies of spending out of refunds (lump sum receipts) and spending out of withholding in the first Reagan tax cut found that 35% to 60% of refunds were spent but 60% to 90% of the withholding was spent (See Nicholas Souleles, "The Response of Household Consumption to Income Tax Refunds," *American Economic Review*, vol. 89 (September 1999), pp. 947-958; and Nicholas Souleles, "Consumer Response to the Reagan Tax Cuts," *Journal of Public Economics*. Vol. 85, pp. 99-120.). This research suggests a significant fraction of a temporary tax cut is spent, but that the lump sum has an effect that is about two thirds of the effect of withholding. This comparison is, however, somewhat clouded by the possibility that individuals may use tax refunds as a method of forced savings and not intend to spend them. In both cases, however, there is evidence of an effect for temporary tax cuts. Research on the 2001 rebate also indicates a significant amount was spent: David S. Johnson, Jonathan A. Parker, and Nicholas S. Souleles, Household Expenditures and the Income Tax Rebate of 2001,"*American Economic Review*, Vol. 96, December 2006, pp. 1589-1610 find over two thirds spent within two quarters. For other research see CRS Report RS21126, *Tax Cuts and Economic Stimulus: How Effective Are the Alternatives?*, by Jane G. Gravelle. Not included in that discussion are survey data asking individuals about their spending, as individuals themselves may not know what they spent. A preliminary study of the 2008 rebate also found significant spending: Christian Broda and Jonathan Parker, "The Impact of the 2008 Tax Rebates on Consumer Spending: Preliminary Evidence," Mimeo, University of Chicago and Northwestern University, July 29,2008: [http://online.wsj.com/public/resources/documents/WSJ2008StimulusStudy.pdf]

[26] Christina Romer and Jared Bernstein, "The Job impact of the American Recovery and Reinvestment Plan, Chair, Nominee Designate Council of Economic Advisors and Office of the Vice President Elect, January 9, 2009, [http://otrans.3cdn.net/45593e8ecbd339d074_l3m6bt1te.pdf]; Mark Zandi, "The Economic Impact of the American Recovery and Reinvestment Act," January 21, 2009, [http://www.economy.com/mark-zandi/documents/ Economic_Stimulus_House_Plan_012109.pdf].

and employment by a range of 0.8 million to 2.3 million compared to what it otherwise would have been. In 2010, CBO projects that the ARRA would boost GDP by 1.1% to 3.3% and employment by 1.2 million to 3.6 million in 2010 compared to what it otherwise would have been. Starting in 2014, CBO projects that the ARRA would cause GDP to be slightly lower than it otherwise would have been due to "crowding out" effects described in the section titled "Long-term Effects".

ISSUES SURROUNDING FISCAL STIMULUS[27]

The Magnitude of a Stimulus

The most important determinant of a stimulus' macroeconomic effect is its size. The 2008 stimulus package (P.L. 110-185) increased the budget deficit by about 1% of gross domestic product (GDP). In a healthy year, GDP grows about 3%. In the moderate recessions that the U.S. experienced in 1990-1991 and 2001, GDP contracted in some quarters by 0.5% to 3%. (The U.S. economy has not experienced contraction in a full calendar year since 1991.) Thus, a swing from expansion to recession would result in a change in GDP growth equal to at least 3.5 percentage points. A stimulus package of 1% of GDP could be expected to increase total spending by about 1%.[28] To the extent that spending begets new spending, there could be a multiplier effect that makes the total increase in spending larger than the increase in the deficit. Offsetting the multiplier effect, the increase in spending could be neutralized if it results in crowding out of investment spending, a larger trade deficit, or higher inflation. The extent to which the increase in spending would be offset by these three factors depends on how quickly the economy is growing at the time of the stimulus—an increase in the budget deficit would lead to less of an increase in spending if the economy were growing faster.

Thus, if the recession is mild, additional stimulus may not be necessary for the economy to revive. If, on the other hand, the economy has entered a deeper, prolonged recession, as some economists believe to be likely, then fiscal stimulus may not be powerful enough to avoid it. Since the current recession has already lasted longer than the historical average, it may end before further fiscal stimulus can be enacted. Economic forecasts are notoriously inaccurate due to the highly complex and changing nature of the economy, so there is significant uncertainty as to how deep the downturn will be, and how much fiscal stimulus would be an appropriate response.

The American Recovery and Reinvestment Act of 2009 will increase the budget deficit by about 1.3% in 2009 and an additional 2.2% (or 3.5% overall) in 2010. Some believe that circumstances warrant a larger stimulus – GDP in FY2009 is expected to contract by more than size of the stimulus in 2009. Others have expressed reservations that the deficit is already too large and, at least with respect to spending, it would be difficult to spend such large amounts without financing wasteful projects. Although the Act authorizes $379 billion of spending in 2009, CBO estimates a outlays of only $120 billion because it does not project that executive agencies can spend the total amount authorized in this fiscal year.

[27] This section was prepared by Marc Labonte, Government and Finance Division.

[28] See, for example, "Options for Responding to Short-term Economic Weakness," Testimony of CBO Director Peter Orszag before the Committee on Finance, January 22, 2008.

Bang for the Buck

In terms of first-order effects, any stimulus proposal that is deficit financed would increase total spending in the economy.[29] For second-order effects, different proposals could get modestly more "bang for the buck" than others if they result in more total spending. If the goal of stimulus is to maximize the boost to total spending while minimizing the increase in the budget deficit (in order to minimize the deleterious effects of "crowding out"), then maximum bang for the buck would be desirable. The primary way to achieve the most bang for the buck is by choosing policies that result in spending, not saving.[30] Direct government spending on goods and services would therefore lead to the most bang for the buck since none of it would be saved. The largest categories of direct federal spending are national defense, health, infrastructure, public order and safety, and natural resources.[31]

Higher government transfer payments, such as extended unemployment compensation benefits or increased food stamps, or tax cuts could theoretically be spent or saved by their recipients.[32] While there is no way to be certain how to target a stimulus package toward recipients who would spend it, many economists have reasoned that higher income recipients would save more than lower income recipients since U.S. saving is highly correlated with income. For example, two- thirds of families in the bottom 20% of the income distribution did not save at all in 2004, whereas only one-fifth of families in the top 10% of the income distribution did not save.[33] Presumably, recipients in economic distress, such as those receiving unemployment benefits, would be even more likely to spend a transfer or tax cut than a typical family.

The effectiveness of tax cuts also depends on their nature. As discussed above, tax cuts received by lower income individuals are more likely to be spent. Some economists have also argued that temporary individual tax cuts, such as the 2001 and 2008 rebates, are more likely to be saved; however, evidence on the 2001 tax rebate suggests most was eventually spent, and debate continues on the effect of the 2008 rebate. Most evidence does not suggest that business tax cuts would provide significant short-term stimulus. Investment incentives are attractive, if they work, because increasing investment does not trade off short term stimulus benefits for a reduction in capital formation, as do provisions stimulating consumption. Nevertheless, most evidence does not suggest these provisions work very well to induce short-term spending. This lack of effectiveness may occur because of planning lags or because stimulus is generally provided during economic slowdowns when excess capacity may already exist. Of business tax provisions, investment subsidies are more effective than rate cuts, but there is little evidence to support much stimulus effect. Temporary bonus depreciation is likely to be most effective in stimulating investment, more effective than a

[29] There may be a few proposals that would not increase spending. For example, increasing tax incentives to save would probably not increase spending significantly. These examples are arguably exceptions that prove the rule.

[30] Policies that result in more bang for the buck also result in more crowding out of investment spending, which could reduce the long-term size of the economy (unless the policy change increases public investment or induces private investment).

[31] For the purpose of this discussion, government transfer payments, such as entitlement benefits, are not classified as government spending.

[32] Food stamps cannot be directly saved since they can only be used on qualifying purchases, but a recipient could theoretically keep their overall consumption constant by increasing their other saving.

[33] Brian Bucks et al., "Recent Changes in U.S. Family Finances: Evidence from the 2001 and 2004 Survey of Consumer Finances," *Federal Reserve Bulletin*, vol. 92, February 2006, pp. A1-A38.

much costlier permanent investment incentive because it encourages the speed-up of investment. Although there is some dispute, most evidence on bonus depreciation enacted in 2002 nevertheless suggests that it had little effect in stimulating investment and that even if the effects were pronounced, the benefit was too small to have an appreciable effect on the economy. The likelihood of the remaining provisions having much of an incentive effect is even smaller. Firms may, for example, benefit from the small business expensing, but it actually discourages investment in the (expanded) phase out range.[34] Net operating losses carrybacks do not increase incentives to spend, but do target cash to troubled businesses.

Table 1. Zandi's Estimates of the Multiplier Effect for Various Policy Proposals

Policy Proposal	One-year change in real GDP for a given policy change per dollar
Tax Provisions	
Non-refundable rebate	1.02
Refundable rebate	1.26
Payroll tax holiday	1.29
Across the board tax cut	1.03
Accelerated depreciation	0.27
Extend alternative minimum tax patch	0.48
Make income tax cuts expiring in 2010 permanent	0.29
Make expiring dividend and capital gains tax cuts permanent	0.37
Reduce corporate tax rates	0.30
Spending Provisions	
Extend unemployment compensation benefits	1.64
Temporary increase in food stamps	1.73
Revenue transfers to state governments	1.36
Increase infrastructure spending	1.59

Source: Mark Zandi, Moody's Economy.com

Mark Zandi of *Moody's Economy.com* has estimated multiplier effects for several different policy options, as shown in Table 1.[35] The multiplier estimates the increase in total spending in the economy that would result from a dollar spent on a given policy option. Zandi does not explain how these multipliers were estimated, other than to say that they were calculated using his firm's macroeconomic model. Therefore, it is difficult to offer a thorough analysis of the estimates. In general, many of the assumptions that would be needed to calculate these estimates are widely disputed (notably, the difference in marginal propensity to consume among different recipients and the size of multipliers in general), and no macroeconomic model has a highly successful track record predicting economic activity.

[34] For more information, see CRS Report RS21 136, *Government Spending or Tax Reduction: Which Might Add More Stimulus to the Economy?*, by Marc Labonte; CRS Report RS21 126, *Tax Cuts and Economic Stimulus: How Effective Are the Alternatives?*, by Jane G. Gravelle; CRS Report RL3 1134, *Using Business Tax Cuts to Stimulate the Economy*, by Jane G. Gravelle; and CRS Report RS22790, *Tax Cuts for Short-Run Economic Stimulus: Recent Experiences*, coordinated by Jane G. Gravelle. Also see *Fiscal Policy for the Crisis*, IMF Staff Position Note, December 29, 2008, SPN/08/01 [http://www.imf.org/external/np/pp/eng/2008/122308.pdf].

[35] Mark Zandi, "Washington Throws the Economy a Rope," *Dismal Scientist*, Moody's Economy.com, January 22, 2008.

Thus, the range of values that other economists would assign to these estimates is probably large. Qualitatively, most economists would likely agree with the general thrust of his estimates, however—spending provisions have higher multipliers because tax cuts are partially saved, and some types of tax cuts are more likely to be saved by their recipients than others. As discussed above, a noticeable increase in consumption spending has not yet accompanied the receipt of the rebates from the first stimulus package. (Note, however, that these effects do not account for the possibility of extensive delay in direct spending taking place.)

The CBO rankings of multipliers are similar to Zandi's.[36] For government purchases and transfers to state and local governments for infrastructure, their multipliers are 1.0 in the low scenario and 2.5 in the high. For transfers to state and local governments not for infrastructure, the multipliers are 0.7 and 1.9. CBO sets the multipliers for transfers at 0.8 to 2.2, for temporary individual tax cuts at 0.5 to 1.7, and the tax loss carryback at 0 to 0.4. As with Zandi, these effects do not incorporate differentials in the rate of spending, however. In particular, they note that infrastructure spending will likely be delayed, while transfers would occur very quickly. Unlike Zandi, CBO emphasizes the broad uncertainty inherent in estimating multipliers.

Table 2. Timing of Past Recessions and Stimulus Legislation

Beginning of Recession	End of Recession	Stimulus Legislation Enacted
Nov. 1948	Oct. 1949	Oct. 1949
Aug. 1957	Apr. 1958	Apr. 1958, July 1958
Apr. 1960	Feb. 1961	May 1961, Sep. 1962
Dec. 1969	Nov. 1970	Aug. 1971
Nov. 1973	Mar. 1975	Mar. 1975, July 1976, May 19
July 1981	Nov. 1982	Jan. 1983, Mar. 1983
July 1990	Mar. 1991	Dec. 1991, Apr. 1993
Mar. 2001	Nov. 2001	June 2001

Source: Bruce Bartlett, "Maybe Too Little, Always Too Late," New York Times, Jan. 23, 2008.

Timeliness

Timeliness is another criterion by which different stimulus proposals have been evaluated. There are lags before a policy change affects spending. As a result, stimulus could be delivered after the economy has already entered a recession or a recession has already ended. First, there is a legislative process lag that applies to all policy proposals—a stimulus package cannot take effect until bills are passed by the House and Senate, both chambers can reconcile differences between their bills, and the President signs the bill. Many bills get delayed at some step in this process. As seen in Table 2, many past stimulus bills have not become law until a recession was already underway or finished.[37]

[36] Congressional Budget Office, "The State of the Economy and Issues in Developing an Effective Policy Response," Testimony of Douglas W. Elmendorf, Director, House Budget Committee, January 27, 2009.

[37] The International Monetary Fund recently analyzed the "timeliness, temporariness, and targeting" of U.S. tax cuts from 1970 to 2008 in International Monetary Fund, *World Economic Outlook*, Washington, D.C., Oct. 2008, p. 172.

Second, there is an administrative delay between the enactment of legislation and the implementation of the policy change. For example, although the 2008 stimulus package was signed into law in February, the first rebate checks were not sent out until the end of April, and the last rebate checks were not sent out until July. When the emergency unemployment compensation (EUC08) program began in July 2008 there was about a three week lag between enactment and the first payments of the new EUC08 benefit. Many economists have argued that new government spending on infrastructure could not be implemented quickly enough to stimulate the economy in time since infrastructure projects require significant planning. (Others have argued that this problem has been exaggerated because existing plans or routine maintenance could be implemented more quickly.) Others have argued that although federal spending cannot be implemented quickly enough, fiscal transfers to state and local governments would be spent quickly because many states currently face budgetary shortfalls, and fiscal transfers would allow them to avoid cutting spending.[38] ARRA granted $379 billion of budget authority in 2009, but CBO projects that only $120 billion will be outlayed in 2009.[39]

Finally, there is a behavioral lag, since time elapses before the recipient of a transfer or tax cut increases their spending. For example, the initial reaction to the receipt of rebate checks was a large spike in the personal saving rate (see above). It is unclear how to target recipients that would spend most quickly, although presumably liquidity-constrained households (i.e., those with limited access to credit) would spend more quickly than others. In this regard, the advantage to direct government spending is that there is no analogous lag. Although monetary policy changes have no legislative or administrative lags, research suggests they do face longer behavioral lags than fiscal policy changes because households and business generally respond more slowly to interest rate changes than tax or transfer changes.

Long-term Effects

A main factor in another round of fiscal stimulus may be the size of the current budget deficit. The 2009 stimulus package is relatively large, and CBO projects the deficit will already exceed $1 trillion in 2009. Deficits of this magnitude would set a peacetime record relative to GDP. Although current government borrowing rates are extremely low (because of the financial turmoil), there is a fear that a deficit of this size could become burdensome to service when interest rates return to normal. A larger deficit could eventually crowd out private investment, act as a drag on economic growth, and increase reliance on foreign borrowing (which would result in a larger trade deficit). By doing so, the deficit places a burden on future generations, and could further complicate the task of coping with long-term

[38] Transfers to state and local governments could be less stimulative than direct federal spending because state and local governments could, in theory, increase their total spending by less than the amount of the transfer. (For example, some of the money that would have been spent in the absence of the transfer could now be diverted to the state's budget reserves.) But if states are facing budgetary shortfalls, many would argue that in practice spending would increase by as much as the transfer.

[39] Congressional Budget Office, *Cost Estimate for the Conference Agreement for H.R. 1*, Letter to Honorable Nancy Pelosi, Feb. 13, 2009.

budgetary pressures caused by the aging of the population.[40] In the highly unlikely, worst case scenario, if too much pressure is placed on the deficit through competing policy priorities, then investors could lose faith in the government's ability to service the debt, and borrowing rates could spike.

Many of these issues could be minimized if the elements of the stimulus package are temporary – an increase in the budget deficit for one year would lead to significantly less crowding out over time than a permanent increase in the deficit. There is often pressure later to extend policies beyond their original expiration date, however. Among policy options, increases in public investment spending would minimize any negative effects on long-run GDP since decreases in the private capital stock would be offset by additions to the public capital stock. Also, tax incentives to increase business investment would offset the crowding out effect since the increase in aggregate spending was occurring via business investment.

The direct effect of the American Recovery and Reinvestment Act on the budget deficit is relatively small after 2011, although it leads to a permanent increase in interest payments on the national debt if not offset by future policy changes.

Should Stimulus be Targeted?

It is clear that the slowdown has been concentrated in housing and financial markets to date. Some economists have argued that as long as problems remain in these depressed sectors, then generalized stimulus will only postpone the inevitable downturn. For example, as long as financial intermediation remains impaired, access to credit markets will be limited and it will be difficult for stimulus to lead to sustained growth. (As noted above, separate legislation to support housing and financial markets was enacted in 2008.) If so, fiscal stimulus may, at most, provide a temporary boost as long as those problems are outstanding, but cannot singlehandedly shift the economy to a sustainable path of expansion. For example, the first stimulus package, enacted in the first quarter of 2008, did not prevent the economy from deteriorating further in the third quarter of 2008. Other economists argue that if the current housing bust is being caused by the unwinding of a bubble, then the government could be unable to reverse unavoidable market adjustment that is bringing those markets back to equilibrium. But some would argue that the best way to help a troubled sector is by boosting overall demand.

Is Additional Fiscal Stimulus Needed?

The economy naturally experiences a boom and bust pattern called the business cycle. A recession can be characterized as a situation where total spending in the economy (*aggregate demand*) is too low to match the economy's potential output (*aggregate supply*). As a result, some of the economy's labor and capital resources lay idle, causing unemployment and a low capacity utilization rate, respectively. Recessions generally are short-term in nature—

[40] See CRS Report RL32747, *The Economic Implications of the Long-Term Federal Budget Outlook*, by Marc Labonte.

eventually, markets adjust and bring spending and output back in line, even in the absence of policy intervention.[41]

Policymakers may prefer to use stimulative policy to attempt to hasten that adjustment process, in order to avoid the detrimental effects of cyclical unemployment. By definition, a stimulus proposal can be judged by its effectiveness at boosting total spending in the economy. Total spending includes personal consumption, business investment in plant and equipment, residential investment, net exports (exports less imports), and government spending. Effective stimulus could boost spending in any of these categories.

Fiscal stimulus can take the form of higher government spending (direct spending or transfer payments) or tax reductions, but generally it can boost spending only through a larger budget deficit, as is the case with ARRA. A deficit-financed increase in government spending directly boosts spending by borrowing to finance higher government spending or transfer payments to households. A deficit-financed tax cut indirectly boosts spending if the recipient uses the tax cut to increase his spending. If an increase in spending or a tax cut is financed through a decrease in other spending or increase in other taxes, the economy would not be stimulated since the deficit- increasing and deficit-decreasing provisions would cancel each other out.

How much additional spending can stimulate economic activity depends on the state of the economy at that time. When the economy is in a recession, fiscal stimulus could mitigate the decline in GDP growth by bringing idle labor and capital resources back into use. When the economy is already robust, a boost in spending could be largely inflationary—since there would be no idle resources to bring back into production when spending is boosted, the boost would instead bid up the prices of those resources, eventually causing all prices to rise. The recession appears to have deepened in the fourth quarter of 2008. By historical standards, the recession would be expected to end before fiscal stimulus could be delivered, but forecasters are predicting this recession will be longer than usual. Most of the stimulus provided by ARRA will be delivered by 2011, and CBO is projecting that there will still be a significant output gap at that point.

Because total spending can be boosted only temporarily, stimulus has no long-term benefits, and may have long-term costs. Most notably, the increase in the budget deficit "crowds out" private investment spending because both must be financed out of the same finite pool of national saving, with the greater demand for saving pushing up interest rates.[42] To the extent that private investment is crowded out by a larger deficit, it would reduce the future size of the economy since the economy would operate with a smaller capital stock in the long run. In recent years, the U.S. economy has become highly dependent on foreign capital to finance business investment and budget deficits.[43] Since foreign capital can come to the United States only in the form of a trade deficit, a higher budget deficit could result in a higher trade deficit, in which case the higher trade deficit could dissipate the boost in spending as consumers purchase imported goods. Indeed, conventional economic theory predicts that fiscal policy has no stimulative effect in an economy with perfectly mobile

[41] For more information, see CRS Report RL34072, *Economic Growth and the Business Cycle: Characteristics, Causes, and Policy Implications*, by Marc Labonte.

[42] Crowding out is likely to be less of a concern when the economy is in recession since recessions are typically characterized by falling business investment.

[43] If foreign borrowing prevents crowding out, the future size of the economy will not decrease but capital income will accrue to foreigners instead of Americans.

capital flows.[44] Some economists argue that these costs outweigh the benefits of fiscal stimulus.

Policies Previously Adopted

Stimulus has also been delivered from other fiscal changes and monetary policy. First, the federal budget has *automatic stabilizers* that cause the budget deficit to automatically increase (and thereby stimulate the economy) during a downturn in the absence of policy changes. When the economy slows, entitlement spending on programs such as unemployment compensation benefits automatically increases as program participation rates rise and the growth in tax revenues automatically declines as the recession causes the growth in taxable income to decline.

Second, any consideration for additional stimulus has to include the effects of stimulus previously enacted. According to the Congressional Budget Office (CBO), the total deficit in FY2008 was $455 billion, or 3.2% of gross domestic product, sharply higher than the FY2007 deficit of $162 billion. In January 2008, CBO had projected that under current policy the budget deficit would increase by $56 billion in 2008 compared to 2007. When the cost of the February 2008 stimulus package and part of the cost of financial market intervention in the fall of 2008 is added, the increase in the deficit for one year rose by nearly $300 billion. CBO projects the deficit will increase further in 2009, to $1.2 trillion or 8.3% of GDP, in the absence of additional stimulus. These increases in the deficit would also be expected to have a stimulative effect on aggregate spending.

Third, the Federal Reserve has already delivered a large monetary stimulus. By the end of April 2008, the Fed had reduced overnight interest rates to 2% from 5.25% in September 2007.[45] On December 16, the interest rate was lowered to a targeted range of 0% to 0.25%. Typically, lower interest rates stimulate the economy by increasing the demand for interest-sensitive spending, which includes investment spending, residential housing, and consumer durables such as automobiles. Yet, the potential for stimulus caused by lower interest rates can be limited if tight credit markets constrain borrowing. In addition, lower interest rates can stimulate the economy by reducing the value of the dollar, all else equal, which would lead to higher exports and lower imports.[46]

One might take the view that the Federal Reserve has chosen a monetary policy that it believes will best achieve a recovery given the actions already taken. If it has chosen that policy correctly, an argument can be made that an additional fiscal stimulus is unnecessary since the economy is already receiving the correct boost in spending through lower interest rates and through the first stimulus package. In this light, additional fiscal stimulus would be useful only if monetary policy is unable to adequately boost spending—either because the Fed has chosen an incorrect policy or because the Fed cannot boost spending enough through lower interest rates and direct assistance to the financial sector to spark a recovery, and direct

---

[44] For more information, see CRS Report RS21409, *The Budget Deficit and the Trade Deficit: What Is Their Relationship?*, by Marc Labonte and Gail E. Makinen.

[45] For interest rate changes see CRS Report 98-856, *Federal Reserve Interest Rate Changes: 2001-2009*, by Marc Labonte.

[46] For more information, see CRS Report RL30354, *Monetary Policy and the Federal Reserve: Current Policy and Conditions*, by Gail E. Makinen and Marc Labonte.

intervention in financial markets is not adequate.[47] (Now that interest rates have fallen to zero, the Fed can no longer reduce rates to stimulate the economy, but it can increase – and has increased - its direct assistance to the financial sector.)

INTERVENTIONS FOR FINANCIAL FIRMS AND MARKETS

A number of direct interventions in the economy occurred in 2008 which could be seen as a type of stimulus, in part because of credit problems. One indication of restricted credit despite stimulative Federal Reserve monetary policy was the failure of mortgage rates to fall significantly. Instead, the spread between Treasuries and Government Sponsored Enterprise (GSE) bonds remained elevated over the summer. The newly created Federal Housing Finance Agency (FHFA) cited the persistence of this wide spread as a major factor in its decision to place the GSEs in conservatorship in September. During the week of September 15-19, financial markets were further disturbed by the bankruptcy of investment bank Lehman Brothers and Federal Reserve intervention on behalf of the insurer AIG. These actions eroded market confidence further, resulting in a sudden spike of the commercial paper rate spread from just under 90 basis points to 280 basis points, a spike that in times past might have been called a panic. If financial market confidence is not restored and private market spreads remain elevated, the broader economy could slow more due to difficulties in financing consumer durables, business investment, college education, and other big ticket items.

In September 2008, Administration and Federal Reserve officials with the bipartisan support of the Congressional leadership, announced a massive intervention in the financial markets, requesting authority to purchase up to $700 billion in assets over the next two years. The Treasury had also provided insurance for money market funds, where withdrawals have been significant. Congressional leaders and other Members raised a number of issues and made some additional proposals, which included setting up an oversight mechanism, restrictions on executive compensation of firms from which assets are purchased, acquiring equity stakes in the participating firms, and allowing judges to reduce mortgage debt in bankruptcies (not included in the final Act).

Later, in October 2008, legislation (P.L. 110-343) was enacted to allow an initial $250 billion of financing with an additional $100 billion upon certification of need, with Congress allowed 30 days to object to the final $350 billion. The plan has oversight by an Inspector General, audit by the Government Accountability Office, setting standards of appropriate compensation, and providing for equity positions in all participating companies. The final package also added an expansion of deposit insurance coverage. There remained, however, concerns about how to price acquired assets in a way that balances protection of taxpayers with providing adequate assistance to firms. The Treasury had indicated use of a reverse

---

[47] Fed Chairman Ben Bernanke may have hinted at the latter case when he testified that "fiscal action could be helpful in principle, as fiscal and monetary stimulus together may provide broader support for the economy than monetary policy actions alone." Quoted in Ben Bernanke, "The Economic Outlook," testimony before the House Committee on the Budget, January 17, 2008.

auction mechanism to purchase mortgage backed securities, where companies will bid to sell their assets. It is not clear how well such an auction would work with heterogeneous assets.[48]

The Treasury subsequently announced that it would use the first $250 billion authorized to purchase preferred stock in financial institutions and has now indicated it will use subsequent funds for capital injections, consumer credit (such as auto loans, student loans, small business loans, and credit cards) and mortgage assistance.[49] Congressional leaders urged Treasury to provide $25 billion in aid to U.S. auto manufacturers.[50] On November 10, a restructuring of government assistance to AIG was announced which increased the amount at risk from $143.7 billion to $173.4 billion, extended the loan length and reduced the interest rate. The Federal Reserve also announced on October 14 that it would begin purchasing commercial paper.[51] News reports indicated the Federal Deposit Insurance Corporation (FDIC) had a plan, supported by many congressional Democrats, to offer financial incentives to companies that agree to reduce monthly mortgage payments, but that this plan was opposed by the Bush Administration.[52] On November 23, the government announced a plan to assist Citicorp, and on November 25 the Federal Reserve revealed plans to purchase $200 billion in asset backed securities through the Term Asset-Backed Securities Loan Facility (TALF); these securities are based on auto, credit card, student and small business loans.

Much of the intervention up to this point had been in the financial markets. However, the Detroit automakers (GM, Ford, and Chrysler) asked for $34 billion in loans to forestall bankruptcy. After Congress did not adopt an emergency loan of $14 billion in a special post-election session in December 2008, the Administration announced, on December 19, that it would provide $17.4 billion from TARP: $9.4 billion to GM and $4 million to Chrysler. An additional $4 billion would be made available for GM if the remaining $350 billion in TARP funds is approved. On December 30, $6 billion in TARP funds were provided for GMAC, the auto financing company.

The Federal Reserve has also announced purchases of commercial paper, $200 billion of asset backed securities, and $600 billion of mortgage-related securities; the government has also announced a plan to guarantee certain assets of Citigroup and Bank of America. On March 18, the Federal reserve announced plans to purchase over $1 trillion in assets, including $750 billion in mortgage backed securities and $300 billion in long term Treasury debt. On March 23, 2009 the Treasury announced a plan for a public-private partnership to purchase troubled assets, including one part that uses the Federal Deposit Insurance Corporation (FDIC) to insure loans and another part that would allow access to the Federal Reserve's Term Asset-Backed Securities Loan Facility (TALF).[53]

Legislation has been introduced (H.R. 384) by the Chairman of the Financial Services Committee to regulate the spending of the final $350 billion, but many of the provisions could also be achieved through an agreement between the Congress and the Administration.

---

[48] See CRS Report RL34707, *Auction Basics: Background for Assessing Proposed Treasury Purchases of Mortgage-Backed Securities*, by D. Andrew Austin.

[49] Testimony of Interim Assistant Secretary for Financial Stability Neel Kashkari before the House Committee on Oversight and Government Reform, Subcommittee on Domestic Policy, November 14, 2008.

[50] David M. Herszenhiorn, "Chances Dwindle on Bailout Plan for Automakers," *New York Times*, November 14, p. A1.

[51] Federal Reserve Board Press Release, October 14, 2008.

[52] Buinyamin Appelbaum, FDIC Details Plan to Alter Mortgages, Washington Post, November 14, 2008, p. A1.

[53] For further discussion see CRS Report RL34730, *Troubled Asset Relief Program: Legislation and Treasury Implementation*, by Baird Webel and Edward V. Murphy.

There is interest in directing some of the funds to directly aid mortgage holders to avoid foreclosure and small business loans, as well as considering oversight issues. Congress could have enacted legislation to disallow the release. However, on January 15, the Senate defeated a proposal to block the spending of the additional funds.

Among the issues of concern with financial interventions is whether an ad hoc, case-by-case intervention is likely to be a successful strategy. A case-by-case strategy can create uncertainty and also moral hazard (causing firms to undertake too much risk if they expect to be rescued). The creation of TARP represents a shift to a more broad-based approach. The approach of a broad based intervention could take the form of the purchase of troubled assets (as originally proposed or through a "bad bank") or the injection of capital (such as the Treasury's decision to purchase preferred stock).[54]

[54] These issues are discussed in more detail in CRS Report RL34730, *The Emergency Economic Stabilization Act and Current Financial Turmoil: Issues and Analysis*, by Baird Webel and Edward V. Murphy.

In: The Financial Crisis
Editors: Barbara L. Campos and Janet P. Wilkins
ISBN: 978-1-61209-281-2

Commentary

GLOBAL OPERATIONS MANAGEMENT

*Rui Yang Chen**

ARCHITECTURE OF CCPUL

This section presents the Customer Complaint problem of Product Usage Life cycle (CCPUL). The motivations, scope, goals, contribution and thesis architecture of this research are also discussed in this section.

Research Motivation and Goal

The development and design for a product is the most important thing in a competitive market. The forward design is the key on the RandD department. Which a new product is successful or fail, is related to the customer complaint about product problems. So we can track the problem and clarify the responsibility for efficient performance management. We can accumulate experience and feedback to design origin so that mechanisms such as design guidelines/checklist can be developed to prevent problem reoccurrences in the future. This is a thought which establish a reverse design by reverse thinking (Youngsup and Russell, 1995; Sheu and Chen, 2006). The customer complaint users here may be extended to mean manufacturers, channels, ODM customers, and end users.

When a product occur problems, it is usually a user brings up the problem and gives the product to the buying source to handle. Normally, the product will be sent to the original buying sales agent or the sales agent which is a chain retail store, and then the sales agent will send it to the proxy agent to recondition. If the proxy agent doesn't have a qualified technician, it will be sent to the maintenance center of the manufacturer of origin to recondition.

The process is a long, complicated and not efficient. Because a proxy agent may not have these service experience and capability, it has to rely on the product technique archives to supply easy maintenance service for customers. Because which a manufacturer face is proxy agent, not a downstream sales agent or customers, when a customer encounters problems, the

* E-mail: a168.jacky@msa.hinet.net

first thing he demands is the after sales service from the store / sales agent from where the product is bought from.

However, in the complicated and longwinded flow path, they usually don't have an efficient way to utilize the past information well. So that when the problem occurs next time, they will spend much time on the investigation and analysis for the problem again. Besides, analyze and investigate over and over not necessarily can find out the genuine cause of the quality problem. In addition, in the complicated and large information, the person in charge of the quality problem usually can not promptly and properly detect the extraordinary cause which may lead to the bad product quality by his professional knowledge and experience. He leans to instincts and random variable to work.

From the above description, we can make a little question and discussion: how to maintain properly and promptly the customer complaint, in order to respond to the customer as soon as possible, avoid occurring mistakes again, and feed back to RandD for product improvement.

Problem Statement

Traditionally, the customer complaints have only been processed by the RMA department, where identification of problem is vague and thus can not prevent problem reoccurrences in future from the upstream.

Two problems were identified from the above statements. First problem was a reformulation of the backward design from customer's complaint with the consideration of all the downstream relational attributes such as product design, manufacturing, sales, and so on.

As timely new product development becomes critical due to shorter product life cycle, the respond time from the customer complaint to product design must be shorter than ever.

For this purpose, the concept of design for X (DFX) plays a key role by considering the most important X item constraints synchronously in the design stage and integrates process through feedback relationships for new product development.

More recently, for manufacturing, quality, maintainability, reliability, and assembly, researchers have focused their key point on design for X item [2, 5, and 13]. Beside this, a comprehensive information management system was necessary to implement these two key functions: design for manufacturability and manufacturing information feedback to design.

Since the 1990s, also speed and flexibility in the new product development had received increased priority. Although the above literature is widely distributed over many different disciplines, most studies had concentrated on a specific "X" topic such as DFM, etc and manufacturing information feedback to design.

Two issues which usually present the problem:

1. DFX only focus on a specific "X" item such as DFM, etc. This has meant that do not consider other process multi-attributes simultaneously, and do not capture enough structured and relational information feedback through product formation and usage life cycle.
2. Customer's complaint usually does not connect with seamless operations of the downstream functions. Some researchers demonstrated that the formation of inter-firm new product development networks was linked to both internal organizational

and external factors. This means that the product problems do not map the cause and responsibility, of department relationship.

To address the first problems, this section proposed an integrated framework for product forming and usage life cycle which includes:

(1) The section will provide an integrated framework for customers and downstream organization or individuals such as end users, ODM/OEM customers, manufacturing, logistics, etc., to feedback knowledge seamless and relationship in the product forming and usage life cycle.
(2) The section will build and store a many to many relationships from product problems to mapping the cause and responsibility department relationships.

Second problem was automated mapping cognitive uncertainties attributes with differential process stage thinking and perception, which involved in classification problems were explicitly measured, analyzed, and tracked into the knowledge induction process.

Product problems submitted by customer maybe observation error, uncertainty, subjective judgments, and so on, many data occurring in real world was presented in fuzzy description. Fuzzy sets and membership function allow the modeling of uncertainties, while providing a symbolic method for knowledge comprehensibility.

Another, product problems usually occur at downstream stages of the product forming and usage cycle, so there are no classified attributes felt by new product development. There is no incentive for product design to apply the priority on others' relational attributes. Decision trees are one of the most useful approaches for learning and classified from feature-based examples, but they do not undergo a number of alterations to deal with perception vagueness and measurement uncertainties. Accordingly, fuzzy decision tree representation is becoming increasingly approach in dealing classification with problems of uncertainty, and inexact data. One issue is usually present about literature in this problem:

(1). Most of existing algorithms for constructing fuzzy decision trees focus on the selection of the attributes. They attempt to improve the classification accuracy for unknown cases. But, an important point is how to identify suitable for the attributes.

To address the second problems, this section proposed a database base fuzzy decision tree with multi-attributes.

Our fuzzy decision tree differs from traditional fuzzy decision trees. It let identification more suitability usage cause of past validation result by continue learning.

Result and Contribution

(1) Establish an integrated feedback framework for the product usage life cycle.
(2) Propose an automatic cause identification methodology for product problems with fuzzy symptoms by using the fuzzy decision tree method.
(3) Establish an intelligent diagnose system of product problems.

Architecture of CCPUL

Architecture

Reference Figure 1-1, this study is from customer complaint acceptance, analysis, and cause attribution to the problem resolving and the responsible department, and then responds to customers and attributes the causes for the RandD reference. According to the Cooper's study (1994), the forward design of a new product development process is divided to seven steps, such as an idea beginning of a product, early estimation, a concept design, product development, product test, pile run, and mass production. At this section, the backward feedback means starting at users, and feedback to market, RandD, origin, manufacture, channels etc. six areas in the enterprise function process. These become a trace process for product problems.

INDEX

A

access, 18, 20, 29, 35, 40, 110, 113, 121, 149, 150, 151, 153, 162, 163, 167
accountability, 3, 129
accounting, 3, 119, 122, 128
accounting standards, 3
actual growth rate, 141
Adam Smith, vii, 9, 10
adjustment, 163, 164
Administrative Procedure Act, 110
adverse effects, 107
Afghanistan, 140
agencies, 3, 5, 6, 13, 14, 23, 41, 45, 47, 139, 158
aggregate demand, 54, 55, 67, 151, 156, 163
aggregate supply, 163
aggregation, 12
Alexander Hamilton, 13, 16
allergic reaction, 49
allergy, 49
alternative energy, 152
alters, 156
American Recovery and Reinvestment Act, ix, 128, 140, 142, 147, 148, 153, 155, 157, 158, 163
American Recovery and Reinvestment Act of 2009, ix, 128, 140, 142, 147, 148, 155, 158
appraised value, 124
appropriations, 107, 134, 136, 156
arbitrage, 13
arms control, 17
Asia, 2
assessment, 5, 41, 43, 44, 103, 104
assets, 13, 14, 23, 72, 73, 76, 77, 78, 79, 81, 84, 85, 104, 105, 106, 107, 108, 109, 110, 112, 113, 114, 117, 118, 119, 120, 121, 122, 123, 124, 138, 139, 147, 149, 150, 151, 152, 166, 167, 168
asymmetry, 64
Atlas Shrugged, 9
ATO, 106
attribution, 172
audit, 166
Austria, 17, 50
authorities, ix, 19, 20, 22, 23, 29, 33, 37, 41, 47, 50, 109, 149
authority, viii, 1, 5, 6, 28, 103, 104, 105, 106, 107, 108, 109, 110, 112, 113, 120, 122, 123, 133, 134, 137, 147, 149, 151, 162, 166
automate, 39
automobiles, 165
aversion, 98
Ayn Rand, 9

B

balance sheet, 3, 4, 75, 79, 84, 97, 124
balanced budget, 156
bankers, 42, 119
banking, ix, 3, 4, 17, 71, 109, 110, 117, 118, 119, 123, 139
banking sector, ix, 71, 117, 118
bankruptcies, 115, 118, 166
bankruptcy, 70, 79, 100, 106, 108, 109, 111, 112, 113, 115, 121, 151, 166, 167
Bankruptcy Code, viii, 103, 104, 105, 106, 109, 112, 113, 115
banks, 2, 3, 4, 5, 6, 75, 99, 101, 103, 104, 105, 106, 109, 110, 115, 117, 118, 119, 120, 121, 122, 123, 124
barriers, 7, 79, 124
base, 171
basis points, 77, 78, 80, 81, 84, 88, 90, 166
BBB, 79, 85, 90, 96
Beijing, 2
Belgium, 99
benefits, 10, 12, 13, 15, 31, 128, 133, 138, 147, 148, 152, 153, 154, 155, 159, 160, 164, 165

blame, 1, 118
bond market, 70, 71, 73, 74, 86, 88, 101
bondholders, 73, 86
bonds, 3, 13, 54, 55, 58, 70, 73, 74, 75, 79, 80, 84, 85, 90, 96, 99, 100, 121, 130, 152, 154, 166
bonuses, 6, 10, 122
borrowers, 4, 70, 118, 120, 150
breakdown, 3, 20, 132
Brownian motion, 76, 77
Budget Committee, 135, 161
budget deficit, 55, 127, 131, 140, 141, 148, 158, 159, 162, 163, 164, 165
budget resolution, 127, 128, 135, 136, 137, 138
budget surplus, 58, 133, 141
Bush, President, 136
business corporation crisis, vii, 48
business cycle, 149, 163
businesses, 21, 38, 105, 106, 123, 154, 156, 160
buyers, 15, 70, 120

C

candidates, viii, 53, 56, 58, 61, 65
capital flows, 165
capital gains, 138, 152, 156, 160
capitalism, 9
cash, 14, 71, 79, 84, 107, 121, 128, 129, 135, 160
cash flow, 14, 129
census, 130
central bank, 2, 122
central planning, 11
certification, 166
challenges, 138
Chernobyl accident, 23
Chicago, 6, 16, 67, 109, 111, 112, 157
China, 2, 10
Civil Service Retirement accounts, 128
classes, 84, 89, 108, 111, 113, 118
classification, 171
collateral, 109, 112, 120, 121
colleges, 153
commerce, 12
commercial, 106, 121, 123, 151, 166, 167
commodity, 111, 112, 113
common sense, 5
communication, 23, 29, 33, 34, 35, 36, 42
communities, 120
community, 33, 35, 40
compensation, 6, 10, 70, 73, 76, 85, 122, 123, 147, 148, 152, 155, 159, 160, 162, 165, 166
competition, 10, 59, 61
competitive advantage, 23
competitiveness, 18
competitors, 25
complex market system, vii, 9
complexity, vii, 1, 5, 24, 103, 104
conference, 128, 134, 135, 137, 138, 140
conflict, 22
Congress, ix, 103, 104, 107, 117, 119, 120, 121, 123, 127, 129, 130, 131, 133, 134, 135, 136, 137, 138, 139, 140, 141, 142, 147, 148, 150, 152, 166, 167
Congressional Budget Office, 133, 135, 138, 139, 140, 156, 161, 162, 165
consensus, 11, 15, 28, 148, 149
conservatorship/receivership authority, viii, 103, 105
constituents, 29
Constitution, 66
construction, 72, 154
consumers, 13, 123, 164
consumption, 55, 56, 61, 137, 151, 157, 159, 161, 164
contingency, 19, 50
cooperation, 13, 17, 38
coordination, 28, 38, 39, 112
corporate fraud, 15
corporation, vii, viii, 17, 18, 19, 20, 21, 22, 23, 25, 26, 27, 28, 29, 30, 31, 33, 34, 35, 36, 37, 38, 39, 40, 41, 42, 43, 44, 45, 46, 47, 48, 49, 50
correlation, 86, 88, 90, 95
corruption, 10, 15
cost, 10, 13, 14, 44, 64, 79, 107, 111, 119, 139, 140, 148, 153, 154, 155, 156, 165
cost saving, 153
covering, vii, 17, 18, 49, 71
credit default swap, viii, 69, 70, 98, 99, 100, 101
credit market, 2, 5, 14, 89, 117, 121, 123, 137, 150, 163, 165
credit rating, 3, 71, 74, 75, 100, 109
creditors, 42, 76, 107, 108, 109, 111, 112, 113, 115
creditworthiness, 4, 70
crisis, vii, viii, 1, 2, 3, 4, 5, 6, 7, 9, 14, 15, 17, 18, 19, 20, 21, 22, 23, 24, 25, 26, 27, 28, 29, 30, 31, 32, 33, 34, 35, 36, 37, 38, 39, 40, 41, 42, 43, 44, 45, 46, 47, 48, 49, 50, 69, 70, 71, 72, 75, 80, 81, 82, 84, 86, 88, 89, 90, 91, 92, 95, 97, 98, 107, 134, 142, 151
crisis management, vii, 17, 19, 23, 24, 25, 26, 27, 28, 29, 31, 32, 33, 35, 36, 37, 38, 39, 40, 41, 42, 43, 45, 48, 50
crisis response phase, viii, 18
crowding out, 158, 159, 163, 164
cumulative distribution function, 76
currency, 6, 128
current limit, 140, 142
Customer Complaint problem of Product Usage Life cycle(CCPUL), ix

customers, 19, 25, 33, 35, 36, 38, 50, 169, 171, 172
cyclical unemployment, 164

D

damages, 70, 111, 114, 115, 147, 148
Darwinian evolution, 10
data set, 71
database, 49, 171
debt issuance policy, viii, 53
debtors, 108, 112
debts, 106, 108, 128, 132
decision makers, 20
decision trees, 171
decomposition, 14
deduction, 154, 155
deficit, ix, 55, 128, 129, 133, 137, 138, 139, 140, 141, 142, 148, 158, 159, 162, 163, 164, 165
delinquency, 1
denial, 19
Department of Homeland Security, 155
dependent variable, 86
deposit accounts, 110
depository institutions, viii, 103, 104, 105, 107, 113, 123
deposits, 14, 103, 104, 105, 106, 107, 108, 110, 113, 115
depreciation, 152, 153, 154, 156, 159, 160
derivatives, 1, 4, 6, 70, 71, 74, 75, 106, 118, 119
destruction, 10, 18, 22, 49
detection, 38, 39
developed countries, 13
directors, 108, 111, 115
disaster, 19, 22, 23, 30, 38, 40, 42, 45
disclosure, 5
dissenting opinion, 15
distortions, 131
distress, 159
distribution, 6, 53, 55, 61, 113, 159
diversification, 74, 103, 104
diversity, 11, 24
draft, 37, 50

E

early warning, 39
earnings, 152, 153
earthquakes, 22
economic activity, 69, 89, 91, 98, 149, 160, 164
economic consequences, 54
economic fundamentals, 150
economic growth, 140, 148, 149, 162
economic growth rate, 140
economic incentives, 109
economic indicator, 149
economic performance, 141
economic progress, 13
economic sectors, vii
economic stimulus, vii, ix, 138, 139, 148, 149
economic theory, 5, 164
education, 40, 153, 155, 156, 166
educational institutions, 21
election, viii, 53, 56, 60, 127, 136, 154, 167
emergency, 29, 31, 41, 42, 49, 107, 151, 162, 167
Emergency Economic Stabilization Act, ix, 117, 121, 122, 128, 139, 142, 149, 168
emergency preparedness, 31
emergency response, 29
empirical studies, 72
employees, 15, 19, 21, 23, 26, 33, 35, 36, 38, 42, 133
employers, 152
employment, 148, 149, 158
endowments, 55
energy, 17, 138, 151, 152, 153, 154, 156
energy consumption, 151
energy efficiency, 153
energy prices, 151
enforcement, vii, 9, 13, 14, 15, 29, 153
engineering, 6, 15, 42
enlargement, 23
environment, 11, 15, 20, 23, 25
equilibrium, viii, 12, 53, 54, 56, 60, 61, 62, 64, 163
equipment, 42, 140, 164
equities, 138
equity, 4, 54, 71, 73, 74, 75, 76, 77, 78, 79, 84, 85, 86, 89, 98, 101, 120, 122, 150, 166
equity market, 75, 79, 85
erosion, 14
Europe, 2, 10, 12, 71, 108, 111, 115
European Central Bank, 70, 100
evidence, 4, 56, 71, 75, 97, 156, 157, 159
evolution, vii, 10, 17, 20, 26, 29, 35, 40
exclusion, 154, 155, 156
execution, 115
executive branch, 122
exercise, 110, 114, 122
expenditures, 12
exports, 164, 165
exposure, 46, 70, 117

F

fairness, 13
faith, 4, 107, 163
families, 21, 152, 156, 159

family members, 13
Fannie Mae, 4, 104, 120, 139, 150
FBI, 15
FDI, 106, 107, 108, 109, 110
FDIC, viii, 103, 104, 105, 106, 107, 108, 109, 110, 111, 112, 113, 114, 115, 120, 123, 124, 149, 151, 167
fear, 3, 6, 117, 162
federal agency, 106
federal assistance, 109
federal funds, 150
federal government, 106, 107, 127, 128, 129, 130, 133, 138, 139, 141, 151
Federal Government, 113
Federal Home Loan Banks, 104, 115, 120
Federal Housing Finance Agency (FHFA), 120, 139, 166
federal law, 103, 104
Federal Reserve Board, 167
finance, vii, 3, 4, 5, 14, 54, 119, 120, 121, 127, 129, 164
financial condition, 114
financial crisis, iv, vii, 1, 2, 9, 15, 75, 84, 89, 98, 151
financial incentives, 167
financial innovation, 15
financial instability, 147
financial institutions, 1, 3, 4, 6, 103, 104, 106, 112, 117, 121, 122, 137, 150, 151, 154, 167
financial intermediaries, 105, 106
financial markets, 1, 7, 13, 14, 15, 78, 119, 121, 130, 133, 136, 139, 142, 147, 148, 150, 151, 163, 166, 167
financial regulation, 6
financial resources, 21, 38, 127
financial sector, 120, 121, 148, 151, 165
financial stability, 1, 100, 107, 122
financial support, 120
financial system, 1, 2, 118, 119, 122, 148, 150
firm value, 73
first generation, 54
fiscal deficit, 141
fiscal policy, 120, 147, 148, 156, 162, 164
flexibility, 130, 134, 136, 141, 170
floods, 22
food, 42, 49, 138, 147, 148, 152, 153, 156, 159, 160
Ford, 23, 167
foreclosure, 120, 123, 168
formation, 54, 159, 170
fraud, 15, 119
Freddie Mac, 4, 104, 120, 139, 150
Friedrich Hayek, 11
funding, 22, 120, 124, 155, 156
funds, 4, 5, 6, 14, 107, 110, 115, 118, 120, 121, 123, 124, 127, 128, 129, 134, 141, 150, 151, 154, 156, 166, 167, 168

G

GAO, 129, 134
GDP, 105, 106, 131, 132, 133, 138, 140, 148, 149, 150, 157, 158, 160, 162, 163, 164, 165
General Accounting Office, 129, 134
Gephardt rule, 135, 136, 137
Germany, 2, 100
global business, vii
global economy, 2, 11
global operations management, vii
goods and services, 138, 150, 159
government expenditure, 58
government intervention, 46
government securities, 128, 133
government spending, 55, 128, 159, 162, 164
governments, 41, 45, 47, 58, 61, 105, 106, 154, 156, 160, 161, 162
government-sponsored enterprises (GSEs), 120
Gramm-Leach-Bliley Act, 4
grants, 152, 154, 155
Great Depression, 2, 106, 131, 149, 150
greed, vii, 9, 10, 11, 14
gross domestic product, 131, 158, 165
growth, 7, 13, 14, 54, 133, 140, 141, 142, 147, 148, 149, 150, 158, 162, 163, 164, 165
growth rate, 7, 140
guidance, 115
guidelines, 19, 25, 29, 169

H

harmful effects, 64
harnessing greed, vii, 9
health, 55, 152, 153, 155, 156, 159
health information, 153, 155, 156
health insurance, 155, 156
hedging, 70
higher education, 153
highways, 153, 155
hiring, 154
history, vii, 4, 54, 141
holding company, 5, 103, 104
homeowners, 122
homes, 14, 153, 154
homogeneity, 11, 61, 74

House, 3, 5, 7, 123, 127, 128, 134, 135, 136, 137, 138, 139, 140, 142, 148, 150, 152, 153, 154, 155, 157, 161, 166, 167
housing, 1, 2, 3, 4, 5, 14, 42, 118, 120, 133, 137, 147, 148, 150, 151, 152, 153, 154, 155, 163, 165
Housing and Economic Recovery Act (HERA), 120
Housing and Economic Recovery Act of 2008, ix, 110, 120, 128, 139, 140, 142, 150
Housing and Urban Development (HUD), 120, 139
human, 5, 10, 12, 21, 22, 45, 46
human nature, 10
hurricanes, 22

I

identification, 28, 49, 98, 170, 171
idiosyncratic, 11, 74, 89
illiteracy, 13
image, 19, 31, 34, 38, 41
imbalances, 2
imitation, 155
imports, 164, 165
incentive effect, 160
income, 4, 5, 55, 56, 99, 119, 129, 138, 149, 153, 154, 155, 156, 159, 160, 164, 165
income distribution, 159
income support, 138
income tax, 138, 153, 160
independence, 130
individual character, 98
individual characteristics, 98
individuals, vii, 3, 11, 14, 17, 31, 40, 55, 105, 106, 137, 152, 153, 155, 156, 157, 159, 171
induction, 171
industries, 114
industry, 15, 46, 107, 121
inflation, 1, 55, 138, 158
information technology, 153, 155, 156
infrastructure, 5, 41, 42, 147, 148, 152, 153, 155, 156, 159, 160, 161, 162
initiation, viii, 104, 105
injections, 123, 167
injuries, 19, 21, 31
institutions, viii, 1, 3, 4, 6, 12, 13, 21, 31, 103, 104, 105, 106, 107, 109, 112, 113, 115, 117, 121, 122, 123, 137, 150, 151, 154, 167
insulators, 11
integrity, 14
intelligence, 12
interbank deposits, 105
interest rates, 2, 5, 54, 55, 73, 85, 89, 91, 118, 120, 138, 148, 150, 162, 164, 165
intermediaries, 105, 106
Internal Revenue Service, 120
International Monetary Fund (IMF), 89, 100, 124, 160, 161
international relations, 17
intervention, vii, 17, 46, 107, 117, 139, 147, 151, 164, 165, 166, 167, 168
investment, 4, 5, 6, 54, 99, 106, 107, 119, 120, 150, 158, 159, 162, 163, 164, 165, 166
investment bank, 4, 5, 6, 119, 120, 166
investment incentive, 160
investments, 3, 4, 5, 134, 156
investors, 3, 5, 6, 13, 70, 71, 74, 85, 89, 97, 98, 117, 118, 119, 121, 124, 154, 163
invisible hand, 11
Iraq, 11, 16, 140
Iraq War, 11, 16
isolation, 152
issues, vii, 3, 33, 58, 70, 75, 127, 130, 163, 166, 168, 170
Italy, 53, 69, 100

J

Japan, 2, 6
journalists, 19
jurisdiction, 1, 6
justification, 10

K

Keynesian, 54

L

lack of confidence, 117
law enforcement, 29, 153
laws, 3, 4, 109
laws and regulations, 3
lawyers, 13
lead, 11, 36, 43, 71, 104, 111, 133, 138, 140, 158, 159, 163, 165, 170
leadership, 134, 151, 166
learning, 11, 39, 43, 171
learning process, 39
legislation, ix, 103, 104, 105, 117, 128, 130, 134, 135, 136, 138, 140, 142, 147, 148, 149, 151, 152, 162, 163, 166, 168
leisure, viii, 53, 55, 56, 57, 59, 61, 62, 64
lending, 1, 2, 4, 14, 118, 119, 137, 150
Lexicon Communications Corp, 35
life cycle, 170, 171

linear model, 84, 85, 89
liquid assets, 121
liquidate, 108, 114
liquidity, 4, 70, 73, 74, 86, 89, 97, 120, 121, 122, 150, 162
litigation, 111
loans, 2, 3, 4, 5, 105, 115, 117, 118, 119, 120, 121, 123, 124, 130, 149, 150, 151, 167, 168
local conditions, 22
local government, 154, 156, 161, 162
logistics, 171

M

macroeconomic policies, 120
macroeconomics, 119
Madison, James, 110
magnitude, ix, 19, 21, 75, 149, 152, 157, 162
major decisions, 111, 115
majority, 56, 115, 128, 155
man, vii, 9, 10, 11, 12
management, vii, viii, 1, 5, 6, 17, 18, 19, 20, 21, 22, 23, 24, 25, 26, 27, 28, 29, 30, 31, 32, 33, 35, 36, 37, 38, 39, 40, 41, 42, 43, 44, 45, 46, 48, 50, 104, 105, 108, 109, 111, 112, 115, 119, 129, 130, 169, 170
Man-made disasters, 22
manufacturing, 170, 171
mapping, 171
market capitalization, 78, 79, 81, 84, 85
market discipline, 4, 118
market failure, 2
market share, 21
marketing, 119
marketplace, 5, 10
Markets, vii, 2, 4, 5, 9, 115, 118, 121, 166
marriage, 152
married couples, 152
mass, 35, 42, 155, 172
mass care, 42
materials, 82, 83, 97
matrix, 62
measurement, 171
media, vii, 17, 18, 19, 20, 23, 25, 29, 30, 33, 37, 41, 46, 47, 48, 49, 50
Medicaid, 148, 152, 153, 155
medical, 42, 48, 49
medical care, 42
Medicare, 127, 128, 140
membership, 28, 171
Merton model, viii, 69, 71, 72, 73, 76, 77, 78, 79, 81, 84, 85, 88, 89, 97, 98
messages, 34, 35, 37, 48
methodology, 43, 44, 61, 72, 79, 171
middle class, 147, 148, 152
military, 15, 140
Missouri, 9, 16
Mitigation, 40
models, 1, 3, 5, 61, 72, 73, 74, 75, 79, 85, 86, 88, 89, 97, 100, 101
modern capitalism, 9
modernization, 152, 153
modifications, ix
monetary policy, 118, 120, 147, 150, 156, 162, 165, 166
moral hazard, 13, 168
mortgage-backed securities, 3, 118, 150, 151
multiplier, 54, 62, 158, 160
multiplier effect, 158, 160

N

Nash equilibrium, 12, 56
national debt, 163
natural disaster, 19, 42, 45
Natural disasters, 22
natural resources, 159
negative consequences, 19, 31, 34, 45
negative effects, 19, 20, 64, 163
negative relation, 84, 91
net exports, 164
neutral, 55, 73
new media, vii, 17
null hypothesis, 86

O

OAS, 85
Obama Administration, 140
Obama, President, 140, 142, 147, 148, 155
Office of Management and Budget, 131, 140
officials, 45, 47, 118, 151, 166
oil, 151
open economy, 156
operations, vii, 18, 19, 21, 26, 27, 29, 30, 31, 38, 40, 42, 44, 46, 50, 129, 134, 139, 170
opportunities, 39
optimization, 59, 60, 65
organize, 110, 120
output gap, 164
oversight, viii, 7, 104, 105, 111, 113, 122, 166, 168
ownership, 15, 76

P

Panama, 130
paper money, 14
paralysis, 14, 30
participants, 1, 3, 6, 11, 13, 14, 65, 75, 139
payroll, 128, 152
penalties, 12, 152
pensioners, 155
Pentagon, 140
per capita income, 131
performance rate, 118
permit, 4, 110, 112
personal benefit, 10
personal responsibility, 3
planned economies, 12
police, 13, 49
policy, viii, 2, 15, 29, 43, 53, 55, 56, 58, 60, 61, 62, 64, 70, 103, 104, 118, 120, 121, 147, 148, 150, 156, 159, 160, 161, 162, 163, 164, 165, 166
policy instruments, 64
policy options, 156, 160, 163
policy responses, 2, 118, 120
policymakers, 1, 120, 121, 122
political power, viii, 53, 61
politics, 10
population, 11, 15, 22, 54, 55, 163
portfolio, 74
positive relationship, 84
positive social transfer, viii, 53
post-crisis phase, viii, 18, 36, 41, 42, 50
potential output, 163
poverty trap, 13
pre-crisis phase, viii, 18, 20, 36, 38, 50
preparation, iv, viii, 18, 20, 31, 36, 37, 38, 43, 50
preparedness, 31, 38, 46
present value, 58
President Obama, 140, 142, 147, 148, 155
prestige, 18, 49
prevention, viii, 2, 18, 36, 38, 43
principal component analysis, viii, 69, 75, 86, 91, 92
principles, 24, 27, 28, 29, 107
private investment, 4, 54, 107, 159, 162, 164
probability, 22, 43, 53, 56, 58, 60, 62, 65, 72, 74, 85
producers, 13, 49
product design, 170, 171
product life cycle, 170
production function, 64
professionals, 20, 28, 48
profit, 13, 37
profitability, 85
project, 118, 158
proliferation, 17
property taxes, 152
proposition, 54
protection, 39, 70, 107, 113, 115, 166
public capital, 163
public debt, vii, viii, 53, 54, 57, 64, 122, 128, 130
public housing, 153, 155
public investment, 159, 163
public opinion, 18, 49
public safety, 21, 24, 42

Q

quartile, 93, 95, 97

R

rating agencies, 3, 13, 14, 99
reactions, 10, 34, 47
reading, vii, 2, 12
real estate, 13, 14, 118, 123
real property, 111
reality, 24, 58
recall, 38
recession, 103, 104, 118, 133, 137, 138, 147, 148, 149, 150, 151, 158, 161, 163, 164, 165
recognition, 156
recommendations, iv, 25, 28, 141
reconciliation, 127, 136, 137
reconstruction, 10
recovery, 14, 23, 30, 36, 42, 74, 122, 124, 140, 154, 157, 165
recovery plan, 42
recovery process, 42
redistribution, 62
redistributive effects, 54
reform, ix, 3, 5, 7, 113, 117, 123, 141, 167
regression, 84, 86, 88, 89, 91, 92, 95, 97, 100
regulations, 3, 110
regulatory bodies, 25
relevance, 41, 74, 75, 77, 89
reliability, 170
relief, 45, 156
remediation, 29
renewable energy, 152, 153, 156
reparation, 37, 43
repo, 70
reputation, vii, 17, 19, 21, 23, 47
requirements, 29, 36, 114, 128, 156
resale, 14, 150
researchers, 71, 157, 170
reserves, 162
residuals, 75, 86, 91, 92

resilience, 15, 150
resistance, 152
resolution, viii, 60, 61, 65, 104, 105, 107, 110, 111, 112, 113, 127, 128, 135, 136, 137, 138
resources, 21, 28, 38, 39, 41, 42, 43, 44, 45, 46, 127, 157, 159, 163, 164
response, viii, 18, 19, 20, 23, 24, 25, 29, 31, 33, 35, 36, 37, 38, 39, 40, 41, 43, 45, 46, 49, 50, 132, 148, 150, 158
restrictions, 130, 166
restructuring, 70, 123, 167
retail, 169
revenue, 135, 147, 148, 153, 154, 155, 157
rewards, 12
Ricardian Equivalence, 54, 55, 67
rights, viii, 104, 105, 110, 111, 114
risk, 1, 3, 4, 5, 6, 7, 15, 23, 36, 37, 42, 43, 44, 49, 69, 70, 71, 72, 73, 74, 75, 76, 77, 78, 79, 80, 84, 85, 86, 88, 89, 91, 97, 98, 99, 100, 101, 103, 104, 107, 108, 119, 121, 122, 167, 168
risk assessment, 5, 43, 44
risk aversion, 69, 88, 91
risk factors, 70, 71, 72, 73, 74, 89, 91, 98
risk management, 1, 6, 36, 43, 44, 119
risks, 1, 5, 24, 29, 36, 40, 43, 44, 70, 74, 75, 89, 101, 119, 130
risk-taking, 1, 4, 122
roots, 1, 48, 86
rules, 12, 14, 24, 25, 29, 38, 120, 122, 123

S

safe haven, 14
safety, vii, 4, 17, 21, 24, 31, 42, 48, 159
sanctions, 13, 14
savings, 1, 54, 107, 109, 153, 157
school, 152, 153, 154
science, 15, 153, 155, 156
scope, vii, ix, 12, 17, 23, 169
Second Liberty Bond Act, 127, 129, 130
Secretary of the Treasury, 107, 122, 127, 135, 136, 137
securities, 3, 13, 79, 85, 111, 112, 113, 118, 120, 121, 123, 128, 130, 133, 134, 139, 149, 150, 151, 167
security, viii, 10, 13, 44, 53, 54, 62, 64
seigniorage, 128
self-interest, 10, 11, 46
self-regulation, 4
sellers, 370,
Senate, 122, 128, 130, 134, 135, 136, 137, 138, 139, 140, 141, 142, 148, 154, 155, 161, 168
Senate Finance Committee, 136, 137
separate insolvency regime, viii, 103, 105
services, 21, 45, 105, 138, 150, 153, 159
shareholder value, 20, 117
shareholders, 36, 73, 76, 86, 111, 112
short-term interest rate, 150
showing, 74, 132
signals, 86
signs, 85, 88, 89, 161
simulations, 54, 61, 62, 63, 64, 66
small businesses, 38, 123, 156
social behavior, vii, 9
social benefit, vii, 9, 10
social benefits, 10
social construct, 12
social costs, 15
social group, 61
social security, viii, 53, 54, 62, 64
Social Security, 66, 67, 127, 128, 133, 141, 155
social structure, 12
social transfers, 61
social welfare, 11
society, 10, 11, 12, 13, 20, 21, 22
solution, 11, 25, 62
specialists, 11
speech, 33, 34
spending, 55, 120, 128, 129, 134, 135, 137, 138, 139, 142, 147, 148, 152, 153, 154, 155, 156, 157, 158, 159, 160, 161, 162, 163, 164, 165, 167
spontaneous order, vii, 9, 12, 14
Spring, 5, 106
SSI, 155
stability, 1, 107, 122, 139
stabilizers, 138, 165
stakeholders, viii, 17, 20, 23, 24, 29, 35, 36, 42
standard error, 86
state, ix, 13, 19, 22, 108, 109, 110, 115, 147, 149, 152, 153, 155, 156, 160, 161, 162, 164
states, 20, 54, 55, 61, 110, 152, 153, 155, 162
statistics, 75, 82, 84, 88
statutes, 110
statutory authority, 5, 134
stimulus, vii, ix, 118, 120, 138, 139, 147, 148, 149, 151, 156, 157, 158, 159, 161, 162, 163, 164, 165, 166
stock markets, 100
stock value, 85, 90, 150
strategic planning, 23, 31
stress, 2, 5, 6, 28, 38, 40, 72, 91, 98, 118
structure, viii, 12, 19, 28, 53, 100, 104, 105, 124
structuring, 108
subgroups, 86
subjective judgments, 171
subprime loans, 2, 3, 5, 119

substitutes, 14
substitution, 154
supervision, 110, 111
supervisors, 4
suppliers, 33, 35
surplus, 58, 128, 129, 133, 141
surveillance, 39
survival, 12, 18, 21, 47
symptoms, 171
systemic risk, 6, 15, 89, 103, 104, 107, 108

T

tactics, 19
target, 35, 150, 159, 160, 162
tax cuts, 139, 147, 148, 152, 153, 154, 155, 156, 157, 159, 160, 161
tax deduction, 152
tax incentive, 159, 163
tax rates, 53, 58, 61, 73, 160
tax system, viii, 53
taxation, 54, 55, 57, 58, 61, 62, 63, 64
taxes, viii, 53, 55, 58, 62, 70, 73, 86, 120, 128, 131, 138, 152, 164
taxpayers, 107, 139, 153, 155, 166
teams, vii, 17
technician, 169
techniques, 1, 33
technological change, 15
technologies, 20
technology, 26, 36, 153, 155, 156
telephone, 49
temperature, 22
testing, 72
The Road to Serfdom, 11, 16
Third World, 13
thoughts, 12, 34, 48
threats, 21, 24, 29, 39
thrifts, 103, 104, 105, 106, 107, 109, 115, 124
time series, 86
Timothy Geithner, 103, 104
total revenue, 58
trade, 10, 158, 159, 162, 164
trade deficit, 158, 162, 164
trade-off, 10
training, 10, 36, 38, 40, 155, 156
trajectory, 140
transaction costs, 13, 73
transactions, 4, 5, 6, 12, 13, 14, 107, 108
transfer payments, 153, 159, 164
transference, 44
transmission, 151
transparency, 20, 48, 119
transportation, 42, 155
transportation infrastructure, 42
Treasury, 4, 6, 14, 74, 103, 104, 107, 118, 120, 121, 122, 123, 124, 127, 128, 129, 130, 132, 133, 134, 135, 136, 137, 138, 139, 141, 144, 147, 149, 150, 151, 154, 166, 167, 168
Treasury bills, 14, 130
Treasury Secretary, 103, 104, 139
treatment, 49, 55, 109, 148
Troubled Asset Relief Program (TARP), ix, 117, 121, 122, 155
trust fund, 127, 128, 129, 134, 141
Trust Fund, 128
tuition, 154
Turkey, 7

U

U.S. Department of the Treasury, 127, 129, 132, 134, 139
U.S. economy, 103, 105, 148, 158, 164
U.S. Treasury, 6, 107, 136, 139, 144
UK, 6, 99
unemployment insurance, 138, 152
unemployment rate, 148, 149
uninsured, 107
United States (USA), 1, 9, 70, 103, 104, 105, 107, 108, 110, 111, 115, 124, 128, 129, 130, 131, 137, 142, 164
universities, 153

V

validation, 171
valuation, 76, 100
variables, viii, 69, 71, 72, 73, 74, 75, 77, 78, 83, 84, 85, 88, 90, 91, 95, 98
variations, viii, 12, 69, 71, 75, 84, 91, 92, 97, 98, 124
vector, 56, 58, 60, 61, 62
vehicles, 4, 23
Vice President, 157
volatility, viii, 69, 71, 73, 74, 75, 76, 77, 78, 79, 81, 84, 85, 88, 89, 90, 96, 97, 98, 99, 101
vote, 28, 56, 61, 107, 112, 134, 138, 139
voters, 53, 58
voting, viii, 28, 53, 61, 111
vulnerability, 44

W

wage rate, 55

wages, 56
waiver, 107
Wales, 12
war, 13, 22, 140, 141
War on Terror, 142
warning systems, 39
Washington, 4, 5, 103, 104, 129, 130, 151, 160, 161, 167
water, 42, 148, 153
wealth, 54, 64, 105, 106
welfare, 10, 11, 54
Western Europe, 108, 111, 115
workers, 42, 55, 56, 58, 61, 64, 152, 153, 155, 156
working families, 152
World War I, 129, 130, 151

Y

yield, 70, 74, 85, 88, 90, 91, 94, 118